UNHOOKED

Clare Gee was born in Africa in 1977 and was sent to live in Yorkshire with her English father when she was five. Aged 16, she moved to the capital, where she descended into a life of drink, drugs and prostitution. After a period of rehabilitation, she has rebuilt her life in London. She is also the author of *Hooked*.

UNHOOKED
THE REHAB OF A
LONDON CALL GIRL

Clare Gee

MAINSTREAM
PUBLISHING

EDINBURGH AND LONDON

First published in Great Britain in 2012 by
MAINSTREAM PUBLISHING COMPANY
(EDINBURGH) LTD
7 Albany Street
Edinburgh EH1 3UG

ISBN 9781845967963

This book is a fictional account loosely based on the life, experiences and recollections of the author. Dates, places, sequences and the detail of events have been changed for artistic purposes and to protect the privacy of others. Most of the people in this book are entirely fictitious.

A catalogue record for this book is available
from the British Library

Printed and bound by
CPI Group (UK) Ltd, Croydon, CR0 4YY

1 3 5 7 9 10 8 6 4 2

To Rex Bilton.
For everything – thank you.
I shall never forget.

Unhooked. *v. to have detached as if by releasing*

PART 1

CHAPTER 1

'I'm going to make you gush all over this, little girl.' *Dirty old bastard.* 'Look at me. I want you to watch me as I make you come.'

I opened my eyes and was met by the saggy skin and grey hair of a grandad, and the buzzing of a vibrator. My heartbeat thumped in my skull. His skinny lips parted as he raised the plastic cock to his mouth in what I supposed was meant to be a seductive move. I felt a rush of anxiety and my head slumped back onto the already soiled sheet.

'You like that, don't you?' he hissed. I wanted to squeeze his windpipe in my hands and stare into his eyes as he died slowly.

He must have been 60 if he was a day. I was three weeks off my twenty-seventh birthday.

My 300-quid cash payment momentarily raped my mind; I felt disgusted by the thought of it. The pensioner clamped his mouth onto my clit and began sucking. He grunted. Suddenly, my adrenalin levels rocketed and I burst upright and pushed him backwards with the full force of my legs. I jumped off the bed and started frantically getting dressed.

'I can't fucking do this.'

'What the hell are you playing at? What's wrong with you?'

'Are you fucking serious? *This*. This whole thing is what's wrong, you fucking prick. Just stay away from me. I'm going. I'm fucking going! I'm leaving all this. I can't do this any longer, I just can't fucking do it!' My heart was booming. I wanted to grab his coarse hair and bash his face into my knee, splattering his nose across it, then set him alight for fun.

'I should have known. You black bitches are so pissing unreliable.'

'Oh, fuck off, you stinking piece of shit,' I spat.

'Don't you dare swear at me, do you hear me? Or I'll call your agency.'

'Do you really, honestly believe I actually give a flying fuck if you do?'

'I should have known not to book a nigger again. You're all the –'

Two strides and I smacked his face. Hard. He squealed. I hit him again, harder. He squealed louder. 'How dare you? Get out of here, you dirty black whore! Get out now!'

FIVE DAYS LATER

The moment the train pulled out of Waterloo, heading for a residential drug rehab centre in Weymouth, I shut down. I knew that I was heading towards my last chance.

I was ashamed of what I'd become: a 26-year-old coke-whore shitbag loser. That was how I perceived myself, and I was convinced that was how others viewed me too. I'd fucked up. Badly.

I'd existed in London as a cocaine-addicted, alcoholic hooker for most of my 20s, and now, finally, I'd waved the white flag; I needed to escape the chaotic existence I'd created. Swapping my gash for cash was no longer a viable option and banging shit up my snout had turned me into a paranoid, frightened, angry mess. I knew I required help to change, and Bringing Counselling Home, who were militant with their rules, promised to provide a zero-tolerance environment. This I needed, but spending time with druggie tossers I didn't. I'd been to rehab years before, spending several months in a different residential facility. So why try again if it hadn't worked the first time? Because the problem had not been the process. When I'd first tried to get clean, I was a 20-year-old girl and I clearly hadn't been fully ready to change. And now? Now I was different: I'd finally realised that *every* aspect of my life was in shreds. Everything was controlled by my use of substances and by men. I had become a slave. Nothing was right and, simply put, I was not coping. Not one bit.

- *addiction* = a set of compulsive behaviours, attitudes and thought processes; a sickness of the mind that manifests itself in the abuse of mood-altering substances and in obsessions that are used as a means of coping with everyday life.

- *addict* = a person who suffers from the above symptoms. It is about attitude, not necessarily the use of substances.

Jim, who'd travelled from Yorkshire that morning to take me to rehab, was sitting opposite me, talking animatedly about God knows what. I wasn't listening. Nevertheless, it was reassuring that the only person who'd retained even a scrap of faith in me was there.

Although we'd been sexual for two years, that was history. Our relationship had altered over the time we'd known each other, but our love had not diminished. The idea of it being severed altogether was impossible to imagine. Jim had become my family, an honorary father, the brother I'd never known, a perfect partner but without the sex, and the only person who I knew for certain loved me.

When we'd first met I was 20 years old and had recently left rehab after completing my first stint. Jimmy was 27 and, in my eyes, a fully fledged man. He was articulate, knowledgeable about art, history, current affairs. These things mattered to me. My father was an intellectual, and his influence on my upbringing couldn't be totally wiped out, hard as I'd tried to do so. I admired Jimmy hugely and was soon rewarded with his sturdy, nurturing love.

At that time, narcotics had taken a back seat; he wasn't into 'that scummy bollocks', he'd tell me whenever I suggested we take some Ecstasy or speed together. But alcohol is legal and acceptable, so we drank. The pair of us could drink, that was obvious. And drink and drink and drink. We were young; everyone does that. Don't they?

I doubted that my dad, who'd raised me by himself, still loved me. I'd hurt him too much.

Until I turned 14, on the surface life was normal. Maybe not conventional, but Dad and I were a family. I wanted for nothing – except, occasionally, my mum. But I kept that to myself. She was my secret. Dad and I never discussed my silly, slutty, selfish mum, who'd been married to an African man when she had a liaison with my English father. My mother is black, her husband was black, but it was obvious that 'their' child was half white. Her husband buggered off and left her shamed and exposed, with a mixed-race baby as a stark reminder to herself and her community of her mistake.

In 1982, my father returned to Britain after having spent 20 years teaching in Zambia, and what did Mum do? Sent me to England in a bid to hide the evidence.

I was dragged off by an air-hostess to sit on a plane, alone, aged five. I remember I turned round to look at my mum and she was crying and waving a white tissue in my direction. I turned round again and she was gone. For good.

That was the last time I ever saw her. I don't know at what point I realised that I was never going to see her, touch her or smell her again, but I instinctively knew she wasn't coming back.

As a result of this, I became fixated on the idea that my dad would vanish equally as suddenly, without warning, so it made sense to me to do everything within my power to prevent this from happening and to encourage him to want to stay with me. I set about being the exemplary daughter, focusing entirely on pleasing him. I tried and tried, all the time, and I cried if I was anything other than perfect.

But my persistent negative thoughts about my mother leaving me turned into self-loathing, and my deep feelings of inadequacy became the rumblings of a distant storm.

On that train to that place on that day in May, Jim joked about the irony that he was taking me to rehab as the 'appropriate adult'. After all, when we'd been in a relationship we'd spent more time drunk than sober. We'd been inseparable and during that time had managed to get ourselves barred from numerous bars and clubs in the town in which we lived. I could barely find the energy to smile. All I wanted was to sleep and sleep and sleep, and for everything to be changed when I woke up.

The hum of Jim's boyish voice was neither irritating nor comforting; it was just there. Occasionally, I'd hear him giggle and I'd open my eyes and look at him. His bulky body filled the seat opposite and his blue eyes waltzed under heavy brows as he tried to gauge what to say next to ease my pain.

'Give me your hand.' He reached across. 'What can I do to make you feel better, Katie?'

I didn't know what to say. I shook my head slowly from side to side and tears ran down my spotty face.

'Everything might feel like a big fucking cesspit of horrors, right now, kidder, but it'll be all right, you'll see. Look, just don't forget it's only temporary, OK? Nothing is permanent. Things change all the fucking time, whether you want them to or not.' He was rubbing my hand firmly. 'But choosing to alter a fucked-up situation of your own accord takes fucking cojones, don't forget that, sweetheart. You're still young, and you've still got that cute round arse, so it's not all bad, eh?' He chuckled. I didn't. I hated my behind.

'And let's face it, as long as you're not rotting in a casket in the ground, it's never too late.' I could hear him, but I couldn't believe in what he was saying.

'Look, I know for a curious little bear like you who wants to taste everything that life has to offer it's difficult to avoid a spot of bother here and there, isn't that right?' He tittered and I smiled, but nothing seemed funny.

I'd chucked everything away. The one thing I had yet to abandon was my mind – although I wondered if I'd tossed that aside when I'd committed bigamy. How did that happen? Simple. I was permanently off my face on drugs and alcohol. Three years ago, I'd married Sam – whom I'd left after two weeks – and I went on to have a holiday romance with Hassan while in Africa trying to escape London, cocaine and hooking. I married him without having divorced Sam. I did this to try to help him get a British visa. I'd hoped that if I ignored the problem it would evaporate into the ether. It didn't. Not an ideal situation, it has to be said.

'Do you trust me?' Jimmy asked. I did. 'Well, I can promise you this, Kate: as long as you haven't killed anyone, there's hope, OK, darling? Do you hear me?' He shook my hand from side to side. 'Look at you, pet. You're still bloody breathing. You're alive – for God's sake, be grateful for that! Come on! You're fucking alive! Not everyone gets a chance to change, so stop fucking wallowing in this, find that African spirit and fight!'

I was definitely still alive – I could feel my heart thumping – and I'd definitely managed not to bump anyone off. But I knew this would not be the last time I'd think about killing myself.

CHAPTER 2

RULE

- Clients must not use alcohol or narcotic drugs of any kind.

The number-one principle for anyone trying to recover from a substance addiction: abstinence – from all things mood-altering, including alcohol.

Sounds obvious? Not when dealing with people who appear continually to want to sabotage themselves. Believe me, addicts, whether or not in recovery, are brilliant at making the irrational sound absolutely plausible. And most never overcome being manipulative, lying fuckheads.

When I arrived at the centre, there were thirty-five men and five women in primary care. The total number of inmates in the rehabilitation centre (aka plain old 'rehab', or 'treatment', as snobs amongst us preferred to call it) was always fluctuating as people came into the first stage (primary) and left to go on to the second stage of their treatment (secondary) – or decamped to go and get wasted somewhere. In the secondary stage, the rules were less rigid, but *whatever*. I didn't have to concern myself with that; I'd done secondary during my earlier stint in another centre. Anyone returning to rehab after a relapse – a regression into his or her old habits – was not expected to stay beyond primary care. Or so I was led to believe.

Charge sheet: the main players – women
Tessa, my best buddy – heroin and crack.
Stacey, the grumpy dyke – alcohol.
Sabrina, the innocent doll – alcohol.
Camille, the odd, frail one – anorexic alcoholic.
Lisa, the pensive, willowy model – cokehead anorexic.
Yours truly, the party-girl coke-whore alcoholic.

Charge sheet: the main players – men
Leon (we'll come to him later) – crack.
Simon, the posh boy – heroin and crack.
Daryl, the peacemaker – heroin.
Austin, the ageing white Jamaican gangster – crack.
Billy, non-stop-talking nice guy – barbiturates and alcohol.
Alan, the over-zealous newcomer – anything and everything.

The counsellors and adjudicators – that is, the Powers That Be (PTB)
Lenny, the camp head honcho.
Maggie, his annoying sidekick.
Nick, the young, good-looking one.
(Plus three others.)

On the sidelines:
Magda, the gentle receptionist.
Antonia, the housekeeper and cook.

Jim had left with a soft tug on my cheek and a wink. His

words 'Chin up, kid' nearly made me want to hang on to his leg and never let go.

'You know, there's very little you can get away with not telling us here, Katie, so for your own benefit you might as well get involved in a spot of honesty as quickly as possible. Know what I mean?' the counsellor said the moment she'd closed her office door.

A 'spot' of honesty – my fucking arse!

'So who's Jim?'

'I've known him for years.'

'Really? In what capacity?'

She sounds like a copper. 'What do you mean? He's a really close friend.'

'Right. So he's a *friend*, is he?'

'Well, he's more than a friend, he's like –'

'I'm sure he is. Look, we have a few minutes. Is there anything you want to tell me?'

I'd been in rehab 30 minutes, if that, and already I was being interrogated. I stared at this woman's nest of dyed blood-red hair and wished she'd just vanish.

'You've been in rehab before, Katie, so you must remember that honesty is the backbone of recovery.'

Why is she tilting her head, raising her eyebrows and grinning so sarcastically?

'So, this Jim fella, is he a client?'

She can't mean what I think she means, can she? A client? I wanted to punch her in the mouth.

'He seemed like a mensch, a real decent guy.'

OK, so now she was being nice about him, but it was too late. The damage was already done. She sat very still and so did I. Sweat blitzed my skin. *Don't look at her. No, look at her, look at her. She'll think you're hiding something if you don't. Why*

the fuck is she still staring at me? Hang on – maybe she thinks
I run a legitimate business and that Jim is a company client. She
couldn't possibly have thought I was a hooker, could she? Me? OK,
I didn't present like a typical businesswoman, but neither did
I look like the archetypal call girl. I've never worn heels – I'm
5 ft 10 in. – I never wore revealing or designer clothing and
I rarely used make-up.

'Jim's a friend, as I said.'

'Ah-ha, well, he clearly cares a lot about you from what
I could see.' She paused and peered at me through bright-
coloured rectangular glasses, the type that people wear as a sign
of their individuality, ignoring the scores of others wearing
exactly the same thing. 'I'm going to keep this simple, Katie,
OK? It's easier for both of us if I do. Know what I mean?
Look, a lot of the women who come through here have worked
as prostitutes, you know . . .'

She'd said it. She'd used *that* word. And to my face! 'What
do you mean by that?' I barked. But I knew what she meant.

Sadistic Fantasy: I reach over the desk, grip her hair and hear
a crack when I head-butt her straight on her nose.

For most people, getting accused of being a hooker within
minutes – hell, hours, days, years – of meeting someone would
most definitely be a punchable offence. But I had admitted myself
to rehab. Most women with drug problems have sold themselves
– it goes with the territory – and the woman across the desk was
a counsellor. She knew the coup. But I was still livid that she'd
suggested that I was, or more accurately had been, a whore.

'Sorry, what's your name again?'

'Maggie.'

'Well, *Maggie*, I don't know what you want me to tell
you.' I couldn't believe that this trollop, who, judging by her
appearance, had been round the block more times than I cared

to think about, was trying to imply that she knew everything about me. How dare she accuse me of selling my arse, as casually as if she were asking whether I took sugar in my tea? I wanted to knock her out, I really did. Yeah, I'd sold my body, but that was my business, and if she thought I was about to tell her that detail then she could do one.

'I've told you that I drank a few bottles of wine a day, and –' I visualised myself wobbling around The Pelican, a members' club, holding hostage anyone I could and talking at them endlessly, trashed on vodka, champagne, wine and cocaine.

'And the rest,' Maggie gestured impatiently, pushing the glasses that I wanted to shove up her arse back onto her beak. She clearly wasn't listening to me. Suddenly, an image of my nose bleeding during a session on the marching powder flicked into my mind like a subliminal message.

'Yeah, OK . . . I drank vodka as well as sniffing coke. So what's the big deal about that?'

'How much charlie?'

'A couple of grams a day, OK? I've also told you Jimmy is a really good friend. Now what? I've nothing else to say.' I wanted to add *to you, you nosy bitch*, but didn't. 'Although I can tell you this much, I feel . . . dirty. I feel . . . disgusting.' I averted my eyes. I started removing bits of fluff that weren't there off my jeans. 'I keep getting hot sweats, and I feel as though every organ in my body is contaminated and my blood saturated with toxins. I can feel it in my system. I can literally feel something swirling inside me and it's rotten. It's fu– it's nasty, grimy and it's everywhere.' I kept nearly swearing and then catching myself, thinking it would be inappropriate. 'Every single day is the same. I wake up, my skin is sticky, I'm sure I stink, I sweat all the time and my nerves are shot to fu– to pieces until I get on it again. I've been like this for years, and you know something?

Unless I'm out of my head, I'm a twitchy fu– a mess. I feel polluted. I really, really do.' My heart was racing.

'I do und– '

'I'm shattered. I'm so, so, so tired. Of everything. Tired of thinking. I'm fu– I'm exhausted . . . I'm worn out, do you understand? I mean, do you *really* understand what I'm talking about?'

'I've been –'

'And my mind . . . my mind is, well . . . I don't even know about that. It's easier to say that I've got a few issues and . . .' I looked at her and shrugged. 'I just don't know what to do. I can't cope. I just cannot cope. With being alive, with anything, and . . .'

'You'll be all right now. You're a tough shiksa.'

'A what?'

'Well, I'm presuming you're not Jewish, right?'

'Uh-uh.'

'Well, I am and to me you're a shiksa who's found her way to the right place.'

'But what if I'm not?'

'In the right place?'

'Yeah, what if I'll never be all right? I'm not well . . . I, I can't seem to live. I just can't seem to do anything right, ever. I'm not doing OK at all.'

Maggie's arms were crossed. 'I do unders– '

'Please . . . please, don't . . .' Tears were gliding down my cheeks. 'I so desperately want to get this next three months over with so I can make a new start with my life, but I've got to tell you, I feel insulted that you've asked me if I'm some sort of hooker.'

'I didn't say that. I asked if there was anything you wanted to get off your chest.' She handed me a tissue.

'Look, I know what you meant, OK? God, I've just walked through the fu– through the door, and you . . .'

'It's all right, Katie, you can swear, you know. It's good to let your anger out,' she said with an over-egged serenity. Next she'd be making me hug trees and chant mantras.

'Breathe. Take slow, deep breaths.' She sang this. *Literally.* What. The. Hell?

'I feel like I haven't slept for years . . . I am totally fucking wiped out. I don't even know how I've made it this far.' Adrenalin surged through my body and whenever I moved my hand towards my face I could see strobes of light – like I'd taken acid, but without the full-on hallucinations. It was really bad when I hadn't done any drugs for a few hours.

'Katie, I do know how you're feeling. I've sat where you're sitting now.' *Here we go, her pointless attempt to bond with me.* 'I came in here 12 years ago, not wanting to say anything about my life to anyone. I thought I'd try to wing it by minimising the rubbish I used to get up to.' I cringed when I heard: 'You know the drill. Being open is the only way people get better.'

I thought 'wing it' had been bad enough, but with the addition of 'you know the drill' my patience was nearly dead. I thought she was using expressions that she felt made her sound 'down with the youth'. I knew exactly what she meant, but my face told her that I couldn't give a toss about winging it or drills, and as for the two of us uniting in some sort of sisterhood of ex-junkies, she could piss off.

'We need to get to the crux of why you use drugs and alcohol, Katie. What is it you're trying to escape from? Here we're going to help you delve into the causes of your problems, so honesty and open-mindedness and, number one, being willing to help yourself will aid your recovery. The sooner the better, know what I mean?'

I didn't respond. I was staring at the faded tattoos on the tops of her arms and thanking God and all that was good in the world that, unlike her, I didn't have the voice of a chain-smoking man inside a woman's body.

'Substance misuse is a symptom of underlying problems and through 12 simple steps we look intensely at these. So the more you put into this the more you'll –'

'Get out of it,' I said in unison with her. *Zzzz* . . . I knew the patter.

'Any idiot can stop using drugs and drinking. It's *staying* stopped that's the problem, girl. I mean, let's face it, you stopped before, didn't you? But if it was that easy to not go back to what you knew, you wouldn't be here now, would you?' *Thanks for reminding me.* 'Just remember to take one day at a time.' *Fucking clichés.*

I zoned out and watched her lips move, her face framed by her red mane. I was desperate to sleep but I knew I wouldn't be allowed to. On the outside, I always had things to do – money to make, drinks to drink, powder to sniff – so afternoon snoozing was never part of my repertoire. But now I could relax a little because:

1. I was away from London.
2. My mobile phone had been confiscated and therefore no punters or dodgy 'friends' could contact me.
3. On that day, for the first time in years, there was bugger all for me to do. Nothing at all except pretend to listen.

CHAPTER 3

RULE
- As far as possible, clients must remain with the group at all times.

The house I was to live in for my three-month stay was called Avalon, a mixed-sex house. Avalon was where the less roguish guys were. These men were seen as sexually less enticing to the women, who were unrealistically expected to stick together. The other primary-care house was Hazelwood, a male-only house: eight shared bedrooms of testosterone-fuelled angst. Lovely.

Maggie explained the basics of the routine I had to look forward to over the coming twelve weeks: 'Two group therapy sessions a day, which last for ninety minutes each, and they'll be held here, in the centre. This is where you'll come every day from 8.45 to 4.45.'

- *group therapy* = participating in the therapy process *as a group* and not individually.

The group sessions were supposed to help create camaraderie, trust and identification with other users, which would serve to ease feelings of alienation and shame. We were all the same – *apparently*. We came from varied backgrounds and had had experiences that had occurred in different places. That was very obvious very quickly, but, we were told, our feelings and behaviour had mirrored one another's. *Right*. 'Look for the similarities and not the differences,' we were advised. But similarities were hard to find at times in that place.

Maggie continued: 'Every weekday morning, the first group therapy session begins at 9.30 a.m. That will be held in the main group room or one of the two upstairs offices. A counsellor will come into the group room before each session, after we've done the daily meditation reading from the *Just for Today* book, and call out names so you know where to go. In a little while, after we've done your bag search, you'll be going into the main room so you can reacclimatise. During the time you're not in therapy sessions, you'll be in the group room, OK, Kate?' *Yes, OK, OK!*

'And you're expected to have mini-groups then.'

'Yeah.'

'Oh, and the afternoon session begins after lunch, at 2 p.m.'

- *mini-group* = individual patients get four or five others together to discuss something. This is not facilitated by a therapist.

'On Saturday, you'll be here at the usual time, but you'll leave to go back to your house for lunch at midday. In the afternoon, you'll go for a walk and chill out in the park.'

Chill out? Does she have to use that expression? Guess she's trying to sound cool, so, yes, she does.

27

'Sunday is another visit to the park for you lucky people.' She grinned, I guessed, at the ridiculousness of what she was saying, and so did I, to humour her. 'And then . . .' (drum roll) ' . . . in the evening you'll have a homemade buffet to which you all help yourself. Antonia, the cook, will prepare it all for you while you're enjoying yourselves outside.'

Am I meant to get excited by this?

'Tell me something,' I interrupted.

'What do you want to know?'

'Do you do confrontation letters?' These were a type of therapy I'd come across during my first spell in rehab and which I'd found particularly difficult.

'Of course. They're a vital part of the process.'

'Right.' *Shit.* 'OK, sorry I disturbed you. Carry on. What were you saying?'

'They're hard to deal with, I know. But the life story and confrontation part of the treatment is vital for each of us to come to terms with who we really became during those lost years. Know what I mean? They're designed to strip us of any delusions about ourselves: you can't kid a kidder, kinda thing . . .'

'Yeah, but they're so harsh. And my lost years only came to an end . . . er, less than an hour ago.'

'By the time you do your life story, you'll have more time behind you, if that's any consolation.'

'Well, it's not really.'

'Anyway, don't think about all that for now, Kate. Don't forget that these confrontation letters are simply feedback. The name implies something more worrying than the reality, but –'

'You've got to be joking! From what I remember, they're absolutely fucking horrendous and people should be worried about them.'

'Worry gets you nowhere. It's just one day at a time, remember?'

'Yeah, but . . .'

'No buts. Just get through today and don't worry about what's to come.' I felt anxious. 'Right, OK, where was I? So you must always stick with the group, Katie. Always.'

I was distracted by thoughts of how I'd stop myself from murdering someone in the middle of the room while getting the feedback regarding my life story.

'There may be times when you need to go into town to buy something, toiletries, new knickers, etc.'

Was I meant to smile again? She did, so I tried to.

'But that won't be any time soon, by the way, so don't start planning your shopping spree just yet, OK?'

I wasn't! Hurry up! Let's just get this bollocks over and done with and get on with the fucking 'treatment', please.

'Eventually, you may well be able to go out of the centre with just two other girls. But at all times you'll be accompanied – except for when you go to the toilet.'

She clearly thought she was being funny, but I didn't have the will to humour her again.

'All the rules are the same for everyone. You're not being singled out, all right?'

I hadn't thought I was. I nodded.

'Where was I?'

'I don't know.' *I can barely hear what you're saying; I'm fucked.* I'd have paid money or even screwed a stranger to earn a nap on that chair right there.

'That's it, on a Saturday evening, if you've all been behaving yourselves, you can watch a film. It won't take you long to get to grips with it . . . By the way, do you prefer to be called Katie or Kumba?'

'Sorry, what was that?'

'Well, I keep calling you Katie, but I read in your admission notes that your real name is Kumba or Kombi, isn't it? Where's that from?'

'It's Kumba. My mum's Zambian, and, yeah, it's the name on my passport and stuff, but people just call me Kate or Katie.'

'Oh, right . . . so even your mum doesn't call you Kumba, then?'

'No.'

'Oh, OK . . . But you were born and brought up in England?'

Here we go . . . 'I was raised here, but born in Africa.'

'In Zambia?'

'Yeah.'

'Do you ever go to visit?'

'No,' I sighed. I'd been through this conversation too many times in my life. 'I don't know my mum. There was just me and my dad at home.' I found anything relating to my mother hard to talk about, but people were always intrigued and to shut them up I usually gave them something. 'My mum, who's black, was married to a Zambian bloke, who was also black and, to cut a tedious story short, Mum had a one-night stand with my dad, who's white, and got pregnant by him while still married to her husband.' You couldn't make it up. Maggie's face fell. And that was that. Job done. I'm not sure if the look was of empathy or shock because I'd told the story robotically. But where would it stop if I started expressing emotion? I wasn't even sure how I felt about the saga.

I was asked more tedious questions, about where I lived and with whom: Putney, with no one.

'How do you pay your rent?'

'I just do.' I wasn't going to give her more than I already

had. Not then. I didn't care if she was a therapist or an ex-smackhead-oompa-loompa; I was keeping it zipped.

'Ain't nothin' goin' on but the rent, eh? Gwen Guthrie.' She burst into song.

Cheeky cow.

'God, I love that song. Do you know it?'

'I've heard it, yeah.'

'That was my era, that was . . . So, it's your birthday next week?'

'In just over a week, yeah.'

'You're going to be 28?'

'I'll be 27, but, please . . . I don't want people to know. I just want to forget about it. Is that OK?'

'Well, if that's how you feel, all right. But let's put it in perspective: we're hardly going to arrange for you to have a huge shindig with a band thrown in for good measure, now, are we, eh?' I liked her Scouse accent, even when she was being sarcastic.

'I know that. But I just don't want people knowing about it.'

'So you don't even want a birthday cake and candles? Antonia makes a mean cake.'

'No. Honestly, I want to forget about it.'

'As you wish.'

The inquisition over, she said that the doctor would be in to see me.

'Sign your name here.' I didn't read her scrawlings; I just signed.

Someone knocked on the door and came straight in. 'Oops, sorry. I thought you were alone in here. Excuse me.'

'I'll only be a few minutes, OK, Nick?'

The guy apologised and left.

'So, does your dad know that you're here then, Katie?'

'Who was that?'

'Nick is one of our more recent recruits.'

'Oh, right . . . a patient?'

'No. He's a counsellor and he's married. I saw that look in your eye.'

'You're wrong. He's not my type. Gosh, he looks too young.'

'To be a counsellor or to be married?'

'Both.'

'Well, I was first married at 21. An attempt at keeping myself off the streets after my parents kicked me out. Yeah, I suppose he does look young. He's 25, mind you. But how lucky he is that he's got clean at such a young age. He found his recovery through the rooms. I bloody wish I'd got to grips with all this before I did. I was 37. And look at you – your whole life is in front of you, sober and well, if you want it.'

- *the rooms* = NA and AA meetings.

'So anyway, yeah, does your family know you're here?'

'No. No one knows. Only Jimmy. My dad and I haven't spoken for months, but that's not uncommon. We've gone for more than two years with no contact before now.'

'Really? I went for 12 years with no contact with my father, and then next thing he'd dropped down dead from alcoholism.'

'Right, well, my dad isn't an alcoholic. He just has a very domineering wife. Oh, and I'm really sorry to hear about your dad.'

'It happens.'

'Well, both my dad and his wife are bonkers, unfortunately, and to be fair I don't blame my dad for being freaked out by my behaviour. But his wife hasn't encouraged a reconciliation. Besides, they've spent most of their marriage slating me. That's how they bonded. Elaine believes she "rescued" my dad from me, when they met when I was 17. By then I'd become rebellious. I was pretty bad in many respects, it has to be said. I just wouldn't listen to anyone.' I could have talked endlessly about this situation.

'You're bitter, then?'

'Damn right I am. My dad let me down by turning his back on me when he met his "saviour" Elaine, and that fucking arsehole only added fuel to an already troubled situation.'

'You have your part to play in this, though, Katie.'

'I know I do. I know that . . . And I know I behaved badly, just as they did.'

'Resentment will rot your insides, you know that? And it's a sure way to find yourself back on drugs if you don't deal with those feelings.'

Whatever.

CHAPTER 4

RULE

- Clients are not permitted to self-prescribe. Any concerns about health problems should be referred to a doctor, who will decide whether medication is required.

The doctor, an overweight, bespectacled man in his mid-50s, greeted me with a bored 'Hello-how-are-you?' to which I wanted to reply, 'Well, as I'm sure you can imagine, taking into account that you've found me here on my first day of rehab . . .' But since I knew that he wasn't really asking me how I was, I gave him an equally banal answer: 'Fine.'

I felt like a 12-year-old child self-consciously catching my teacher's eye when I met Maggie's smile with my own as she left the room. The doctor walked round the desk and sat where she'd been sitting.

'So, Katie,' he said, breathing loudly, holding the form close to his eyes. I nodded. Something about him disgusted me. As I sat staring at him, I realised why I'd taken an instant dislike to the man: *he used call girls.* I could spot a whore from across the street and I could do the same with punters. He glanced at me and scribbled something. No questions, no chitchat, just tablets. I was surprised at the brevity of the 'consultation', but didn't have any incentive to say anything. I knew I'd be getting some drugs regardless. Dr Punter babbled inaudibly and left the room.

Maggie re-entered. 'We've got a lot of work to do here. You know that, don't you?' she said. That was *clearly* a rhetorical question. 'Don't worry. We'll help you.' This was all I wanted to hear.

'You're not bad, remember that, my girl. You've been unwell.' I knew that all too clearly. 'And the good news is that you *can* get better. From this day forward, you never need to think of yourself as a using addict. But understand this – nothing at all and no one can come before this. Protecting yourself must come before everything, otherwise you don't need me to tell you that this won't work.' She sounded like a religious zealot.

- *a using addict* = a person in the throes of an active addiction.
- *in recovery* = the process of being abstinent and supposedly trying to live better.
- *a recovering addict* = a person whose addiction is no longer part of their daily life.

'This is Sabrina.' A squat, acne-infected blonde girl offered three limp fingers for a handshake. She made no eye contact, twitched her nose and looked down. Bit self-conscious, I decided.

'I'm Stacey,' said a dark-haired, moustached, lesbian-type tracksuit-wearing girl, who tried to assert her authority with a firm, full-palm grip.

'I know you!' I couldn't believe it. She froze. 'You're from Yorkshire, aren't you?'

The blood ran out of her cheeks. I could tell that for a microsecond she contemplated lying. 'How do you know that?'

'I've been following you,' I said, teasing her.

She scanned my face, looked towards the door, then at Sabrina, and broke into a trying-to-look-relaxed smile, not convincing anyone, when she realised that what I'd said was absurd.

We were roughly the same age and she'd lived in the same town as me. Like me, she used to hang out by the beach and amusement arcades, smoking, drinking and trying to be cool.

'You went to my school. I'm sure you did.'

'Oh my God, that's so weird. I don't remember you. But I was only there for two years before me and my mam and dad moved to Peterborough.'

Maggie was perched on her throne behind her desk, faffing in a drawer while listening to every word. 'You can't escape your past,' she chipped in, trying to be philosophical. 'That's why we help you to learn to accept it while you're here.'

Sabrina was standing silently with her hands folded in front of her, smiling meekly, her lips smothered in pink lipstick and heavily lined in a darker colour. She was a bit bland, but inoffensive. She had a pretty, doll-like face with round blue eyes. When she caught me looking at her, she rubbed her nose as though there was something itching it, an absent-minded habit. I got the impression she carried a lot more sadness than her bright-coloured clothes and fixed smile implied. She wasn't the kind of girl with whom I would normally associate, I could see that immediately. She didn't seem sassy or clever, although I was sure she thought she was both. Her clothes were cheap but trendy, and her hair resembled straw – bleached nearly to death. But she tried. She was overweight, no doubt describing herself as 'big-boned', despite being petite, and carried what I soon found out was an *après*-baby tummy, which she attempted to keep hidden by continually pulling down her top. Yeah, I was opinionated. So what? I knew they'd be judging me, too.

'You haven't got anything sharp in here, have you?' Maggie asked as she peered into the only piece of evidence to show I had an even remotely glamorous past: the Chloé bag that Joel, my sugar-daddy ex-boyfriend, had bought me.

'I don't jack up, ya know. So, no, there's nothing sharp.'

'So you've no tweezers or anything in here? That's all I meant,' she countered.

Like any non-intravenous user, I resented any implication that I might inject my drugs. Elitist bullshit that also worked the other way: needle-using junkies thought that people who didn't do as they did were spineless. I, well, I just pitied them and thought they were scum, in spite of our emotional lives being pretty much on the same level, so I was told.

As I sat on the plastic chair staring at Maggie, who was busily poking through my bag, I thought about where I was and what I was about to do for the next three months and what a contrast this was with my old life. My mind suddenly flashed onto the time I'd been involved with the son of a Middle Eastern president. I'd been asked by a friend of mine, Henrik, who owned two members' clubs in town, if I'd join his friend for dinner. Apparently, the 34-year-old fella hadn't had the nerve to ask me out himself, even though we'd smooched as we'd danced together a week or so earlier. I had no recollection of this, however, or of who he was, until I saw him again in the flesh. The dinner date wasn't a job; Henrik didn't know I was a hooker. I agreed to go, but only if he agreed to be there too, at least initially, until I'd established a rapport – or not – with the mystery man. I was picked up from the flat in Putney that I was living in at the time by a driver in a Bentley and taken to the Windows Bar at the Hilton Park Lane, where I nervously met the two men, who stood as I approached. I grinned as soon as I realised who my date was; I remembered him immediately.

I was dressed in jeans, a coral-coloured silk top and white leather Converse. I hadn't been told at that stage who his father was, but president's son or not, I wasn't about to start wearing designer clothes. I didn't have any, for a start, and as for a dress and heels, that wasn't my style.

Henrik soon left the two of us necking champagne. My date was a 'Friday Muslim', it seemed: mosque once a week, and wine and women the rest. I secretly sniffed coke in the toilet, but the long jokes he told didn't seem to get any funnier the buzzier I got.

Nothing out of the ordinary took place until we were leaving the bar to go to the last place on earth I wanted to be after whacking nearly two grams of charlie up my snout: a restaurant. He wrapped his arm around my waist and we strolled towards the lifts. From nowhere, three men huddled up close to us, and by that I mean it suddenly got very cosy. I panicked and thought we were getting mugged, yet the guy I was with seemed at ease. It all happened very quickly. I asked him what was going on and he muttered something about 'security' and told me that they'd been in the bar for the whole duration. This made me shudder. I'd been spied on and hadn't had a clue. All five of us stood in the lift in silence. I felt more than a tad peculiar about the whole set-up. We went to Henrik's club, where we were fussed over to the point where it was annoying. Later, when I came to leave, I was offered my date's American bodyguard's phone number, not his own, for 'security purposes'.

I felt like I was involved with the Mafia, and what were my thoughts on the matter? The only thing I cared about was whether, through them, I might get hold of some cocaine of a higher calibre than I'd ever tried before.

Sabrina and Stacey were doing and saying nothing as Maggie was rummaging around in my bag like an old fogey at a jumble sale, taking out my belongings, shaking tobacco flakes off them and questioning me about her findings. At the time, I couldn't understand why the girls were there. Witnesses, I later decided, to make sure that I didn't try to accuse Maggie of stealing anything. Feeling stressed as I moved my arse around my seat, I took my brown hair extensions out of their ponytail and put them back up in exactly the same way.

'Can I do anything?' asked Stacey.

'Get us a bin bag, will ya? You've a right load of trash in here, Katie.' I guessed what she was going to say next. 'You can tell a lot by the state of a woman's bag.' *So predictable.* 'Messy bag, messy mind.' *Not very original. Two out of ten, Maggie; try harder.*

I wasn't concerned about what she would find. There wouldn't be any drugs; they were always used on the night they were bought. Worst case? Empty cocaine wraps. But what did she expect? I was a cokehead. In fact, if she *didn't* find any, I'd feel a fraud being in a rehab.

I smirked in Sabrina's direction, but she seemed oblivious

to everything. Stacey was stony-faced and looking right at me, which gave me the creeps.

Then she said, 'How old are you, if you don't mind me asking?'

Why do people say, 'If you don't mind me asking?' They're about to ask anyway, so just get on with it. And why does anyone get offended if someone asks their age? It's a perfectly reasonable question.

'Ask me anything – if things here are anything like the last place I was in, you're going to know what my favourite sexual position and my bra size are soon, anyway,' I smirked.

'What is it?' Stacey probed.

'Very funny. So, moving quickly on' – we all laughed – 'I'm 26.' I wasn't about to mention my upcoming birthday.

'You're, like, three years younger than me,' said Sabrina, which surprised me and clearly her also. She seemed younger.

'Are you saying I look old? Actually, don't answer that!'

'You won't need these,' Maggie held up two unopened condoms.

'I might if I get lucky.'

'Fat chance,' Sabrina said. We held eye contact for longer than was necessary, then she pulled away.

'I can assure you that you won't be getting shtupped round here, girl.'

There was more chance of my falling through a crack in the floor than getting rogered. Rules and routine were paramount to achieve an ordered life, so we were told, and, to be fair, I've never heard of an active drug user whose life was organised. The BCH ship was run on a 'Follow the rules or get out!' basis – no exceptions, and this meant absolutely no sex. Apparently.

I looked at the clock. It was 11.30 a.m. It seemed the bag

search was going to take some time. 'Can I use the toilet, please?' I asked Maggie.

'One of you take Katie to the bathroom, will you?'

Sabrina stood up and I followed her.

CHAPTER 5

I could hear voices coming from the main room as I entered the toilet.

'It's all right, I'll just wait for you here,' my blonde chaperone informed me. *Is she actually going to stand and wait for me outside the door?*

I pulled the light on, imagining the drawstring was riddled with bacteria. I checked the toilet seat, pulled down my jeans and sat. I was too knackered to hover above the seat as I usually did in a public toilet. My eyes darted around. Was there dirt lurking in the corners? My mind was rattling with minutiae. The air felt heavy. One deep breath and I could easily have thrown up. The irony was that I often lived in squalor. I wouldn't do the dishes for days, and sometimes I'd even thrown away plates rather than wash them up.

Suddenly, from nowhere, I had a vision of myself sniffing and drinking. *You'll never get through 12 fucking weeks of this shit. Why bother trying?* my internal goblin began. 'Don't fuck this up, Kate,' I said out loud.

Drugs were how I usually quietened my mind, but I didn't have any and I wouldn't be having any anytime soon. *No more powder? No more vodka? Ever? I can't do it. I can't do this*. This was my life now. It was my choice, I knew, but in that moment it terrified me. I wanted to scream. I flushed the loo and stared into the mirror at someone I didn't recognise. I was facing a future I knew nothing about.

I was into my second hour, and had more than 2,000 left to get through. Would I feel like this every day for the next few months? If so, I wouldn't make it.

I found Sabrina, true to her word, outside the loo. We shuffled back towards Maggie's office.

'Oh, excuse me!' said a skinny ginger guy, who flung his arm dramatically in front of the fella he was with to prevent us all from bumping into one another. How gallant. *Twat*. Sabrina teased him, he 'touché'd her, but the guy he was with didn't make a sound and neither did I.

The boring bag search was over and Maggie told me to go with the girls into the inner sanctum: the group room. I felt like vomiting. No doubt people would be in my face, asking my name, where I was from and what I was on. Just like the '90s rave scene, except that here we referred to drug use in the past tense.

'I still can't believe you recognised me from Yorkshire,' said Stacey suspiciously. As far as I was concerned, that conversation was over. My sole focus was on entering the new arena.

I felt I was moving in slow motion. I could hear noise – other people. I wished they'd fuck off; I wished I could disappear. The girls already had, into the room. I stopped. I wanted to run. My heart was racing. I'd messed up *again and again*, and here I was *again* facing the consequences.

Sabrina popped her head round the corner. I was rooted to the spot. Somebody passed me. 'How do?' I didn't answer.

'Come on,' Sabrina said, beckoning to me.

'Uh-uh . . . no, I can't,' I said, blinking ferociously. I wanted my dad; I wanted Jim; I wanted to cry.

'OK?' Sabrina asked.

Do I look O-fucking-K? I sniffed.

'You've made it this far, Kate, babe. Come on now. You owe it to yourself to take this final step.'

My legs were wobbly. Blondie said something else. She sounded far away. I was about to collapse. I brushed along the wall as I tried to get back to Maggie's office, barely feeling the floor underneath my feet.

'I can't go in there. I'm going to throw up . . . I think I'm going to pass out and, er, I don't know what to do.' I sat on the floor, then stood up again. 'Everything is . . . er, I've ruined my life and . . .' I bent over, trying to catch my breath.

Sabrina caught up with me. 'Are you OK, Katie?'

No! No! No! I'm NOT OK. Nothing is OK, OK?

'Come with me. You'll be fine,' Maggie said.

'I can't, I can't do it. I can't move. I just can't go in there.' I must have looked in pain; I was in pain. 'My head's all over the place. Maggie? *Maggie?* Please . . .' I whimpered. 'Oh my God, oh my God. Please. Please can someone help me? I don't know what to do. I'm losing it. I don't know what to do.' I held my head in my hands. I sat back down on the floor.

'Slow, deep breaths, Katie. Come on, girl, get up, you're going to be all right.'

No I'm not. No I'm not. No I'm not!

'Kate, come with me. Stand up.'

'No, no, no, I can't. What's happening to me? I feel really fucking odd. I don't think I can stay here.' I started beating my clenched fists on the wall.

'Stop that! Stop that!' Maggie yanked my arm and dragged me to my feet. I burst into tears.

'I need to leave. I'm going to leave. I want to go home.'

'Deep breaths, Katie.'

'No, I can't!'

'Right, come on.'

'I'm going to fall over.'

'You're going to be all right. Remain focused, Katie. Breathe. Atta girl! Come on. Slow, deep breaths. Let's get you into the bathroom, get some tissues, blow your nose and put some cold water on your face, eh? That's going to help. You'll be OK. Now go on in there.' It sounded simple. 'Off you go.'

'Someone's in there,' I panted, wiping my eyes.

'No they're not. Go on!' Maggie's hand fluttered towards the door, and her jangling silver bracelets shooed me away.

I chanted out loud, with each blast of water that hit my face, that I was going to be OK. My tears had stopped. I came out to Maggie, who told me to 'come along'. I did, following straight behind her into the smoky room. She ordered me to sit, so I sat. Any attitude I'd previously given her had gone down the pisser along with my stinking urine (courtesy of a kidney infection).

I cowered in the corner and focused on the carpet. I'd managed stage one. Stacey pulled a chair close; Sabrina made me a cuppa. I lit a cigarette and another girl, Camille, who was scarily anorexic, came to introduce herself with a handshake. I couldn't help but stare at her. I'd seen more meat on a butcher's pencil. The poor lass looked lifeless, completely asexual, and her age was impossible to guess. What was clear, though, frighteningly clear, was that she was banging on death's door.

I carefully peered around and began to feel calmer. Much calmer. More people ignored than acknowledged me. Good. Sabrina made chitchat about my journey there and whether it was cold outside. I wasn't interested and neither was she, but it was better than being asked personal questions. Within moments, two blokes nodded hello and another girl waved at me. Thankfully, they all kept their distance, and judging by the look of them, I was glad that they did.

CHAPTER 6

RULES
- Sexual contact of any kind and sexually suggestive behaviour are not permitted.
- Clients must always be accompanied by a counsellor or another client when leaving the centre and may not leave without permission.

'There are no fit guys here! Is this everyone?' The moment I opened my mouth, I regretted it. My other addiction was sexual attention.

'Yeah, just about,' replied Sabrina.

'So is this all the girls?'

'Yeah,' Stacey nodded.

'With all these guys you'd think there would be at least one that was half-decent-looking, wouldn't you? They're all pretty grim.' I was now definitely feeling better.

Sabrina twitched her nose. Stacey gave me a look of displeasure. I was only trying to have a laugh. She needed to get fisted to take that miserable look off her face. But it was good to learn quickly the stances that people took on various issues.

Camille's response to my faux pas? Nada. She seemed introverted yet intense, coming across as wholly inaccessible, emotionless and isolated.

OK, before arriving at BCH I'd spent too much time having too much sex with too many strangers, so wasn't I sick of men? Not in this context. A bit of flirting would be the only aspect of 'normal' life I'd be able to replicate within the confines of this unnatural environment. Despite my nerves feeling destroyed, my habit of surveying my surroundings for suitable males remained intact. Rules or no rules, at some point I had to find a distraction. My fragile ego needed this. It was all I had left.

In rehab, expressing an interest in sex was frowned upon. It was a dangerous form of escapism, apparently, a distraction from the reasons we were in there. However, annoyingly, some people behaved as though they were virgins and had never in their lives thought of doing anything illicit. This stank of being a diversionary tactic to avoid scrutiny and keep the focus on the 'naughty ones' who weren't playing nicely. But avoiding scrutiny in BCH was like avoiding indigestion after eating tarmac. And the reality was that quite a few of my new comrades had come straight from prison, and others had fucked men and women, or both, for cash and drugs.

I'd nearly lost my mind, but not my eyesight. I wanted to find something to occupy my mind other than myself. What harm would that do? I still had a few days' grace before I was expected to follow the protocol, so my lustful comments, although I'm certain they were noted, were dismissed.

Moments later, Maggie, with her huge hippy mane, came into the room and called my name. Like an obedient puppy,

I clambered out of my nest and followed her to the kitchen. Medication time. Instantly, I felt alive – just as, when I was using drugs, from the moment I was on my way to score I didn't feel a fraction as rough as I had done before I was on my way to get what I needed.

Two blokes were doing the washing-up and bantering with Maggie, but I ignored them, opting to focus on the pills. My plan was to neck them, sit down, not talk to anyone or have anyone talk to me, and wait for the drugs to kick in.

No chance.

'Pass us a glass of water,' Maggie chirped.

The ginger washer-upper, one of the guys whom I'd nearly bumped into in the corridor, had pre-empted her request. Clearly, I wasn't the only one with my mind on the drugs.

'Nice to meet you. I'm Simon.' He sounded posh, which surprised me.

Maggie randomly started singing. 'I love Billie Holiday,' she said. 'And that song is one of my all-time favourites. "Summertime" – do you know it?' I did, but that was the last thing on my mind. One swig of council pop and the Librium was gone.

'Open your mouth.'

'Are you joking?'

'If I was, I'd say, "A horse walked into a pub and ordered a pint of . . ." Of course I'm not joking,' Maggie answered.

I was in rehab for a cocaine problem. A pill freak I was not, but a buzz is a buzz. Even so, I couldn't help but think that if I wanted drugs I'd have paid for them, stuffed them into my vagina and brought them in that way. What I wouldn't have done was sneakily collect soggy tablets that I was meant to have swallowed for a cheap thrill later. Besides, let's face it, why choose to go into rehab in the first place if you don't want to change? I could think of more fun ways to while away a few months of my life.

Group therapy: 'The members of this group all share the same problems: alcoholism, chemical dependency and eating disorders. Through these sessions we share our experience, strengths and hopes, so that we may help each other through identification and understanding and the realisation that we are not alone.'

My first group began. After that, I remember nothing – for days. Librium is powerful stuff. *You think you can use drugs? Bang! OK, I'm going to show you.* Even heroin addicts with collapsed veins were slammed sideways by this shit, which is used to relax muscles and encourage sleep – in elephants, I'm guessing. The impact was massive: unsteadiness, confusion and blurred vision. The pills were to depress overactivity in the brain and to prevent the addict noticing that the chemicals they'd become accustomed to were no longer entering their system. In case this wasn't enough, for the first seven nights I was also given sleeping pills fifteen minutes before bedtime at 10 p.m. Bedtimes were between 10.30 and 11.15, except for people on detox. Some had detoxed before they arrived. The people doing detox questioned those who claimed to have already done one before arriving. Although no one admitted it, seeds of doubt sprouted – were they legit or were they just claiming to be addicts to justify their lives and relationships being wrecks?

During those first days, when I wasn't in group I slept and slept and slept, trying to recoup the rest that I'd failed to acquire over the preceding years. This was the only time during rehab that I was pretty much left alone.

I had nightmares most nights, and not just during the detox.

I'd wake up crying, shaking and wet with sweat.

I put on more than a stone in weight within the first two weeks.

We all, except Camille, troughed unashamedly. The thing that Camille both loved and detested was not only everywhere, but was seen by most people not only as normal but as something to look forward to, healthy and utterly essential in order to exist. She was withholding from herself one of the very few primary requirements in order to remain alive. How much must she have hated herself?

I hadn't eaten properly for years, certainly not the type of home-cooked fodder that was being prepared for us by Antonia, the comfortingly motherly cook-cum-housekeeper. The reason we didn't have to cook for ourselves was so that we could focus solely on our mental health. I knew that shutting up the barrage in my head would indeed be a full-time job. However, in the centre we all did chores such as dusting and hoovering. Easy as this may sound, a holiday camp this was absolutely, categorically not.

CHAPTER 7

RULE

- Clients are not permitted to be alone in their bedrooms
  for more than ten minutes at a time.

Of course, some clever arses would have their ten minutes, loiter downstairs for five, then go back to their room for another ten. This wasn't allowed, and you could count on some tool noticing and then grassing you up in a group.

Initially, I shared an en suite room with Sabrina, who'd already been there for a month: two single beds, two sets of drawers and matching wardrobes, made from the same wood as school furniture.

'What brought you here?' I asked her.

'I was drinking too much,' she answered. 'No, nothing else,' she confirmed when I asked if there was anything more. I didn't get it. How could a girl like her be in a rehab for 'just' alcohol? *Fucking lightweight.* Now, if she'd been drinking meths, fair enough. But she hadn't. The culprit was cider.

'I reckon I'm starting to feel a bit better, you know. I can remember what happened yesterday,' I laughed as we got ready one morning. I'd been inside just over a week. It was an appropriate day for me to be entering my new beginning, my 27th birthday, but I'd kept quiet about that.

'It takes a while until you start coming round. I was out of it for a couple of weeks after I got here. My life's in such a state, I reckon I didn't want to properly wake up cos I didn't want to face it. I've got a daughter . . .'

'Really?'

'Yeah, she's three, bless her, and if I don't sort myself out I'll lose her. And believe me, I'll do whatever I have to do to stop that from happening.'

'I can imagi– '

'Anyway, listen, I want to tell you something.'

'Shit, what is it? That sounds –'

'No, don't worry. It's nothing serious – I'm just saying, OK?'

'Oh no. What are you going to tell me? Urrgh, what's that on your arm? That looks painful.'

'It's nothing.'

'It doesn't look like nothing. It looks nasty.'

'It's just a scar. Please don't talk about it,' she said dismissively and turned away.

'How did it happen?'

'I'll tell you later . . . Anyway, look, as I was saying, do you remember standing up in the group the other day and telling Daryl that he didn't know what he was talking about?'

My heart rate instantly soared. Panic.

'Oh my God, are you serious? Did I? I don't even know who Daryl is. Oh, please say you're joking.' She wasn't. 'When was this exactly?'

Did she really have to tell me this? It felt like when you've been pissed and someone says, 'Ooh, you'll never guess what you did last night!' Fucking sanctimony. Hate it.

'I wasn't in the group. I was told about it, that's all.'

'So people have been talking about it? Haven't they got enough of their own problems to think about instead of talking about me, for fuck's sake? Was I that bad?'

'If you'd really been troublesome, I don't think you'd still be here, so I wouldn't worry too much about it.'

'How can I not, now you've told me? Is this Daryl in this house?'

'He's in Hazelwood, the fellas' house. Anyway, come on. You ready?' My mind was buzzing with apprehension. 'Let's go downstairs. We can't be late or we'll have to cop for it on Monday morning.'

• *to cop* = to declare what rules have been broken.

'You've straightened your duvet, yeah? You don't want them on your case about having a scruffy bed.'

'Hold on a minute, let me just get an iron to make sure it's really smooth,' I said with a wry grin. She didn't know whether or not I was joking.

'At least you'll be able to call your mum and dad or boyfriend or whoever, now you've finished your detox. Bet they're dying to hear from you,' Sabrina said enthusiastically as we all sauntered quietly down the street from the house where our rooms were towards the centre HQ. The residents of Weymouth knew who we were. There were numerous drug rehabs in the small town and our reputation preceded us. This made me self-conscious. I hated being seen as part of the group and being judged badly for it.

We arrived a few minutes after Hazelwood. Every day, the

ritual was this: whichever house arrived at the centre first would sit and wait for the rest, who would then walk in single file around the room greeting the group that was already there. We could usually manage this without too much monkeying around, but Neanderthal thwacks on the back were, of course, obligatory. Within a few minutes, a counsellor would enter, shout out our names and tell us which room we should be in for our 9.30 session.

We'd then trot off to our relevant rooms and pull our seats into a circle. The preamble would be read out. This was a basic explanation about what was about to happen.

In turn, we'd introduce ourselves by name and state the nature of our addiction: 'I'm Katie, an addict alcoholic.' Saying 'I'm an addict alcoholic' might have stuck in my throat had I not accepted that this was my truth; still, if I'd thought about the words I'd have grinned like an idiot, cos I felt like one, sticking a big fat label on myself. The scary thing is that admitting to this comes with responsibility: the responsibility to change. That's the reason the admission is such a seminal part of the 12 Steps. Aligning myself with the stereotypical view of an alkie – a bed-wetting, bedsit-dwelling, white-cider-drinking drunk who pisses and craps in public – was not at all sexy.

After this, the counsellor would ask one of us to read a short daily meditation, which always ended with the words: 'Just for today I shall . . .' We were expected to have already filled in the blank space that followed and relate it to the reading. 'Just for today I shall hope that these twats I'm here with would disappear' was not the right answer. I felt like a dickhead doing this, and judging by the smirks on some other people's faces they did too.

The counsellor would then start by talking about a specific

aspect of recovery, or the group would be thrown open. This was an opportunity for anyone who had something on their mind to discuss it and, just like in school, if you wanted to contribute you'd raise your hand. The sessions were intense and emotive, and I immediately felt some benefits.

At the end, we would all stand up, link hands and say the Serenity Prayer:

> **God grant me the serenity to accept the things I cannot change, the courage to change the things I can, and the wisdom to know the difference.**

CHAPTER 8

'Kate, please come to reception,' Maggie shouted, like a sergeant major. Was I in trouble? I didn't think I'd done anything wrong, but I couldn't be sure. I was so used to things turning to crap.

There, in front of Magda, were two bunches of flowers. The card on the larger bunch read: 'Happy birthday, keep up the good work, Pet. xxx.' Jimmy. It gave me a much-needed nudge in the right direction. The other bunch was daffodils, my favourite flowers, from Dad and Elaine. Immediately, my eyes filled with tears.

'May the forthcoming year bring you peace and the happiness that you deserve. Many happy returns xxx xxx' *Six kisses!* He hadn't forgotten me; he hadn't forgotten! I wondered how he knew where I was.

Jim I was thrilled to hear from, but when it came to my father any joy was short-lived and always shaded with sadness. I couldn't hide my urge to start wailing. I touched the words, hoping it would make me feel closer to him.

'These are from my dad,' I said proudly to Maggie. I wiped tears from my cheek and Magda reached over to stroke my arm.

*

This was different from the previous year, when none of my friends were talking to me. That included Petra, my former partner in crime, whom I couldn't stand and stomached just cos we were both trapped in the same lifestyle. Then, I'd not heard from my dad for two or so years, and the night before my birthday I'd done my usual and gone out alone in my local area, Putney, chatting to anyone who would talk to me. I'd been sniffing coke and drinking by myself for most of the day. The more fucked-up I felt, the more I wanted to feel a connection with someone – a friend, a stranger, anyone . . .

I texted a punter whom I'd seen twice. He seemed non-threatening, was average-looking, had a nice house in Walton on Thames, a bit middle class for a supposedly single early-30s bloke, but so what? He'd told me he was a copper, which had made me paranoid, in spite of him claiming that he'd done MDMA and pills sometimes when he went out 'partying with the lads'. He replied to my text with a phone call.

I got a taxi to his place. The guy's mate answered the door. There was a lot of booze around, which we all indulged in between dancing and puffing on weed. He told me he had two Ecstasy pills and asked if I wanted him to score some more. I wasn't interested in Ecstasy. I had a bit of coke left and I'd kept quiet about it. I wasn't sure in what capacity I was there, but it didn't take too long before I was watching the guy who'd answered the door sucking off the other. I was mesmerised. Next thing, the copper came over to where I was slouched and started groping my pussy through my jeans. I was compliant and gave it the obligatory groans to placate his ego, but I couldn't feel a damn thing.

'You don't mind my boyfriend joining us while I do you, do you?' he breathed. *Do me? Right. OK.* The boyfriend –

boyfriend! – was standing in the background tossing himself off. I was wasted, more so than I'd expected to be. In fact, I felt oddly out of it. Had my drink been spiked? I tried saying something, but the words wouldn't come out. I was on the sofa with one leg out of my jeans and by now the policeman was fully naked with his head between my legs lapping at my cunt while the boyfriend fucked his arsehole – meaning every stroke, by the sounds of it.

'Are you going to give your father a call this evening?'

'Can I?'

'I don't see why not. Surely you're due a telephone call now?' Maggie grinned. 'You've finished your detox, haven't you?' She knew I had. 'So why not?'

I felt nervous about the possibility of speaking to my dad. I hoped he'd speak to me, now that he and Elaine knew that I was trying to change. His aspirations for me to become an academic like him had long gone. Now he just wanted me to be safe and coherent.

When I went back into the group room, I felt relief and sadness. Dad had made contact. He could have ignored the information he'd got about me being in rehab again so that he wouldn't have to deal with the pain it must have caused him. But whoever had told him – it had to have been Jim – must have presented it in a positive manner.

In a moment of excitement, I told Stacey, who was sitting next to me, that it was my birthday and she took the liberty of shouting this out. Tessa, a mid-30s, short, dark-haired, blue-eyed lairy Londoner who'd arrived three days after me, came over to tick me off for not having mentioned it sooner. We hugged. I liked her. She was very tactile and that suited my need to give affection. We'd had very different upbringings;

both her parents were heroin addicts who had died from overdoses. Neither of us knew it then, but her story was to inspire my recovery more than that of anyone else I met.

Everyone started singing 'Happy Birthday'. I started blushing, but I felt a part of something. I wasn't alone.

RULE
- When making phone calls, clients must be considerate towards others. There is only one phone for clients' use and calls are therefore to be kept to a maximum of ten minutes.

We could make or receive one call a day, lasting no more than ten minutes. This was an area where some people really took the piss and others got jealous because they got fewer calls, or none.

I couldn't remember the last time I'd spoken to my father or stepmum. They usually slammed the phone down and pulled the wire out of the wall within moments. This caused me to feel:

1. A failure
2. Alone
3. Hated
4. Hysterical
5. Resentful/angry
6. Tearful
7. Anxious
8. Betrayed
9. Exasperated
10. Self-blame

UNHOOKED

This is how my father felt about my lifestyle and me while he was slamming the phone down:

1. A failure
2. Alone
3. Hated
4. Hysterical
5. Resentful/angry
6. Tearful
7. Anxious
8. Betrayed
9. Exasperated
10. Self-blame

Stalemate.

I asked five people to join me in a mini-group. Three of them had also been estranged from their parents.

'There's no reason for you to be defensive with your dad, Kate, cos you're not hiding anything about what you're doing. Why would he get angsty with you, eh? You're in treatment now, mate, getting help, and he'll know that. If your pops is anything like my ma, he'll just be pleased that you're not begging money from him every five minutes.' This was Stacey.

I hadn't asked my dad for money since I was 17. I'd turned to shoplifting and later touted my gash for cash so that I didn't ever have to beg from anyone. But I kept this to myself.

'But I feel ashamed, you know . . . I feel that . . .'

'That you've let them down?' Billy chipped in.

I nodded. This was the first time I'd spoken to him. I'd noticed he seemed to spend most of his time with Austin. They were the two oldest clients in there. Billy was an Oxford University graduate, a British Muslim and a chiropodist who'd had a five-year dependency on barbiturates and alcohol that had begun when his wife left him for a younger man. He later told me that as a result of his drinking he'd stopped working, his Highgate house had been repossessed, he'd been banned from driving for speeding. 'Before that I was caught driving after I'd had a drink. They didn't even have the decency to ban me for that. I got a warning and points.'

His parents had disowned him for being 'a drunken buffoon', to quote his father, and his sister had sided with his ex-wife after catching him watching *Anal Bandits Second Cumming* online – in his own house, on his own computer. Her kids could stumble on the file the next time they visited him, she said. 'Not that they did. Visit,' he told me. Apparently, his breaking point had come when his two pet hamsters escaped from their cage. One had been found drowned in a drain outside the hostel he'd been staying at in Westminster and the other was never heard of again. Two weeks afterwards he'd begged the money from his parents to get him into treatment. That was three weeks ago.

In that first mini-group, of course, I didn't know any of that. Billy's response to my admission of my feelings of guilt was to say, 'Darling, we all make mistakes.' That comment didn't seem an adequate response to the situation I was in with my dad.

He continued, 'Look, you've gone off the path that your father wanted you to follow, but that's done now, my love. You cannot change the past.' *Nothing like stating the obvious.* 'You're here to change your future. That's all that matters, surely. Yesterday or an hour ago is gone. It's in this moment where life is happening.'

Sage Billy had spoken. Everyone grunted in agreement. It's true that Dad didn't want me to be publicly persecuted for crimes against humanity – that is, my behaviour towards him – he wanted me to be well, to thrive, to succeed and at least be content with my life, even if I couldn't be truly happy. It was easy for me to feel I needed to be hurt for the pain I'd caused him.

My new housemates, strangers weeks before, were now an integral part of my life. They'd given me a boost of encouragement, so I called my dad.

'Katie, happy birthday! We're pleased to hear from you.' He always spoke as though he were a conjoined twin, with Elaine being his cling-on, and it never failed to get on my nerves. But much more importantly than that, he'd used the words 'pleased to hear from you' – to me!

'Thank you for the flowers. They're really pretty, Daddy. Thanks so much. I really appreciate you sending me them. They're gorgeous . . .' I wanted to thank him a million times for not forgetting me.

'You're most welcome . . . So . . . How are you?'

He hadn't asked me that for a very long time. He'd avoided this question for years, knowing I'd be in a right old pickle. He never wanted to hear it.

'Well . . . I'm back in rehab. In Weymouth this time. I thought it would be better to try a new place.'

'Jim came round and told us,' Dad said. His voice sounded strong.

'Really? I'm surprised. He came to your house? What, just like that?'

'Yes, he did. Of course, initially I thought . . .'

'Bet you thought I'd been found raped in a back alley.'

'Don't say that, Kate, please.'

'Sorry.'

'But you're right; we didn't expect him to be the bearer of good news.'

'Oh, gosh. I'm in a treatment centre for the second time and you're saying this is good news?' I chortled.

'Well, it is good news, Kate. Elaine and I want you to be well. We've talked a lot about this. We're both very happy that you've taken this step to help yourself again.'

'I'm sorry if Jim worried you, Daddy.'

'Not at all. We welcomed him in and he stayed for a cup of tea and some home-made lemon meringue pie, which he seemed to enjoy. Anyway, we both thought it kind of him to let us know of your whereabouts . . .' (Awkward silence.) 'And of course we asked him about his artworks and how his furniture business is doing. It seems to be going very well indeed from what he tells us, Kate.'

'Yes, it is. You know how I've always said how talented he is.'

'Yes, I'm sure he is.' I knew avoiding real issues made things easier for my dad to deal with. He tried desperately to keep my life and struggles wholly separate from his by never speaking about how I was feeling or what was going on with me. Under the circumstances, though, he couldn't really avoid asking about me.

'So how are things in there?'

I half laughed. 'Well, I'm trying, that's for sure. I don't really know what to say, except that things got a bit out of hand before I came back here.' My mind flashed onto Hassan, Sam and the bigamy, and the fact that I'd smuggled three kilos of cannabis from Africa to England in an attempt to get some money while avoiding having to open my legs to a stranger. 'But I'm trying to sort things out again now.'

'You've no idea just how thrilled we are to hear this, Kate.

64

That makes us very, very happy.' Now he sounded fragile. Every fibre of my being was screeching at me to apologise to him for being a failure as a daughter, but I'd said sorry so many times that it was time to prove myself through actions, not words.

Silence.

'I'd better go, I'm sorry. I don't want to, but I only get a few minutes on the phone. They're strict with rules here.'

'Glad to hear it.' He was smiling; I could hear it in his voice.

'Well, anyway . . . I love you,' I blurted out.

'And we love you.' I wished to God he'd just say *he* loved me without including Elaine. But I'd take whatever was given.

'And Dad . . . I'm sorry.' I had to say it.

'It's all right, Kate. Just try this time. Please, for your sake, not mine, just try this time.'

In that moment, I hated myself for the hurt I'd caused him. I managed to get into the bathroom before thumping my head with my fists and calling myself filthy names as I cried.

CHAPTER 9

RULE

- Clients are expected to spend time with everyone in the group and are not permitted to form SRs (special relationships), especially male–female ones.

It was going to be difficult to find a male distraction to soothe me during my 12 weeks of anal law-abiding institutionalisation, but I desperately wanted to find someone to flirt with. I discovered that the guy who'd been walking down the corridor with Simon on the day I'd arrived was called Leon. He was softly spoken, white, a bit skinny, with dark, shaved hair, plump lips and big, dark, almost oriental eyes that made him look extraterrestrial – appropriate since he seemed to be a bit of a space cadet, lost in his own thoughts more often than not. He had that ugly-pretty thing going on; at some angles he veered more to the former than the latter. Since I already had two husbands, I wasn't searching for a third, so it wasn't as if he had to be anywhere close to perfect.

Leon was shorter than me, which I hated, and when he walked it was almost apologetically, hunched slightly forward. I wished he'd stand upright. He needed every millimetre he could get. He told me he was in rehab after being given the choice by a judge to do time either in here or in prison. This was his penance for having burgled a jewellery shop; he'd got caught trying to flog the goods to an undercover cop in a pawnshop. Bad luck. Sounded to me like he'd been watching too many crime dramas on TV. He had a scar on his neck that had apparently been obtained during a previous attempted heist, aged 14; it added character to an otherwise boyish face. Nice. 'A bit of a rude boy,' he said.

I was surprised by his story. He seemed more like a doped-up smackhead than a hyper crackhead, and certainly he seemed too gentle to be a burglar. Not my usual flavour, it has to be said, but a girl's gotta do something for light entertainment.

I knew that sexual activity, even flirting, was punishable by expulsion, so a bit of a clandestine tête-à-tête would have to be executed with precision and utter secrecy, but I was determined to try. Why? Insecurity. I wanted to know that I was still desirable, despite feeling like a dirty, good-for-nothing slapper – and that was before I'd broken any of the rules.

Before arriving in BCH, I'd used sexuality to survive in my lonely and limited world, and to cut that out immediately, like drugs and drink, would have felt beyond weird. Using sex was another dependency I had to work on eradicating, but one thing at a time. My priority was to free myself from chemicals, not male attention.

Cocaine and alcohol had had an extremely destructive impact on my life, while boning, albeit damaging in the way in which I'd participated in it, had been a secondary issue, and I wasn't prepared to go cold turkey.

Leon was twenty-three years old, four years younger than I was. That was OK. For a time, I'd take him under my wing.

I'd soon put an end to his Reebok-wearing habit.

'I thought we were roughly the same age,' I said.

'You said that the other day.'

'Oh God, sorry, I'd totally forgotten. Those pills did me in, you know.'

'No worries. It's cool.'

'Well, it's not that cool, is it? Cos I was out of it for the first few days.'

'And you're complaining about that?' He grinned, glancing at me with feline eyes. He had surprisingly white teeth for a crack fiend. Usually they have no teeth, or black ones if they're lucky.

'Well, you know . . . it's a bit embarrassing when I can't even remember what went on, or what I did, or who I spoke to.'

'Most people are fucked when they get here, babe – excuse my swearing.'

'Oh, fucking swear all you like.' *'Babe', eh? Maybe he's not as shy as he looks.*

'Yeah, I suppose . . . it's rehab, innit?'

'Yeah, we're not exactly in a nunnery, you know.'

'In a what?'

'A nunnery. You know, the female equivalent to a monastery.'

'A nunastery?'

'Oh, nothing, I was only teasing.'

'Fair enough . . . Anyway, from what I've seen, them detox meds are making people more loco than when they arrive, innit?'

We both laughed. I scanned the room and saw Simon, who'd grown one of those stupid strips of facial hair under his bulbous bottom lip, standing with his arms crossed. He smirked at me. I didn't like the way he looked at me.

'Were you in a bad way with them, then?' I asked Leon.

'I'd done a detox before I came here, get me?' he replied sheepishly.

Simon was still watching us. Billy pulled up a chair next to me, said, 'Hello, my love,' and then just sat staring into space.

'Where?'

'My ends. Tooting, innit?'

'In London?' *No, Tooting on planet fucking Mars.*

'Yes, mate, I'm a London boy through and through, innit?'

He sounded like one of those Kray-like geezers who 'treats 'er indoors with the respect she deserves' – before bashing her upside the head after he's had a beer with the boys. *Judgemental? Fuck it.*

'You're Northern, huh?' he asked, suddenly stopping my internal snob in her tracks.

'Yeah.'

'Ah, someone's gotta be, don't worry about it.'

I laughed quietly and so did he.

The way Leon had said 'huh?' reminded me of Hassan, husband number two. I *had* to resolve the mess I was in, but how? I was better able to explain the theory of relativity than answer that, and for now I couldn't dwell on it.

I'd married Hassan in Gambia. I'd gone there to escape London and ended up staying for a year. Most of the local people must have thought I was a nightmare. I wasn't the friendliest or most rational drunk on the block, and there weren't even too many contenders for the crown. Gambia's a Muslim country and most people don't drink alcohol.

Why I'd married Hassan while married to Sam and got myself involved in such a stupid situation eluded, disturbed and shamed me. I knew that what I was doing was wrong when I did it and I was scared, but I still went ahead. When I said the vows in front of Hassan's family while wearing a home-made ivory dress, I was wincing inside. Yet I forged on. Maybe I'd wanted to martyr myself, validate my 'goodness' by trying to help someone get a visa to my own detriment. I could travel freely throughout the world, so why should a small piece of paper dictate Hassan's terms?

I had no problem with helping someone to get a visa, but what drove me to distraction was using marriage to do it. And the fact that I was already married to another person when I got hitched to Hassan caused me immense mental torment. So I turned to my trusted method of attempting to eliminate worry: immersing myself in drink and drugs and sex. I tried desperately to rationalise an irrational action. Utterly futile.

Outside of rehab, I'd rather have offered myself up for a trial lobotomy than have admitted to bigamy or prostitution. But if pushed, I'd have confessed first to selling my arse before admitting to the marriages. However, in treatment, you frequently hear that you're 'as sick as your secrets', which puts a whole new perspective on keeping quiet.

CHAPTER 10

Alcohol is a drug. It kills more people than narcotics. Corrosive and highly addictive, it is usually the first place where recovering narcotic drug addicts go wrong, believing it's not dangerous. For an addict, *any* drug, whether legal or illegal, that can alter your state of mind is equivalent to allowing someone to tie a noose around your neck and attach it to a tree and hoping that you don't hang. This time, unlike after my first spell in rehab, I knew that drinking was not an option for me.

The treatment at BCH, as in the centre I'd been to before, was based on the 12 Steps programme developed by Alcoholics Anonymous (AA), a version of which is used in Narcotics Anonymous (NA). The 12 Steps do not focus on which substance has been abused so much as *why* and how to learn to deal with that. The group you choose to join is less important than the principles of the 12 Steps.

The 12 Steps of Alcoholics Anonymous

1. We admitted we were powerless over alcohol and that our lives had become unmanageable.

2. Came to believe that a power greater than ourselves could restore us to sanity.

3. Made a decision to turn our will and our lives over to the care of God as we understood Him.

4. Made a searching and fearless moral inventory of ourselves.

5. Admitted to God, to ourselves, and to another human being the exact nature of our wrongs.

6. Were entirely ready to have God remove all these defects of character.

7. Humbly asked Him to remove our shortcomings.

8. Made a list of all persons we had harmed, and became willing to make amends to them all.

9. Made direct amends to such people wherever possible, except when to do so would injure them or others.

10. Continued to take a personal inventory, and when we were wrong promptly admitted it.

11. Sought through prayer and meditation to improve our conscious contact with God as we understood Him, praying only for knowledge of His will for us and the power to carry that out.

12. Having had a spiritual awakening as the result of these steps, we tried to carry this message to alcoholics, and to practise these principles in all our affairs.

• *The Fellowship* = all groups that follow the 12 Steps programme.

Groups such as Al-Anon run 12 Steps programmes for people affected by the addiction of a friend or family member. This type of emotional sickness is contagious; whoever spends time around a fucked-up person will turn into one if they don't arm themselves against it.

The Steps are written in the past tense, implying that once addicts have found the 12 Steps they have begun the process of change – if they choose it. As in many spiritual disciplines, the newcomer is virtually absolved of past misdemeanours when they commit to this new way. I was certainly held accountable for my past actions, but not wholly responsible. We were told that until we had gained knowledge of how to manage our thinking, we could not be held responsible for our actions. It is said that no one finds themselves in a 12 Step meeting by accident.

In BCH, as in most 12 Step rehabs, the focus was on Steps 1 to 3, although some also concentrate on Step 4 and Step 5, which go hand in hand. Step 4 is self-reflective written work, based on a series of questions that can be found in the AA and NA literature. Of all the Steps, this is the one that highlights the person's flaws the most, so it takes guts to embark on it. Step 5 is simply reading out and discussing your Step 4 answers to someone, a counsellor or sponsor. What's a sponsor? Someone of the same sex whose recovery you admire and whom you ask to guide you through the practical side of the steps. As a result of this, a sponsor often becomes a sounding board. However, some Fellowship members would say that no one person is supposed to have too much influence over another's recovery.

Since I'd already done Steps 4 and 5 during my first spell in rehab, I didn't have to do them again at BCH. In hindsight, it seems slightly ludicrous that someone returning from a relapse does not have to do Steps 4 and 5 in rehab before they get the all-clear to leave. A number of years had passed since my first time, and I'd gone back into treatment worse than I was the first time. Of course, I said nothing. I didn't want to extend the time of my incarceration.

In any case, the most essential, and most worked on, Steps

are numbers 1, 2 and 3. These are the foundations for change. Without an ingrained belief in these Steps, there will be no recovery.

AA Steps 1 to 3: A Brief Explanation

Step 1: *We admitted we were powerless over alcohol and that our lives had become unmanageable.*

Unwittingly, a person looking to change has already practised Step 1 when he or she first attends a 12 Step meeting or goes into rehab. Here, the focus is on the addict admitting – not necessarily accepting (that comes later) – that they had 'no power', in this case over alcohol. Hence they are 'powerless' and are no longer able to manage their life as a result. Therefore their life has become *unmanageable*.

Step 2: *Came to believe that a Power greater than ourselves could restore us to sanity.*

This Step, as with Step 1, needs no action, just thought. The person must decide to seek help from an outside source that *could* (not will, because that's down to them) restore their wellness. An addict cannot change without help and guidance from others.

Step 3: *Made a decision to turn our will and our lives over to the care of God as we understood Him.*

Step 3 encourages people seeking change to make a decision to do something active about trying to change.

With Step 3, the tricky part is the word 'God'. Are you still there? *Please* don't run off. I freaked out too. The first time I went to rehab, I thought I'd stumbled across a religious cult. I'd been an outlaw and was therefore not willing to be preached to about religion. I wanted to change my life, not my lack of faith, and I wasn't alone in this.

I was advised to choose a 'Superpower', a 'Higher Power' wiser than myself whom I'd be willing to let help me. But finding people I considered wiser than me could be difficult. I, like most addicts, thought I knew it all. Most druggies I'd met I thought were dicks. Most didn't know how to spell the word 'decent', never mind live its meaning, but I had to do something, and the obvious choice was to think of 'God' as just another word for 'group'. Within any group, there is a general consensus, an energy flow, so I went with this.

- *turning over my will* = not jumping in and making decisions alone without consulting my superpower (the group) first.

This took humility. I'd lived all my life dismissing others' reactions to my choices. But now I had to take a risk and try something new, even if initially that meant only pretending to trust what the group was telling me. Let's face it, I hadn't been successful in living my life and being my own counsel, so I had to at least believe in the *possibility* that something good could come from this. There was only one guarantee – change comes via only one avenue: application.

RULE

- Clients will be given written work based on the Steps to complete. This work can be an extremely valuable aspect of the treatment and clients are therefore asked to ensure that it is done in a timely fashion. If this work is neglected, the client will not be permitted to progress to the next stage of treatment.

I had begun to write my life story. I would sit in the spartan dining room (where we'd all do our homework in silence for up to two hours each evening) thinking, writing, cringing and wanting to cry. I was going to keep it as simple and as blame-free as I could, even though I knew that not banging on about my dad's failures and my stepmother's input into the breakdown of our relationship would be difficult. But this was about me, not them, which meant I'd also have to admit for the first time since I'd arrived to being a hooker.

The guys in the group in which I was going to read my life story would then read letters to me that they'd written based on listening to my tale of woe. These were the confrontation letters I'd asked Maggie about when I'd been admitted. They'd slate me about everything and make presumptions, which would more than likely be based on their own lives, rather than listening to what I'd said and how I'd said it. To be fair, they'd probably not be far wrong. But the idea of them wiping the floor with me regarding my past as a hooker, which would have to come out, made me feel sick as a rabid dog.

Preconceptions about hookers and ex-hookers

1. They have abusive boyfriends who beat them and treat them appallingly.
2. They will forever fuck someone if the price is right.
3. They will use whoever crosses their path, particularly for money.
4. They are dirty, grubby, unclean, disease-ridden.
5. They're ready for sex at any moment.
6. They'll give you the best fuck of your life.
7. They're all intravenous drug users.
8. They're untrustworthy, scheming bitches.

9. All they care about is money.
10. You can't trust them with your boyfriend . . . or girlfriend,
    for that matter.

'We don't need *War and Peace*,' Maggie had said. 'Maybe four sides of A4. You know, a bit about your childhood, how life was growing up, the start of your drug use and a bit about life just before you came here, OK?'

'Fine.'

'Is that fine meaning "OK"? Or are you feeling fine as in "fucked-up, insecure, neurotic and emotional"?'

'It's fine as in all right. I just don't like to hear stuff about my own life coming from people who don't actually know me and who quite honestly I don't feel are qualified to comment, since half of them can't even add one plus one together. That makes it harder, but there we go . . .'

'Harsh words, Katie.'

And I hadn't really got started yet . . .

CHAPTER 11

RULES

- Clients are asked not to attract attention to themselves or to the group as a whole when outside of the centre.
- Clients may not go out alone. If you are not in the centre or houses, you must be with someone else. This is for clients' safety and to minimise the possibility of relapse.

Daryl plus one was on the rota to get our daily supply of goodies from the newsagent. I longed for this duty. Not only would I escape the centre for a while, but since this honour was only given to people who had been there for a number of weeks and who were seen as doing well in their recovery, it would also prove that I was inching closer to completing.

I was sitting with my back towards the window, enjoying the warmth from the sun beaming onto my neck and earwigging on Austin's war stories from back in the day, when Daryl hobbled towards me. The poor sod would never walk properly again as a result of a fight he'd got into over some weed. Yes, cannabis, you know the one – that harmless natural herb that promotes peace, not violence. He'd been stabbed several times in his leg while he'd been trying to kick another guy 'around the back of the canister with my Timberlands. But it was me who ended up bang in trouble, like. I lost fucking shedloads of blood after that cunt cut me. Fucking pussyhole.' All this had taken place in front of Daryl's two-year-old son, who'd been left crying in his pushchair.

Although he looked tough – some might say rough – Daryl was in fact a sensitive fella whose usual facial expression was that of a man with the weight of the world on his shoulders. Despite him being built big, there was something totally unthreatening about him. Perhaps surprisingly, considering he had a criminal record as long as Pinocchio's nose, he didn't really look like a thug at all, partly thanks to his wispy blond hair (and the fact that he had some hair and had not shaved it off like most of the men in the centre).

'Are you OK, mate?' he asked me.

'Well, I'm fucking sick of being here, for one, and I'm pissed off at Maggie shouting at me in group again yesterday. So in answer to your question, I've been better.'

'Bet you've been worse, too!'

'I don't know, Daryl. I don't know anything . . . I just can't believe what happened in that stupid women's group. That Maggie gets on my nerves, she does.'

Sadistic Fantasy: Maggie getting a heavy slap around the chops. I snatch the stupid spectacles from off her hooked nose and crush them with my bare hands.

'All I said was that I wanted to leave this fucking shit tip. And that fag-hag responded with, "Why? So you can live the life you were living before and screw a man for your train fare home?" Can you fucking believe that?' This was the closest I'd got to referring to my life in Hookerville to anyone.

'But I suppose one good thing happened – she's spoken to

someone from social services who's going to visit me to try and arrange some funding from the social for the rest of my treatment.'

'Nice one, babes! You must be well buzzing about that.'

'Yeah, but still, sometimes . . .'

'Ignore her, mate. What happened in your past is gone, know what I mean? Fuck, man! We've all done stuff, that's why we're here, innit? You get me?'

Tessa came over. 'What are you talking about?'

'Not much,' I huffed.

She dragged one of the unnecessarily heavy chairs towards me, kissed my cheek, sat down, legs open, and rested her head on my arm. I started stroking her hair. She was sniffing round because Daryl was there.

'Bet you're chuffed about getting some funding, eh, bab?' Tessa always said 'bab', not 'babe'; it made me giggle when I first heard it. 'It's fucking mint, innit?'

'At least your mate Jimmy'll be happy! That'll save him a few quid. Fuck me!' Daryl laughed. He was the man of the moment as people kept approaching him with their orders for the shop.

'It's not confirmed yet.'

Leon came over. 'Get us a Mars bar and a big bottle of Coke and a packet of Rizlas, brother,' he said quietly and then wandered off again.

'You look like a bloke sitting like that, babe,' I teased Tessa.

'I've sat like this all my life, you cheeky cow,' she cackled. 'Give us a snout, will you?' I gave her a cigarette, even though yet another rule was: 'Borrowing anything, including cigarettes, is strictly forbidden.' I lit one myself.

Maggie randomly shouted at Austin to remove his feet from a chair, then a minute later: 'Have you gone deaf, Ozzy?' There was always a lot of nothing going on in the centre at lunchtime, and the nothing was always noisy.

'Oi, Daz, what did I order?' Tessa seemed miffed at his lack of attention.

'I wrote down what you told me you wanted, babes. It's all under control. I'm off.' Daryl fake-yawned; I'm not sure why. It wasn't exactly a chore getting out of the centre for half an hour. Maybe he guessed (correctly) that Tess and I could have used a trip into the outside world. We were staying put, though. This was life. No, this was *my* life: chocolate with negligible amounts of cocoa in it, cigarettes instead of rolling tobacco only if you were feeling flush, and therapy that drove you to count every second until the return of the bearers of treats.

'Daryl, my friend,' Billy cooed, 'would you be so kind as to please buy me an *Independent* newspaper? Just this once? I know it's against the rules, but I'm really sure that no one would mind . . . I'm hardly asking for a copy of *Razzle*.'

'Come on, don't do this to me, man. You know I can't get papers and that, innit?'

'Well, I'm terribly sorry if you feel I've compromised you.'

'Look, mate, I'm going to have to go, otherwise peeps will start moaning. You know how it is, yeah?' He hobbled off.

'Daz looks fit today! He's bang tidy, that boy!' Tessa said. I repeated it, mimicking her, and started to tickle her.

'Stop it, you silly sod,' she screeched.

'What are you two up to?' Leon asked.

Tessa glanced at him and he glanced at Tessa. She then looked at me and I looked at Leon – who looked at me. He looked at us both looking at him and we both burst out laughing. He then started shaking his head, acknowledging girls' playtime, and wandered off.

'Daryl always talks to you more than me, Katie . . . I reckon he wants to do you.' She took my hand and pretended to slap it.

'No he doesn't!'

Tess and I talked about Daryl: what she liked about him, what I liked about him and why he definitely didn't fancy me. She tutted, snorted, said 'Do you think so?' too many times and nuzzled her head into my armpit. I ruffled her hair and she was happy for the reassurance, which was easy to give.

Leon came back and asked if he could join us.

'Course,' Tess said, standing up. 'Sit here, mate. I'm off. Give us another fag, Katie, bab. I'll give you two back when Dazza brings me some baccy.'

'Here. And you can keep your stinking baccy. It tastes rank. Look, Leon, you're making me nervous standing there like that. You loitering with intent, eh? Why don't you sit down, babe?'

'What?'

'I'll leave you two to it,' said Tess, giving me a comic wink.

The Youth pretended he hadn't seen or heard anything.

'So what's happening?'

'With what? I'm kidding. Yeah, I suppose I'm OK. How are you doing?' I didn't wait for his answer. 'Actually, you know what? To be honest, I'm in a bit of an odd mood today, I really am. I'm sick of being here, like a caged animal. God, it's just all so intense.'

He was leaning forward in his chair, hands clasped together. His arms were lean, no tattoos (which surprised me) and hairless. I like hair.

'I hear you.'

'I mean, I can't even wipe my arse without somebody banging on the door trying to get into the bathroom.'

'I know what you're saying,' Leon said sincerely, then realised what he was agreeing with and half laughed.

'I'm pissed off. I'm writing this life story thing and it's

getting me down a bit, you know . . . I hate thinking about everything that I've put my dad through. I literally feel it, you know. It's here.' I touched the area under my breasts. 'My heart feels like a lead weight when I think about the way I've hurt him and fucked my life up.'

'I'm feeling you.'

'I mean, what the frig is going on here? We just sit here most of the day doing *what* exactly?' I tried to laugh. 'Where's the fucking treatment? Are we supposed to get better by sitting around for hours just staring at each other and wishing we weren't here?'

'We're meant to be having mini-groups, sweetheart. You know that.' Leon was sounding very sensible.

'Yeah, but realistically mini-groups are a waste of fucking time.'

'Well, that's down to you, innit?'

'Whatever. Talk to me, Leon . . . not about treatment or the 12 fucking Steps or the dos and don'ts of pissing recovery. Tell me something different, anything . . . Everything's revolving around this fucking therapy talk these days . . . And that fucking Maggie. She gets on my fucking nerves, she does.' I pouted like a blowfish before breathing out slowly.

'Allow it, man. Forget her, innit, Kate?'

'Do you know why she gets up my nose? When I go into detail about some of the shit I did, I don't expect someone to question every single thing about it and make me feel, well, like I'm a scumbag. I can do that to myself. I mean, I never even thought I'd be able to open up and talk about parts of it, you know?'

In some respects, I wanted Leon to know that I'd been a hooker, to see how much he'd judge me for it. But I couldn't just come out with it.

'I try to be open and that fucking Maggie is always trying to put me down for it.'

'Well, if she's doing that, that's out of order and you'd be well within your rights to tell her to jog on, but I think it's just how you see it. It's up to you how you react to her. Don't forget she can't make you really feel anything – it's up to you. You feel me?'

'No, Leon, come on . . . Of course she can make me feel a certain way.'

'She can affect you, yeah, but if you let her get to you, that's game over, mate.'

'That's what she does all the time. She tries to . . . to bring me down to her level.'

'I think she just makes sure you see things in different ways, you know?'

'What, like you're doing now? Anyway, let's not talk about it any more . . . So what kind of stuff do you lot talk about in men's groups?'

He looked coy. I liked the fact that he wasn't willing to blurt out people's confidences just because I'd asked. 'Same as you lot in your groups, probably. Listen, Katie, man, whatever you do, you don't need me to tell you not to leave here.'

'I'm not leaving. Course not – unless they kick me out. Look, I do want to complete this; I'm not here for a bloody holiday. If that's what I was looking for, I'd have gone to Greece or somewhere. I mean, I want things to change, which is why I'm putting up with this stress, but you know how it is when you're feeling physically better. You just want to get the fuck out of here, and the idea of getting those confrontation letters isn't helping me.'

'Right. You know what they are, then?'

'Yeah, we did all that shit the last time I was in rehab.'

'Forget all that. Look, just get as much out of this experience for yourself as you can, huh? You know anyone can stop using. It's staying stopped that's the hard part . . . And I reckon that's what we're trying to do here – prepare ourselves better for the future, innit?'

'Hark at you! Mr Counsellor-in-Training . . . Come on. I mean, don't you ever get sick of taking orders from people?'

'Who likes taking orders, babes? We're in rehab, not the army, get me? But I know I've got to give this a shot and play it by their rules, know what I'm sayin'? I was cracked out of my nut before I came here, and to be honest I knew that if I'd carried on like I was, I was going to end up like one of my mates, banged up for life. Fuck that. There was a time when it was just me and the boys raving it up, dropping pills and cotching round girls' flats smoking puff, innit? Them were the good days, like, but then it changed.' He looked sad. 'I was pretty mash-up out there, and I know some of my bredrin would take the fucking piss seeing me sitting here talking like this, innit? But let's break it down – it's me that's laughing now, get me? I'm feeling the reason you came in here is cos your head was ragged, right? I can see it ain't your body that was fucked up . . .'

I said nothing.

'I've heard you talking in groups, Katie, man, and giving people feedback and that, and, if you don't mind me saying, it's obvious you've been through the wringer. You've earned your stripes, you know . . . so you may as well give yourself a break, innit? Just chill here, get your head together and make plans, get me? I mean, if you left now, what would you do? Go back and hang out with that bird you've talked about?'

'Which one? Petra?'

'Yeah.'

'Probably.'

'And let's have it right: if it had been that good, then you wouldn't be here in the first place, huh?'

'You're a bit of a clever one, you, aren't you?' I said, and prodded his thigh, just as shamelessly as I'd been trying to check out his packet moments earlier. His legs were solid. 'Anyway, let's talk about something else, eh?'

'Like what?' I knew he knew what I meant by the way he looked at me.

'Oh, I dunno . . . What do you think?'

'Dunno. What are you saying?'

Fuck. He was going to make me spell it out. 'How about something like . . . um . . . sex?'

'Go on, then.' He seemed shy, but he was fronting it out. *Good, good boy.*

I had begun to notice a habit Leon had of licking his bottom lip and raising his shoulders up and down in a swift movement as though he was doing a pre-exercise warm-up. It was almost as though he had a tic.

'Being in here for a while must get to people, don't you reckon? I'm feeling pretty horny, aren't you?' I said, running my nails across my lip and glancing at him sideways. He was still leaning forward.

'Course I am! I ain't got jiggy for . . . I can't even remember! It's been too long, man, too long.' Leon shuffled around, licking his bottom lip.

I was aware that I was breaking the holy code of rehab conduct, but I said, 'I just feel like hopping on board a hard dick, you know, and riding it.' I cackled on hearing myself. 'Is that too much to ask?' I sounded smutty as hell, but to me it was amusing.

'For fuck's sake, Katie, man . . . don't say that,' Leon said awkwardly. 'I've got a stiffy now.'

'Show me.'

'I can't.'

'Show me!'

'Babe, *I can't.*'

'You can. Just show me through your jeans. Come on, I bet you've got a big cock, haven't you?' *You're sounding really slutty now, Kate; pipe down.* The truth was I didn't want to.

'It does the job. You're making me want to do you, you know that, innit?' I loved how he used his eyes.

'Me and the other girls have already discussed your dick, anyway, and we all reckon you've got one of those fat ones that gets Really. Fuckin'. Hard.'

'Kate, stop it! I wish I –'

'What are you two whispering about over there?' Maggie shouted.

'Nothing,' Leon answered quietly, as he did his habitual high-speed shoulder jig: up, down, up, down. I said zilch. She knew what was going on; she'd been there herself.

'It doesn't look like nothing to me,' she continued. *Please just go away. Just this once, would you do me a favour and just piss off?!* 'I'm watching you two.' Thankfully, at that moment someone came up to Maggie and started speaking to her.

'She's an arse, that woman, she does my head in,' I tutted. 'Anyway, carry on . . . What were you saying?'

'I was saying that I want to pull your jeans down, tear your knickers off and stuff them into your mouth –' And I'd thought he was shy. '– then I want to bend you over that chair and fuck you from behind, bareback.' Leon was barely whispering. *Dirty boy.* I liked it; I liked it a lot.

'And I'd be moaning,' I leaned closer to say.

'You'd be fucking screaming, babes.'

'My pussy's throbbing, Leon.'

I was talking under my breath, as though we were wired up and our voices were being transmitted into Len's office, where he and the Vice Squad could listen in to our conversation to ensure sinners were prevented from revolting.

'My pussy's moist. *Fuck*, I wish you could do that right now,' I whispered. 'How big's your cock?'

'Pretty big.'

'Pretty big? How big?'

'Shh . . . it's *big*, babes.'

I didn't doubt him. I scanned the room. I felt we were being watched. We were. Stacey and Simon, the equivalent of community police officers, were standing together glaring. Something would be said in a group about this. I didn't know when, but for sure something would be said.

All I knew was that I was going to keep quiet. Very quiet.

CHAPTER 12

Every misdemeanour was confessed to in a Monday morning 'cop group'. We sat in silence, waiting for the fun to begin so it would finish and we could indulge in the only two drugs that were permitted: caffeine and nicotine.

'You might think these rules are unnecessary or silly, but I cannot, I repeat cannot, stress enough that honesty is the backbone of recovery. If you are not honest, and by that I mean thoroughly honest at all times, you will not change, do you understand this, folks?' Lenny, the scrawny, middle-aged, moustached head counsellor, who usually took the cop group, said theatrically, handkerchief in hand. 'The rules here are for a reason. We take them to extremes because we're well aware that once you leave the rigid, structured environment of BCH, you will immediately stop implementing the majority of what you have adhered to within the confines of this place. It's fair to say that even if you were to take a watered-down version of our rules home with you, you would notice a difference in your lives. So, can someone tell me what exactly is the point of rules? They are about what, people?'

His accent was weird; I couldn't work it out. Posh Geordie, I decided. If there is such a thing.

'Discipline,' someone shouted out obediently.

'What else?' he asked, searching for someone to participate and twiddling his moustache.

Silence.

'Structure,' someone else called out.

'Rules are about discipline, structure and what else? Come on, group! I can't hear you! Oh dear, isn't it ironic that no one has been able to tell me the other reason we are so focused on rules in here? It's about *honesty*, folks, honesty. Remember that? Honesty is the backbone of recovery. I've said this time and time again, and I'll continue to say it until I believe it is sinking in. Here you have an opportunity to follow strict regulations, and you get the chance to admit your transgressions if, and more likely when, you commit them, without the threat of police action or jail.'

Transgressions? Police? Jail? This was hardcore stuff.

'Let's face it, out there,' Lenny pointed towards the window, 'there are rules everywhere, and sometimes . . . Simon, are we keeping you awake?'

'Yes, Len. I mean no. No, you're not keeping me awake.' He propped himself up. I wished he'd shave that silly bit of hair off his chin.

'Well, in that case please at least look semi-awake, if you will. As I was saying, even if you don't get caught for your rule-breaking out there in the big world, that's not the point, because we all have a conscience. Isn't that right?'

No one said anything.

'We don't have any psychopaths in this group, do we?' said Lenny, grinning. *Quite possibly, but unlikely.* 'For those of you who think that you're more messed up than the rest, this is your chance to cultivate a conscience. It's through humility that integrity will grow. I presume you all know what integrity is?' I waited for someone to ask its meaning. No one did. *Pity.* 'Good. Every one of you was once someone's baby, don't forget that. You were once pure, full of love and innocent, believe it or not. Even you, Simon.' Len grinned. *Hardy har har!*

'Maybe that innocent child still lives in all of us as our conscience. And no matter how hard or fast you run, you can never quite get rid of it, cos it's part of you.' Clearly, Lenny was in a philosophical mood.

Throughout my wayward years, lying and scheming to get what I wanted had been part of my repertoire. It takes a helluva lot of conscious effort to try and break a habit that's become ingrained. Only by rigorously communicating facts and untainted truth and by constantly checking your motives for the words you use and actions you take will you have a chance to break the cycle. It takes ages. Most addicts remain untrustworthy manipulators until the day they die. I sat pensively and wondered if I was one of those.

'So, in this morning's cop group, as usual we're going to focus on *dishonesties.*' Emphasis on 'dishonesties', in case we still didn't understand. At school, Len would have been the kid who was always first to answer all the teacher's questions. 'I'd like our newcomers to take particular notice here, OK?' As in many churches, 'newcomers' were always the priority. 'But please take heed: this group is certainly not exclusively for our new folks. It's becoming apparent that a few of you need a prod in the right direction. And about the gripes some of you come to me with, moaning that you think these rules are brainwashing you – may I just take this opportunity to remind you that your brains need to be washed!'

A number of us laughed, and Len sat there straight-faced and calm as anything, twisting his moustache. He was quirky and fey, an unusual specimen. He claimed that he'd been married in his 20s. Yeah, and I was Cleopatra in a past life. He seemed genteel, almost regal, and too delicate to be working in an environment like a residential drug rehab.

'So who wants to start with their misdemeanours during the past week? No doubt a few of you have got one or a few cops you want to get off your chest, eh? Leaving more than two cigarette butts in an ashtray before emptying it out? Maybe you didn't wash your cup within ten minutes of using it?' He drew out each word after 'cup' as though he was stalling for time, in the hope that the guilty parties would jump up, unable to bear the disgrace of their crime for a moment longer, and confess. 'Maybe you were more than ten minutes in the shower, eh, Simon? Were you?'

'No, I wasn't,' Simon said defensively, rubbing his hair nervously.

'Well, if I may say . . .' *'If I may say', my arse. Who's going to stop you, Len? Just get on with it.* '. . . your tone implies that the idea of you being in the shower for more than the permitted ten minutes is a near impossibility, despite this being your usual weekly indiscretion, is it not?'

'Well . . .'

'I may be wrong, but perhaps it takes you ten minutes each day just to groom that landing strip you have below your lip.'

I wanted to sing 'na-na-na-na-na' at the tall, freckled prat. It was about time he got some verbal.

'I suppose it has been an issue in the past, Len,' the accused interrupted, 'but over the past week I've really watched the amount of time I've spent in the bathroom. And now you've brought it up, I'm sure it doesn't take me any longer to maintain this' – he stroked his meagre facial hair – 'than it takes you to do yours.' He grinned.

Lenny smirked, sitting there, legs crossed, both elbows

resting on the arms of his chair, holding a hanky as usual.

'I'm sure by now you all know that dishonesty will kill you, group. This isn't the first time you've heard me say this,' Lenny continued. *How the hell can telling a porky kill you?*

'I don't doubt you get bored with talking about this. I'm well aware that these things which are of such great importance in here are minor elsewhere. Oh, I know this all too well, that they are . . . you know, minor, that is.' He paused before completing his sermon. *Get to the point, Leonard.* 'But if you don't grasp the importance of brutal honesty, starting with yourself, it is well documented, and I've seen it myself, and there have never been truer words said regarding recovery, that without it You. Will. Relapse.' This he said with his voice rising. *Nice. That's not peddling fear at all, is it?*

'OK, so who can tell me exactly why dishonesty kills recovering addicts, huh?' No one spoke. *Just tell us, mate.* This was tedious. At best it felt like a quiz, at worst it was like being back at junior school. Except that I'd enjoyed school, and this type of grilling, and especially the way Lenny presented it, made me want to punch him – in the nicest possible way, of course.

Unless a question was directed at a specific person, it was usually the same people who piped up with answers to the counsellors' often cryptic questions.

'Come on, chop chop.'

I started to think about the expression 'recovering addict'. I'd reached that place. I was no longer a 'using addict'; I was now 'recovering'. I'd ridden through the hand-gnawing periods when I'd wanted to run screaming out of the centre and into the nearest bar to order a pint of brandy and try to fuck my way to a gram of charlie. *I'm in fucking recovery, man!* That was on a good day. The not-so-good days went: *Fuck this fucking, cunting place.*

93

I was aware of Leon, who was sitting opposite me. We'd supposedly agreed that when in the same group we should sit near each other rather than opposite. Otherwise the tension was too much. I was self-conscious and wondered: *Do I look pretty? Do I look hot?* I felt hot, but not sexy, just sticky. I usually did feel uncomfortable in group, until I knew the focus wasn't on me.

'Kate, please tell the group,' said Lenny.

My mind jolted. *Shit, what's he talking about? How is Leon seeing me now?* I'd lost the serene look I'd been trying to cultivate – thanks to Lenny, the bastard. *Think, Kate.* I sat upright. *Calm. Be calm. Dishonesty – why it kills . . .*

'Er . . . honesty kills because . . .'

'Er . . . *honesty* does not kill, Kate,' Len butted in. People laughed and I had to join them. 'I think that was a Freudian slip, my dear. Try again.'

'OK, *dis*honesty kills because . . .' I couldn't think. 'Er . . . because . . .' The room was quiet again. I stared at Lenny and Lenny stared back. I glanced at Tessa, who glanced at me, then I looked at Leon, who was looking at his feet. His hands were clasped in his usual show of 'Hey, I'm calm and relaxed over here – don't mind me'.

'I'm not sure. I do know dishonesty kills, but I'm not sure . . . er . . . well, I'm not sure how to articulate how.' I batted the word 'articulate' at him to try to claw back a small amount of respectability, to prove that I was not as ignorant as I felt.

'Hmm . . . It's interesting that you don't know the answer, or should I say you don't know how to *articulate* the answer?' Lenny mocked me. 'Dishonesty kills recovering addicts –'

'OK, yeah, I know it now! I know why,' I called out. Too late.

'Oh, back from our slumber, are we? The reason is because it will take us straight back where we came from.' At this point, Len raised his voice as though he had just discovered the answer to the meaning of life. 'So why did you forget that?' he asked me. 'You hear it virtually every day. Selective hearing, I suspect, group. We all have tendencies to pick and choose what we might *want* to hear or which parts of a conversation we *choose* to remember, but this doesn't always give us all the information that we need, does it? It's very convenient for you not to remember why not being truthful kills addicts, isn't it, Katie?'

Oh, here we go . . . Lenny's leg started to twitch. His snotrag was being waved about and used to full effect. He was really coming to life. 'So what have you not been honest about, Kate?'

This group was going to focus on me. *Bollocks.* My 'dishonesty' was clearly related to my flirting with Leon and keeping quiet about it. But it wasn't as though I'd been lying about my fledgling romance; I simply hadn't said anything. There was an expression for this: 'dishonesty by omission'. I called it 'my business'.

'I haven't got many cops at all, actually. I mean, I twice stayed in my room more than ten minutes and, er, I closed my eyes while I was on the sofa yesterday, and I'm really sorry about that –'

'Again? This is a regular occurrence for you.'

'I know, I can't help it. I just get really sleepy on Saturday and Sunday afternoons when we're in the house doing nothing, and I –'

'Doing *nothing*? You have time for that? That's interesting. I wish I did. So what about your written work? You're about to read us your life story, aren't you?'

'Yeah, I've finished it.'

'Anyway, I'm not talking about the events or lack of them in the house. Think again.'

'I don't know. I really don't know.' I could have guessed but decided not to. Nothing had happened between Leon and me, but in rehab nothing needed to have happened for questioning like this to be taking place. In fact, if I'd been caught blatantly getting up to no good, I would have been given a single train ticket back to London after having 60 minutes' worth of bag-packing time bestowed upon me.

Lenny's face was expressionless. People coughed and shifted uncomfortably in their seats. 'Leon, perhaps you can help Katie out?'

'I'd love to,' he grinned. Cracking thunder would have been an ideal sound effect here had we been on stage. I wanted to suck him. He wanted to fuck me. He looked at me and let me know so.

'I bet you'd love to. But we're here to save lives, and some folks in this room seem more focused on randy thoughts than on taking recovery seriously. When this happens, it has the potential to rub off on others who actually *want* to change. It's the rotten-apple syndrome, group. One can turn the rest bad.' *Borrrring!* He wanted us to recognise that he was all wise – lest we forget.

'No one can impact on my life in such a dramatic way if I don't let them,' Billy interrupted.

'Who asked you to talk just now? I was in the middle of something.'

'But I think it's fair to –'

'*Excuse* me. I haven't finished yet. But before I do, I'd just like to ask you, Billy, what on earth makes you say that no one can influence you in such a way, hmmm? From what I remember you telling me when you got here, your drinking and pill use went into overdrive as a direct result of your wife leaving you. Please feel free to correct me if I'm wrong.'

Ouch. In a court of law that would have gone like this:

JUDGE: This case is being won hands down by the moustached one.

BILLY: But, Your Honour, he just hit me below the belt!

JUDGE: Sorry, pal, he still gets the point. The truth's the truth and there's no negotiating with that. Extra point to Leonard!

'It didn't help matters, that's right,' Billy said thoughtfully.

'I'm sure it didn't *help* matters one bit. But, for now, would you mind greatly if I continue with what I was saying before?'

'Go ahead.'

'Thank you. So, back to the rotten-apple syndrome. Clearly, we don't want to plant seeds of negativity in vulnerable minds, and we don't want folks to think that behaviours that are against our rules here at Bringing Counselling Home are acceptable. I think you all would agree.'

'Could I go to the toilet, please?' Tessa squeaked in a wispy voice.

'No. You can't leave the group. You should have gone before it started.'

She went red and didn't say another word.

'I'd be doing every one of you a disservice if I allowed this caper you're involved in to carry on. Do you understand, Katie?'

I nodded, eager to shut him up.

'There are people here who could do with your help and not your lust. Do you hear me? You two are playing a very dangerous game.'

Lenny looked at Leon and me in turn.

'So can you shed any light on the point I'm trying to make here, Leon?'

'Well, I'm not sure what you're saying, to be honest. I mean, if you could be a bit clearer, like, and I'll try and help you out, innit?' He hadn't flinched.

'I don't seem to be getting far with these two. Have we all forgotten that the advice we give people is to get a plant and take care of it for a year before getting wrapped up in relationships?'

A plant? What a joke. Sabrina and Daryl started to laugh, and then they both wished they hadn't. When she covered her mouth, I noticed a big bruise on the inside of her arm.

'If either of you finds this funny, then you may be the very people who need to listen. We barely hear a squeak from you, Sabrina, and suddenly this outburst. Do you have something you want to contribute?'

Her face fell and her nose began to twitch. 'No.'

'Daryl?'

'Yeah?'

'Ah, so you have.'

'Have what?'

'You have something you want to say. We're waiting.'

'No I don't.'

'If I may, Lenny . . .' Billy raised his hand.

'No, you may *not*!'

I started sniggering.

'Katie, I don't know how you have the nerve, young lady! So, we suggest that if you can look after a plant, perhaps you are able to think about someone or something else other than yourself. As addicts, we are inherently selfish beings and, believe me, healthy relationships are far harder than you imagine.' I glanced at Daryl, who was clearly thinking the same as me:

How does Len know that relationships are hard to deal with?

'Can someone please remind Leon and Miss Katie what I'm talking about?' These group questions were awkward. He was asking people who'd lived, and often grown up, in a 'never, ever snitch' culture to spill the beans. We had stumbled through our recent past by saying nothing to anyone about anything: hoodlum protocol.

The room was quiet. Billy, whose frown suggested that he felt as though he was shacked up with a bunch of kids, sighed.

Simon spoke. 'Well, I think you might be talking about Leon and Katie always talking to each other and that.'

'And *what* exactly?' Lenny asked.

'Well, you know . . .' He started fingering his hair.

Politically, he was in a tricky situation. Although we were all pushed to live by the laws of the centre, which included pointing out others' misdemeanours, most preferred to keep it zipped. Not everyone, not all the time, but most. We all wanted to be liked. That's human nature, right?

'Well, you know . . . er . . . they keep on flirting, and stuff . . .'

'Surely to God your parents haven't paid astronomical amounts of money for your education for your vocabulary to be this limited, Simon? Get your words out, sonny!' Len snapped impatiently.

Sadistic Fantasy: Tying Simon to the chair, blindfolding him, gagging him, yanking his head back and shearing his ginger locks with a blunt razor.

'Do you keep on flirting "and stuff"?' Len gave me a wry smile.

'I don't *keep on*, but on occasions I've had a bit of a flirt, yeah.' I had to offer something, otherwise it would have seemed as though I was totally taking the piss out of everyone, and everyone already suspected, rightly, that mischief was afoot.

'Well, it's becoming more and more apparent that the two of you are in some form of SR. It's quite obvious when you are constantly whispering in each other's ears, thinking no one's looking, that something's being concocted.'

• *SR* = special relationship, an 'exclusive' friendship.

Lenny clearly thought he was being cool by using this term.

'Really? Well, it's not. I mean, how *could* it be?'

'Nobody here is stupid, Kate.'

Don't bet on that. 'I know that. But look, we don't *whisper*. We might talk quietly, but it's not like we're breathing into each other's ears or anything.'

Tessa started laughing.

'Quiet!' Lenny barked.

'Sorry,' she said, as though she was speaking to her dad.

'So, what have you got to say about this, Leon? Anything?'

'About Tess laughing? Nothing.'

'Oh, very amusing! We seem to have a troupe of jokers here, group. Is there something I'm missing?'

'Nothing's funny,' said Leon, looking annoyed. 'I just don't see what all the fuss is about, to be honest. Allow it, Len. I don't know what Si's going on about, you know. There ain't nothing going on with me and Katie, you get me? I, like, get on well with her, innit, and I don't see what the problem is with that . . . I mean, I converse with Maggie too.' *Con-fucking-verse? Oh dear.* 'So what you sayin'? Something's going on with her and all? Madness, mate, madness.'

'Well, is it?' Everyone except me started tittering.

'NO!'

'So who else thinks Leon and Katie are trying to keep a secret from us?'

Five out of fourteen hands went up. The traitors were noted.

'This is utter bollocks, you know! You're talking rubbish, Lenny. Fu— Can't we just talk about other things? Something important? I have to sit here listening to a kangaroo court. If I'd fu— if I'd slept with Leon, I could see your point, but just cos I've chatted to the guy a few more times than maybe —'

'Pipe down, Kate.'

'To be fair, I've talked to other people, like Billy, and a big deal isn't made about that. And for some weird reason I'm getting accused of fucking sneaking around and lying about stuff that I haven't even done.'

'Please don't swear, Kate. Not in group.'

'OK, but look, Len —'

'Katie, be quiet!'

'Please, for once, could you just follow your own advice?'

'That's enough!'

'You know, I felt all right for once until you come along and —'

'Be quiet this instant!' Lenny yelled, nearly leaping out of his chair.

'Katie, man, shh,' someone said quietly. People were fidgeting in their seats.

'No. I won't be quiet. Listen, Len. It's fucking hard enough as it is in here and then you have to try and dig out information from nothing. I don't get why you're doing it. I mean, I just don't —'

'From this moment, you're on a warning, do you hear me?'

'Oh, you're a —'

'Silence! This instant! There must be limits put on disruption such as this, Kate.'

'But —'

'You have seven days in which to show us that your attitude

is improving. If not, you're out. I'm not going to tolerate this type of rudeness any longer!' Len screamed. I believed what he said.

I didn't hear anything more in that group. The end couldn't come soon enough and I was relieved when we linked hands to say the Serenity Prayer.

I didn't want to be kicked out, but maybe this time I'd overstepped the line.

Fuck their stupid recovery!

Er . . . whose *recovery?*

CHAPTER 13

Drugs kill. In school I'd been told this, but as a young girl I had no understanding of the meaning of death. It was an idle threat that had no emotional impact on me, used by grown-ups to keep me in my place and exercise authority over me. I heard the words but felt nothing. Now I knew that drugs do indeed kill. They can strike you stone dead. One day, a pill, a line, a hit keeps you warm; another day, the same fix can leave you cold.

Yep, drugs do kill and death usually happens quickly. Often it's painful: convulsions, heart attack, brain damage, and gone. If you're lucky, you'll become comatose and not wake before your body packs up. Chances are you'll die alone. Your junkie mates will have done a runner, petrified of facing any penalty, yet ignoring the fact that if they're found they'll be prosecuted for manslaughter for leaving you to rot. Your parents will probably hear the news that you've snuffed it from a police liaison officer, whose overriding memory will be what his colleagues told him of the vile stench you caused after shitting and pissing yourself. Or maybe your family will hear through the local newspaper; if it has nothing else to fill its pages, you might finally gain the recognition that eluded you in life.

I had been aware of the possibility of dying. Especially after sessions that lasted for days, I often wondered how I could still be breathing. I had no gratitude for the fact that I was. I was, and that was that.

So why take the risk of death? Why not? There was an overwhelming and perverse feeling of personal power attached to being able to keep on going and going and going, pushing my body and taking myself to the verge of death. If I survived, then I had an opportunity to play the game again.

I certainly hadn't been brought up by my father, a quiet intellectual, to think it was all right to sell my arse, bang poison up my nose and glug enough vodka to sink a dinghy, but I did it. Being high was being free – of myself, of my worries, of my sadness and insecurities – and once I'd discovered that I could control my feelings with drugs and alcohol and that I didn't have to tolerate the intolerable, I was hooked. I gained confidence and peace from my often negative thoughts. I was better able to say no, so I did. I said no to piano practice, organ lessons, classical music, opera, ballet and homework. I knew I was disappointing my dad by my change in attitude, but I didn't care. I'd spent years obsessively trying to please my father – and now it was time to do something for me.

Life was now doable. I'd found the solution to all my problems. In fact, I believed I had actually found the answer to the entire world's problems. And as for the crap I'd been told at school – 'drugs are bad; drugs kill; drugs will ruin your life and your family's life' – what utter garbage! Drugs were being good to me and were therefore good *for* me, and if someone was going to try and tell me otherwise, they were trying to keep me down, so they could just fuck off.

Most people enjoy altering reality because it feels good, and it's acceptable in our society to do this using alcohol. A couple of wines or a beer after work doesn't necessarily mean that you drink because you're unhappy, does it? Fun is being had and work alliances formed – what's the problem? Everyone seems to be doing it. Without you even noticing, though, the amount of drink consumed can increase for various reasons: peer pressure, an 'occasion', 'just because'. OK, you have a hangover the next day, but you still get up and go to work; you don't do anything out of the ordinary. Life's good. What's the big deal?

If an addiction is going to become part of your life, it will not happen overnight, whatever drug you use. Even frequent use will not necessarily cause dependence. Addiction is not about quantity or even necessarily regularity of use – it's about attitude and *why* you choose to do what you do and why you continue when it has a detrimental impact on your life.

Now mix substances: booze with narcotic drugs. For example, cocaine. What do you get? If you don't get paranoid and twitchy, you'll probably have a damn good time – for 20 minutes or so.

'One line won't do any harm. Sod it.' Besides, you feel tipsy, and apparently it'll sober you up. You think you're more coherent. And now, if you choose, you can drink more. You've replaced a depressant with a stimulant. You're living in the moment, and any ideas about being 'good tonight' get ditched. The new drug user enjoys a zest for living and a feeling that anything is possible. It is at this point that addiction reels you in.

Let us not forget that people often get into drugs because of only one thing: they're fun! Some of the most exciting and exhilarating experiences of my life have happened when I was high. In the beginning, you feel *more* everything. You laugh, mingle, feel more attractive. You're taking your life by the balls and consuming all that God has put on this planet to be used. If it wasn't OK to take this stuff, it wouldn't be here in the first place, right?

You feel in control and more alive than ever before. And that excess weight around your tummy? Gone! You wonder why you didn't start doing this before now. The rest of the world, you feel, is living a sepia existence, while your life is in Technicolor. You have sex that you never imagined was possible with people you wouldn't have thought you'd ever sleep with (both ego boosts and don't-remind-mes; memories of the latter can easily be blotted out, no problem).

One day, you might glimpse the reality that you are drunk or drugging or both every weekend – and more weekdays than you'd want to admit to, even to yourself. But instead of dwelling on this, you call in your friend Denial, who brings her twin sister, Justification, to help combat your concerns.

Your behaviour becomes more unpredictable, your moods more changeable, and you only have enthusiasm for life when you're out of it. You grow suspicious of people who aren't doing the same as you – worse than that, you fear being judged by them. If they question you, you stay away from them or treat them with contempt. Your employers are getting fed up with your lateness, your grumpiness and your inability to concentrate. You feel bad about upsetting people, but you're not even sure you can decipher what's causing the upset.

Denial becomes your new best friend, soon to be the only friend who will put up with you, other than people with the same progressive sickness. You try and ignore your conscience when it whispers that what you're doing is not smart. You forge on, spending more cash on having a good time than you can afford. Money becomes tight and debt looms. A drink or a line helps you forget your stresses. When you're not tipsy, you feel down because your worries are still there. A drink or a line picks you up for a while. Anxiety grows. A drink or a line settles your nerves. At first. If you're lucky, you'll stop what you're doing, now. But what if your predicament and the reasons for it feel more than you can handle? What then? Borrow? Steal? Prostitute yourself to enable you to pay for what you need to forget?

Have you ever noticed how, when people are intoxicated, they always have a messy, stressed appearance? They look physically different. They frown more, their mouths become downturned, their eyes become droopy. They don't look the same. Think about it. The devil is not only in the detail but also in the denial.

CHAPTER 14

During the session where I read my five-page life story, it was weird saying 'I sold my body for money' in front of six of my peers, one of whom was Leon. I didn't feel deep shame; I felt belligerent.

After the words had slipped out of my mouth, I'm not sure what I expected to happen. I just felt like Kate, a girl from Yorkshire who loves her dad, Jim and vanilla ice cream. In that order. And that's exactly who I was. I couldn't associate myself with being a hooker.

In women-only groups, we'd talked about prostitution in its various forms. One of the girls and I had taken cash for sex, and the other girls had also done some bartering here and there to get by, so I knew I wasn't alone.

'How was that?' Maggie asked me in a one-to-one session after the group.

'Yeah, I guess easier than I thought.'

'This is really gonna help you now you've decided to open up. Maybe that seven-day warning has done you good, eh?'

But was it going to help me stop being jumpy? Help me believe in myself and that I had a future really worth striving for? Would it help me find a job when I left rehab? Help my dad grow the backbone required to side with me when I was right and his wife was not? Just one time? Would a seven-day warning stop me wishing harm on my mother or stop me fantasising about my own death? The answer to these questions was an emphatic no.

'Maybe it has, I don't know, but I'll be glad when the seven days are up. I've still got another three, feeling like I've got a ticking time bomb under my feet. But saying that, I've kind of noticed a change in me, yeah.' *And that change is absolute terror about what's to come – tomorrow, with my confrontation letters.*

'Well, that's the purpose of what we do here: to encourage change.'

'To encourage or to force?'

'That's a matter of interpretation, but you know that we can only do so much. Of course, this part of your treatment and sharing your life story is a big step forward. Ultimately, it's down to you and about how much you want to change, you know that. But it's good to see that you're serious about recovering, Kate. Well, most of the time.'

I hadn't been left with much choice other than to change, but how that change was taking place wasn't always obvious. It wasn't as though I was waking up each day feeling like a different woman. I wasn't especially happier and I definitely wasn't excited about my future.

'We haven't had a chance to catch up properly since I came back from my long weekend,' Maggie continued. 'So tell me what Lenny said to you when he gave you the official warning?'

'He was good about it, to be honest. Though I wish I hadn't shouted like that in the group. I feel like a right plonker.'

'Things happen, Katie, but . . .'

'It's a habit when I feel trapped.'

'Old habits die hard, eh? I think Dusty Springfield sang that.'

'Oh, I don't know.'

'If I remember rightly, the album was called *A Very Fine Love*.'

'I've really no idea. The only thing of hers I've heard is "Son of a Preacher Man".'

'Excellent song!' Eight out of ten for Maggie.

'The thing is that I don't always know exactly what I'm doing here. If I'm still yelling at people when I'm in certain situations, and I'm in here, then where's the change?'

'The change happens only when you consciously try to apply what you're learning. You think that just cos you're in the confines of these walls suddenly some magic happens and you become different? Dream on. It takes time. So it's taken a while, but now you've started opening up about the prostitution stuff, this is where you'll really start to notice things shifting positively for you. Soon we'll have you talking about your mum.'

Not if I could help it. Now she was back down to two out of ten.

'One thing at a time, eh?' she said. 'Let's get the next few days out of the way first. You look anxious when I say that, but try not to think too much about it, OK? Look, when I came in here, I'd lost everything, and anyone who was close to me had done a runner. I know how it feels. And I've seen so many girls come through here who were standing on street corners, doing all sorts to men for a tenner bag of smack. I know you don't think you were the same as that, Katie.' *You're right; I don't.* 'But being a hooker is being a hooker, however you want to package it. If you sell your body for 300 quid or a tenner, or a line of coke, or free drinks from someone you don't give a hoot about, you're still selling yourself. I know this may seem hard for you to understand.'

Standing on a street corner is the same thing as going to a swanky hotel? And free drinks? Maggie stared at me, searching for a reaction. I said nothing, deciding to forget that it hadn't been too long since I'd decided to change my life. At that point, I'd been working in a flat and getting banged for less than a hundred quid a time.

'I've got three kids,' she said, changing the subject. 'Have I told you about them?' She hadn't. 'When you start talking honestly, you can see much more clearly how things affected and affect your relationships with other people.' She handed me a photo in a delicate porcelain frame. 'We're just about on speaking terms today. Although my eldest daughter, the tallest one on the right, finds it harder to forgive me for the past than her sisters.' I stared at the photo. 'They don't know the details about everything, but they know that I wasn't emotionally available for them. Know what I mean? It's taken me nearly 12 years of sobriety to gain their confidence so they'll accept regular contact from me. That wouldn't have happened if I hadn't faced up to the things I did and who I'd become.'

Fuckin' great lot of hope that gives me with my dad. As usual, I was thinking about my own situation and was not overly concerned with hers. 'Will it take me years and years, then, to get close to my dad?'

'No, I'm not saying that; everyone's different.'

'How old's your oldest girl?'

'The same age as you.'

It was then that I realised: *I am Maggie's daughter. I'm the patient who keeps her at arm's length, just like her own kid.* For a moment, I thawed. *She's OK.* She was a woman who, like me, had made profound mistakes but, unlike me, because she had children, her mistakes could possibly affect her for life. And she had to live with that. But most importantly, she'd never given up.

If you stop using drugs and alcohol, your world doesn't suddenly become easy. Tidying up the junk from the past can take many years, and most of those years are painful. The emotions that come with that are the biggest challenge you'll ever face in your life.

Being in rehab isn't therapy just for the people who've checked in for 12 weeks. Often the counsellors are recovering addicts, and I was glad that this was the case because they were able to identify with some of the weirdness that comes with addiction in a way that other people couldn't.

Maggie had made some bad decisions in her past, but when making them she hadn't consciously planned to fuck anyone else's life up too. It made me think about how my mum had made choices that had damaged me, but perhaps she hadn't set out to harm me and leave me with a legacy that was the catalyst for some dire choices made by me while I was growing up. The idea was hard for me even to allow myself to think about. Compassion for my mother was alien to me. Who would I be without the hate? I'd spent all my life punishing myself and despising a woman whom I believed had cast me aside like trash. Yet the truth was I'd never known her and, what's more, mistakes are mistakes, no matter how serious the repercussions. Ultimately, I'd avoided the fact that it had been my own choices that had driven me to where I'd ended up. No one else's.

'Anyway, back to you,' Maggie said.

I looked at her. She looked like a mother. She loved like a mother. She *was* a mother, and she yearned for the same admiration from her children that any mother wishes for.

'So, what are you going to do about Jim?'

'Er . . . I don't know. You mean about him paying for my treatment? Don't you think I'll get some funding from the social?'

'Quite possibly. You'll find out tomorrow. But I do think you need to get a mini-group together. There's a lot going on for you at the moment. You've just read your life story – then tomorrow you get feedback.'

'You mean the confrontation letters?'

'Well, that's one name for them, yes. And you should ask the group what they think about the funding situation. Just talk, Katie! I've heard you unable to shut up at times and now nothing? Come on! Get things off your chest. That's the purpose of being here, isn't it? Use this time!'

'I feel embarrassed talking about it; I don't want them thinking that Jim is, well, you know . . .'

'A punter? I know.' I grimaced. 'But remember that most people, especially those out there in the real world, wouldn't ever think you'd been a prostitute. It wouldn't cross most people's minds.' God, I hated the word 'prostitute', but it had to be used. 'Tell it as it is,' Maggie would say.

'Look, if nothing else, Kate, it's good practice for you to be able to be open about your truth. Your reality is your reality, girl, and if someone wants to question it, that's up to them, and there's nothing you can do about that or about your past. It's up to you how you choose to respond to people and their questions, and here you can practise that stuff. You asked how change takes place. Well, use every opportunity to help it happen. This is life, right now. We can put things off, worrying about what people might think about us. But here, not yesterday or tomorrow, is where you live, you know. Now, go on! If you don't feel able to answer a question – just say so.'

I huffed and tutted.

'What happened with your life when you were out there before coming in here, Katie?'

'What do you mean? It crumbled into pieces.'

'Because *you* went to pieces.' *All right, don't rub it in.* 'And whose advice did you follow, eh? Tell me, who did you listen to during all those years?'

'Well . . . no one.'

'Exactly. Now get in that bloody group room and get a mini-group together,' Maggie said firmly. 'It doesn't have to involve many people, just three or four, OK? And find out what advice the group has to offer you regarding Jim. Go on! Scaramouche!'

Dare I say it? Right then I liked Maggie: nine out of ten.

'And you can stop that bloody tutting,' she said sharply. 'How old were you when you started taking drugs?'

'Me?'

'Well, there's no one else here,' she said.

'Around 14 or 15.'

'Ah! I'm sure you know that people stop developing emotionally at the age they start abusing substances.'

'Har har! Yeah, I've heard you say that before. Do you think it's true?'

'Most definitely. So, it seems you're still stuck as a 15-year-old girl in an adult's body.'

My prognosis was looking worse by the day. Surely it could only get better?

CHAPTER 15

Just before the group in which I was to get my confrontation letters, I met with Raj from social services. The discussion about funding was short. He reckoned that if someone voluntarily placed themselves in rehab, he or she was a worthy cause, since this was the only way they stood a chance of changing successfully.

Raj ticked boxes on a questionnaire and asked me how I felt I was getting on.

'Well, I wish I didn't have to go through this. But my life is screwed. I mean, if I think about leaving, I feel I might crap myself, cos I know what I'd be going back to.'

'Many people just carry on and end up on the streets, in prison or, another popular one, they die. So I'm convinced you've made the right decision.'

He told me about how he'd recently done the New York marathon. I was surprisingly interested and not at all cynical, which was a first when it came to small talk for me. It was good to hear about someone living a life that wasn't a total disaster. I signed some forms and within moments Raj left.

I was desperate to tell Jimmy it was likely that I'd managed to save him four grand. This was, of course, *after* he'd already forked out £2,000, plus the cheeky 500-quid fee for Dr Punter. Added evidence, in my mind, of dodginess on his part. Five hundred quid to write a prescription? Come on!

Now, though, I had my confrontation letters to get through.

Tessa, Billy, Sabrina, Stacey, Daryl, Leon, Maggie, Lenny and I were all sitting in a circle in a cramped upstairs office. Two counsellors in one small group. That was saying something. Usually it was one counsellor per group, but in the confrontation group backup was required.

'Please swap seats with Sabrina, Katie,' said Maggie, who was sitting directly opposite Lenny. We moved silently and our shoulders bashed.

'I'm really, *really* sorry,' said Sabrina. *What's she so excited about? It's me who's meant to be nervous.*

I moved onto the only comfy seat in the room. Now I was really scared. I was sitting between the two adjudicators, and in no way was that helping to ease my stress.

I looked at everyone, but not one person acknowledged me. My chest felt heavy, the air was stale, the room was claustrophobic and the faces of my soon-to-be-assassins were bleak. Most had their arms crossed and my fate was sitting on their six laps.

Fuck, fuck, fuck, fuck, fuck, fuck.

'After each letter, I'd like you to thank the reader, OK?' Len said. 'We will not move on to the next letter until you do this. These people have spent most of last night taking the trouble to write these two pages of feedback for you.'

Don't try and patronise me, Len, you wanker. I nodded.

After we'd done the usual preamble, we were straight into it. Tessa began. Her voice was quivering.

Dear Kate,

This is hard for me to write because I've lived as selfishly as you have and so I know all about the things you failed to tell us in your so-called life story. You've deceived and lied your way through your sad little life and blamed everyone apart from yourself along the way. It's disgusting. You didn't give a shit about anyone except yourself throughout your time sniffing drugs and using men for what you could get. Don't think I don't know how gross your behaviour was. I do. You talk about how your dad never hit you when you were little; maybe he should have done to try and bash some sense into that thick skull which was only capable of acts of selfishness and betrayal. The way you treated your dad was hateful – and after everything he'd done for you. How could you fuck him over like you did? He deserved better than your no-good treatment. I've treated my pets better than you treated him.

She never once looked up. My eyes felt as though they were on stalks. I was watching her face the whole time she was reading. She was close to tears on more than one occasion, and so was I. I hated hearing these words from her, and I felt bad for her that she had to do this.

'Thank you,' I said when she'd finished.

Tessa burst into deep sobs and said, 'Sorry.' It was heartbreaking.

'It's OK, it's OK,' I said, as I wiped away a tear that was rolling down my face. I wanted to hold her and tell her it was all right. My head was buzzing; I couldn't decide whether I felt angry or wanted to cry freely.

Daryl was next:

You're a right old tart, aren't you, eh? You think you can pull the wool over my eyes by not coming clean about what a slapper

117

you've been. Get a grip! I've met loads of girls like you, fucking and sucking their way to a sniff, but I'll tell you something, love, I'd never have come near your minge with a bargepole. I've got some self-respect, and if you had, you'd never have been selling your snatch just for a hit, you poxy druggie.

He went on and on before he was finished. 'Thank you,' I said. I wanted to jump up and bite Daryl's nose off before continuously meeting his face with my knee until he fell into a coma.

Then it was Stacey:

Katie, you dirty coke-whore.

What a filthy trollop you've been, eh? All the stuff you didn't tell us about your pathetic life. Do you really think we don't know? Are you trying to mug us all off? Do you believe that I don't know that you were drinking in the mornings and living in a stinking flat that you never kept clean? I noticed you'd forgotten to mention how you'd sucked off taxi drivers when you didn't have the money to pay them. You're nothing but a filthy, sick slut and if you manage to change it will be a miracle.

I zoned out until her lips stopped moving. Next came Billy. At this point, I was in a weird state of partial delirium. Molten hate was surging through my core. I wished I could tie up everyone in that room, gag them and make them watch while I scalped them one by one, before pouring sulphuric acid on their heads and watching their skin pop as they cooked slowly.

Sabrina was next:

Dear Katie, or should I say 'Miss Lie-a-Lot'?

Who the hell do you think you are, trying to tell us a whole pack of shit and bollocks about your so-called life, which wasn't how you'd described it at all? Do you think we're stupid in here, eh? Well, the only stupid person round here is you, you scrubber. You conveniently missed out any detail about your abuse of men, the shame you brought to your dad and your evil behaviour towards your stepmum. You've lived your life not giving a shit about anyone or anything except yourself and opening your legs so you could feed your filthy habit. Do you think you're clever? I don't. I've seen more intelligence in a monkey than what you read to us yesterday. I think you're a dirty pig who would have seen her father dead if it meant getting your hands on some coke. Your mum had a lucky escape when she got rid of you. Otherwise, you'd have abused her in the same selfish way as you did the only man who gave a damn about you. You should have been good to your dad – there isn't another man alive who'd want to be near a self-pitying mess like you. You need to get honest with yourself, and stop trying to be something that you're not. You're a fucking filthy mess. Get real about who you are and what you've become and stop trying to act as though you're better than everyone else, because you're more useless than most other people in here. Get a grip. I don't buy your lying bullshit. You reckon your whoring career started when you were 23 years old. No it didn't; you clearly got some practice in when you were three years old. You reckon those boys used to touch you against your will? Bollocks. You've always loved being abused; that's why you allowed it.

'Thank you.' I wanted to cut her open while she was still alive and shit in her chest cavity before stuffing some of the mess into her mouth.

Leon's letter, which was the last one, went over my head. I'd become cocooned in a mist of dangerous emotions. Sabrina, the fucking cunt, had said that I'd enjoyed being sexually abused as a child. The abuse had been perpetrated by three teenage boys who lived near my mother's compound in our village. I played outside for the most part. There was nowhere else to go, and it was normal for little kids to roam around without a parent on hand. This was Africa. Poverty made us grow up quickly and become quite independent at a very young age. These boys terrorised me from when I was around three years old, making me lie down as they touched me and forced me to touch their private parts. Virtually every day this was happening. I would cry and try to scream from the bushes where they'd take me, but one would cover my mouth to silence me. They threatened me with a beating if I told anyone. It had been extremely hard for me to talk about it. That Sabrina could allow such filth to enter her thoughts, never mind come out of her mouth, was foul. She needed to be dismembered with a hacksaw and reminded with every movement of the blade why I was doing this to her. My eyes were welded to her face.

Tessa began crying again and that suddenly reminded me that there were other abhorrent creatures in the room, too. I'd have been prepared to spend the rest of my life in jail given the opportunity to place an incendiary device under each chair and blow my supposed comrades to smithereens. Yes, including Len and Maggie, and Tessa and Leon – two-faced fucking arseholes, the pair of them. And as for Sabrina – I'd have pulled her eyes out of her severed head with a fork and repeatedly stamped on her skull, just to make sure she was really finished.

'How do you feel now?' Maggie asked.

Was this a trick question?

Because she'd made me go through this, I wanted to grip her cheek between my front teeth and feel her blood cover my lips as I clamped down. I wanted to hear her screams as she wriggled, trying to free herself from my hunger as I bit harder, then harder again, before spitting her rancid flesh into Len's face.

CHAPTER 16

'It's following your own will, Katie, without a thought for rules and regulations, that got you here in the first place,' Lenny said, pouting.

'At least I admitted to it,' I snapped. The whole place could go to hell for all I cared. Confrontation letters and now this crock of shit? There was no escape from having a finger pointed in your direction. This wasn't a cop group, just a bog standard session.

'So, if you tried to rob someone for your next line of cocaine –'

'I've never robbed anyone.'

'Just listen, Kate. And if that robbery went wrong and you ended up killing the person, in court when the judge asked, "How do you plead?" if you said, "Guilty," do you think he'd let you off your prison sentence?'

Totally unnecessary. I hated this kind of overdramatic question. I shook my head. I was hanging on in the centre by a thread and scared of what my response would be if something reignited my anger. I'd been quiet for days after the confrontation group and thankfully I'd been allowed to be so.

The fuss about Leon and me seemed to have taken a back seat with the PTB. But now I was expected to show remorse for having taken a nap. I wasn't sorry and didn't have the will to pretend that I was.

'Well?' said Lenny.

For fuck's sake, can't you just drop it, you anal twit? 'No, Len,' I said wearily. 'I'm sure the judge wouldn't let me off. But I don't think that closing my eyes for a few minutes after dinner can be compared to murder, really, do you?' I felt I was losing it. Rehab was getting too much for me to handle.

'Notice how she's minimising, group. Katie sleeping on her bed has now turned into a minor "closing her eyes". So what happened when Camille confronted you about breaking the rules?'

'I asked her to leave me alone.'

'Why? Why didn't you just get up off the bed when she suggested you should?'

Anger was forcing its way up my throat. 'I was tired, Len. That's why I didn't get up. I was knackered, all right? Absolutely shattered, OK? I didn't do it out of malice, you know. I didn't think to myself, "Right, fuck BCH and Lenny with their stupid over-the-top rules."' I paused. 'I was sleepy and I needed a snooze, that's all. If I'd been able to stay awake, I would have done, but the reality of my situation at the time was that I just couldn't.'

'OK, OK, so what happened after you asked Camille to leave you alone?'

'Well, she wouldn't leave.'

'She?'

Fuck off, Len. 'Oh, sorry, I thought you'd already realised I was talking about Camille. By "she" I meant Camille. You know, that Camille, right there.' I nodded towards her. 'Is that clearer now? You know who I'm talk– '

'Don't get smart with me, Katie. Just tell us what happened

next. You've never really been the same since your confrontation letters, have you?'

'So *Camille* came and stood over the bed, and she, *Camille*, again told me to get up. I said to her *assertively*, not aggressively, to please leave me alone, and that I was tired and I needed to close my eyes for a few minutes.'

'Then what?'

'She wouldn't go.' Like a seraph with a broken wing, the injured party was looking at me through her glasses. 'So I said, "Will you just . . ."'

'Just what?'

'I'm trying to tell you now . . . I said . . .'

'Did you *say* or did you shout?'

'Right,' I said, starting to speak quickly, 'this is what happened. Camille came over to me and told me to get up, so I asked her to leave me alone, and she wouldn't. Then I *told* her to leave me alone, and she still wouldn't. Then I asked her if she'd do me a favour and just fuck off. She refused, so I told her to do one again, and when she still wouldn't fucking leave me to sleep, I yelled at her to get the fuck out of the room.'

'Is that right, Camille?'

'It is, yes,' she answered self-righteously.

'OK, you've got another seven-day warning, Kate. We don't accept threatening or intimidating behaviour here. You know that.'

I started to bite the inside of my mouth. I hadn't noticed anyone else getting even one warning during my seven-week incarceration.

The warning was merely protocol, I decided. Something had changed in me. The incandescent rage I'd previously have felt at a time like this was replaced with a weird, almost placid acceptance of whatever fate had in store for me. I had worn myself out not only with my battle outside of rehab but inside, too. I wasn't sure if I could continue with treatment. I wanted to, but it was all getting too much.

Camille presented as prim and conservative, but this was the woman who'd arrived at BCH just days after she'd been arrested for not turning up in court on a charge of stealing two bottles of vodka from her local Waitrose. She'd said she couldn't face putting her husband through the shame of her appearing in a courtroom because he was a solicitor, but I reckon the damage had already been done. The charge against Camille might have been easier for her husband to deal with had his wife appeared in court when she was supposed to, instead of which he watched her being dragged into a police van one Sunday afternoon when the two of them were taking the dog for a stroll. But we've all been there. Or should I say, I have . . .

After the group, the plaintiff overheard me complaining to Daryl that any noise directed by a person of healthy weight at a five-stone woman would seem like intimidation.

Camille told Maggie, who told me to write her an apology.

I decided to leave.

CHAPTER 17

Three days after scribbling, 'Camille, sorry if I upset you,' on some lined paper, I was just about ready to batten down the hatches and tell BCH to go and screw themselves. If I'd been Maggie, I'd have sung 'Not Sorry' by The Cranberries while brandishing a two-fingered salute at the whole lot of them.

Fuck my Step 4 and leaving when the PTB told me I was ready. I wanted to go home now. Billy, whom I usually enjoyed talking to, had begun to feel like a burden, and most other people weren't worth the effort. I'd never have chosen the majority of them to light my cigarette, let alone spend every bloody waking hour with. When I'd been a teenage toerag, I'd tried to ingratiate myself with crack- and smackhead cons in a bid to remove myself from my suburban roots, but for years now I'd got used to skipping around London with work-shy wannabes who somehow still managed to be covered in gold jewellery and wear Louboutins.

I started to glamorise my past life. Some of the punters I'd fucked were all right; a few were attractive. London seemed so far away that I could barely remember that I'd once had a life there, never mind one that in the early days had felt exciting and which I'd enjoyed. Anything seemed better than being cooped up with people whom I'd never see again after my release, despite our endless chats about eternal friendships, blah, blah.

I was collecting warnings like it was de rigueur; I hated dealing with petty idiots and trivial rules. I felt I was in a vortex where every action, every thought, every desire had to be questioned and the meaning and motive understood. This was my new reality.

The only respite I got was with Tessa, who was growing to be my sister in arms. And there was always Leon . . .

RULES

- Clients are not permitted to keep in the houses items that may be misused, such as mouthwash, aftershave, perfume or aerosols. These are to be stored in the centre and may be used under supervision there. Non-aerosol deoderants may be used in the houses.
- Permission must be obtained from a counsellor if a client wishes to dye his or her hair.

I harboured a nest of matted hair. My top lip needed waxing, my eyebrows plucking, my bikini line felled, my feet pummelled, my nail extensions redone – all of which, of course, I wasn't allowed. Instead I'd been escorted to a nail salon to get my acrylic nails taken off. I was gutted; they'd been part of my body for years.

Meanwhile, I hadn't had a period for ages and I wanted to come on to release some pressure, but all I got was, 'It's normal. Your body's rebalancing,' according to Dr Punter.

The main problem was not my nails, hair, feet or lack of menstruation, but the lack of freedom. When I spoke about this feeling, I was irritatingly reminded that giving it up had been my choice. I'd admitted myself there and no one else was to blame.

Apart from piss, shit and fart, everything I did was scheduled. I couldn't even shave my legs whenever I felt like it. Maggie guarded the razors (in case someone used them to self-harm; I wondered how Sabrina was managing to cut herself) and she didn't think it was necessary to defuzz on a regular basis. I agreed. It wasn't essential for my well-being. But it would have been nice to have the choice. 'It's not like someone's going to be touching you there, now, is it?' Maggie would grin, loving the power she had. That wasn't the point. She'd say no because she felt like it, and she'd get two out of ten for taking a brazen decision to do as *she* liked, regardless of potential aggro.

I was fed up with never having proper time to myself. Even when I managed to sit alone for a moment, some fucker would come bounding over asking if I was all right. I wanted to shout, 'I was absolutely fine before you came poking your nose into my one friggin' moment of peace, but thanks for asking!' The closest I would get to this would be to avoid eye contact and say, 'I'm OK,' in a controlled way. It was a fine line. If I said it too moodily, it was guaranteed that the intruder would pull up a seat and start to probe. But if I said it too heartily, they'd pull up a seat to 'keep me company'.

I was hacked off with wearing the same clothes in rotation and sick of not being able to put stuff in a washing machine whenever I wanted. Instead, we would go in packs of six to the launderette, trudging along the streets of Weymouth like a group of gypsy kids on an excursion.

I was itching to leave and wasn't sure what was keeping me there. My goblin was insistent that I was wasting my time by staying.

I wanted to scream. I hated everyone. I hated my life. Most of all, I despised myself for having got to where I was in the first place.

'This too will pass,' I was told.

Oh. Fuck. Off!

CHAPTER 18

RULE

- Clients are expected to protect their own anonymity and that of others. Therefore, while clients should always be courteous to members of the local community outside the centre, it is advisable not to get involved in conversation.

I relished the two ninety-minute sessions in the park each week, when both houses got together counsellor-free, and when Leon and I would take the last fifteen minutes of this time to get closer than we could ever be in the centre.

Exercise was prohibited. It was imperative that people with eating disorders didn't use fitness as a form of weight control – and for those without an eating disorder it wasn't to be used as a distraction or to get a buzz. But football was permitted. No, I never understood that either.

Tessa and I would usually link arms and watch the fellas in their shorts. Sabrina would join us. She'd stand around neurotically scratching her nose or thoughtlessly pulling her knickers out of her arse, her headphones secured to her large-earring-wearing lugs as indie music pumped directly into her brain. Camille would stand beside us, although she was never there mentally.

The boundaries she had been set were not at all flexible. She was allowed to walk 'at a reasonable pace, but no speed-walking', round the park, once, with another person if she wanted to, but that was it. If she did walk round, she'd go with Stacey, when Stacey wasn't stretching to try to keep herself occupied. If she was confronted about this form of 'exercise' in the cop group, she'd say she had bad circulation and was trying to keep the blood flowing. *Yeah, right.*

Tessa had a crush. Daryl was not my type, but then again neither was Leon. Daryl was unofficially deemed to be 'hers', as Leon was seen as 'mine'.

How I'd gone from screwing the eldest son of a head of state to fantasising about a crackhead short-arse provoked painful questions.

On my first date with the president's son, I didn't screw him. Not because I wanted to be 'good' but because I was too fucked to even try to perform.

Our second date took place in Paris, at the Hôtel Costes. That time, we fucked. Kind of. The guy had got one of his security guards to accompany me on a private jet so I could meet him for dinner in the city. Now, this time, I wore a dress (with flat sandals, but still). On the plane, I drank vodka, ate beluga caviar and tried to find out about my Arabian suitor. I guessed who he was, but the bodyguard refused to confirm my hunch.

When I arrived at the hotel, the guy was waiting for me in the opulent, dimly lit bar. The hotel was exquisitely chic and the company was better than it had been three weeks before.

I'd smuggled an eighth of coke through customs, wrapped

in a condom in my pussy, to do when I got there. First we ate and then we went to our suite. I'd never seen anything like it – luxury in its purest form. From a dinky, scruffy town in Yorkshire to this. I felt quite smug. Sue me.

I asked my date where his security guards were and he reassured me that all was well and no one could hear or see anything that we did. I made us drinks and he ran water and poured scented oil into a bath that we needed to enter via steps. For the first time, we kissed. I was sitting on the edge of the bed, which was a perfect position for me to place his cock into my mouth. I was watching him. He was childlike in his impatience to be sucked. His cock was thick and long, and I grinned.

'Does it make you happy?' he asked me. I nodded. I tugged it and lowered my head and he came – all over my hand. He'd shot his load before I'd even kissed his cock. Now that didn't make me happy at all.

At BCH we surmised all sorts about each other, our pasts and our current flirtations, but with no solid evidence there was little anyone could say.

Rivalries between people could cause havoc, so stepping on someone's toes with regard to a flirtation was a no-no.

'You know, I'm not really that bothered about Daryl, though, eh, Kate?' Tessa cackled defensively when I teased her about him.

'Yeah, course you're not!'

'Don't get me wrong, bab. I'd love to get jiggy with him, but I've got my kids to think about. They'll always come first from now on, always . . . But look at him. He's cute, isn't he?' She was changing the subject to avoid becoming emotional about her kids.

'Er, no, babe. "Cute" isn't the word that springs to mind when I see Daryl.' Whenever he came close, I couldn't help but stare at the scar where a chunk of muscle was missing from his calf.

'You two just never let up staring at the boys, do ya?' Stacey said.

'No, never,' I replied. I could feel a snipe coming from an aggrieved Tessa, so I quickly asked, 'So when do you go to secondary, Stace?'

'Not sure yet. Soon, I think. I'm waiting to –'

'So don't worry about it then, sweetheart,' said Tessa. 'You'll be gone in a minute, eh? And all this will be fuck all to do with you.'

I felt bad for Stacey. Camille stood up. 'There's no need for that,' she said, but Tess ignored her.

Lisa came over. She was a new girl, aged 24, a willowy, gaunt, anorexic cokehead from Bristol. She'd jacked up charlie since leaving home at 15 to work as a model in Milan and then New York. Track marks scarred the inside of her arms. This gave me the creeps. She seemed so fragile. Most people did in the early days, but below that, in most cases, lurked the stamina of King Kong.

It would take Lisa a while to feel at ease and decipher her new regime. At least she wasn't detoxing; she'd done one already. Her Yankee boyfriend had paid for it before packing her off back to Bristol to be near her parents, blatantly not wanting to take responsibility for a life that seemed to be hurtling towards annihilation.

'What do we do here, then?' Lisa asked from behind her shoulder-length dark hair.

'*This*. This is it. This is what we do. We sit here and watch the fellas,' Tessa chortled. I lit a cigarette.

'Do you want to walk around the park?' Stacey suggested. Lisa agreed and they went off together.

The end of the game came and I rushed towards Leon, who was stooped over, panting, alongside Austin. Tessa started taking the piss out of Daryl for being unfit. 'It's all that blubber you've put on in here that's slowed you down, mate! You want to get back on the smack, get some weight off you.'

He was almost too out of breath to respond, but he found it in himself: 'You want to get back on the bench, love, before I body slams you, lairy bitch.'

They both laughed.

'You all right?' said Leon. 'How's it going?' He was giving me the head down, eyes up, 'You're gonna geddit' look.

Things were no longer as bad as they'd seemed during the preceding days. I'd started to thaw. I'd reluctantly decided to stay; I owed myself that much. I'd turned to fantasy during the times I wasn't listening to battle stories about loves lost and crumbled dreams and constipation lasting days on account of heroin use.

I stared at Leon's body. He was thin but strong. Beads of sweat trickled down the middle of his almost hairless chest. I wanted to touch him; he knew it and scrunched his lips into a kiss. Jesus, my heart was thumping.

'Come here, next to me,' I said. We both lay on the grass. 'I want to talk to you about that thing . . .'

'What thing?'

'The thing you found out about me in my confrontation letters group, about how I . . .'

'How you made your money?'

'Yeah.' I started picking at the grass.

'Let's not talk about it. Not now, babes, all right? I want you to know that it don't matter to me, you know what I'm sayin'? We all do whatever to get by, and I'm no angel, get me?'

'Are you serious?'

'Yeah, it don't matter to me.'

'But how can it not? I don't get that.'

'Because you're how you is today, innit? That's who I'm feeling right now, not who you were.'

I could tell I was about to launch into a huge justification of my existence and explanation of how I was brought up well and that Daddy loved me and that I deeply regretted the hurt I'd caused and how it had all been a tragic mistake and . . . and . . . Leon saw this.

'Katie?'

'Yeah?'

'I . . .' He stopped. What was he about to say? 'I care a lot about you. Let's talk about the future, not the past, huh?'

'Right, let's go!' Simon, our house leader for the week, bellowed. That was our signal to go back to our houses for the start of another monotonous evening.

'You know something?' I said. 'I can't believe that for the next week I have to listen to some mummy's boy throwing his eight-stone bag of bones around and telling me what to do.' Leon agreed. I was liking him even more now. Not only was he looking more attractive as time went by – he was also more mature than I'd have guessed.

'Come on, hurry up!' Simon screamed.

'We'd better get going, otherwise he'll have a go and I can't be doing with any bollocks from him. I'll end up telling him to go fuck himself if he gets on that high horse of his.'

Leon's eyes bored into mine. I would have jumped on his cock in an instant had no one been there.

'Where's Lisa and Stacey?' Simon yelled, once he'd taken a headcount.

'They're there!' Tessa screamed back. 'Bet that fuckin' Stacey's trying to turn Lisa into a rug-muncher, you know. It wouldn't surprise me, silly cow . . . As if Lisa would be interested in her even if she was a dyke. But from what I've heard they're all at it at those fashion shows.' She laughed loudly while doing an exaggerated model walk, one arm sticking out at right angles for maximum impact.

Leon and I stood up. He touched my hand and I jumped.

'Come on. People are moving. Let's go,' I said, to cover up my shyness. Neither of us moved.

'I'm going to cop those two in group on Monday,' Simon croaked, referring to Stacey and Lisa.

'Give it a rest' – Daryl.

'You should at least consider not doing that,' Billy added.

'Why? That's what we're meant to do in these situations, aren't we?' – Simon.

'Depends where you're coming from, don't it?' – Daryl.

Billy: 'Well, perhaps according to the laws of our current environment, it may be a –'

'Lisa's just arrived, Si, for God's sake. You can't start fucking pointing the finger at someone who doesn't understand the rules' – Tessa.

'Yeah, but Stacey does. And Tessa, sweetheart, it's not "Si", it's Simon – if you don't mind, thank you.'

'Oh, shut up' – Tessa.

'Yeah, just zip it, fella' – Daryl.

Billy: 'In my humble opinion, guys, it seems as though we're at loggerheads with –'

'And you can shut it an' all' – Tessa.

Billy: 'Excuse me if you feel –'

'Billy, man, fuck's sake' – Daryl.

I began to walk away, but Leon pulled on my arm. I stumbled

backwards into him and just like that he kissed my neck.

'Stop it, stop it!' I said, rushing away. My head was rattling with saucy intentions as I rushed towards everyone else, but I was worried sick in case someone had seen what had just happened. Simon and a few others screamed for Stacey and Lisa to hurry and we began shuffling towards the exit. The girls received a lecture about timekeeping from our pompous house leader. We were 40 adults shuffling along the road, goofing around in double file like a disordered chain gang.

Leon tapped my arse, a signal for me to slow down. 'Hey!' he said. I ignored him. 'I want to taste you,' he grunted. He almost scared me. 'I'll fill you up when we're alone, innit?'

'Shush! For God's sake, don't let anyone hear you.'

'Babes, they've got hearing just like you and me, you know. They might act like robots, but they ain't got sonic ears.'

'Well, I don't know, do I?'

'Look, they can't hear anything. I promise you. No one can . . . only you,' he added directly into my ear. I speeded up to get away from him. I didn't trust myself to not sit on his face until I came on his tongue in a random act of helplessness.

Five minutes later, cheek kisses and attempted gropes were exchanged at the junction where the two groups separated. 'I'm gone, babes. Gonna miss you tonight,' The Youth whispered, pressing his hands into my lower back and pulling me closer. Way too coupley. I pulled away flamboyantly. *Onlookers: if you think you heard something, you're wrong. Saw something? Prove it!*

My once shy soon-to-be-lover was getting confident, maybe too much so. I wanted to complete what I'd started, but the rules of our domicile could not be forgotten.

Would I let myself be thrown out of rehab for the sake of some cock?

Doubt it.

CHAPTER 19

I wanted to be put through my paces physically. I wanted to claw at a hard body, preferably Leon's, as I quivered to orgasm. Yeah, I could get myself off by masturbating, but it wasn't the same. Most of all, I wanted to feel wanted, and I associated sex with feeling loved.

Sex confused me.

OK, so before becoming a whore I'd had a lot of one-night stands, and on the surface this may seem not too dissimilar to paid sex with strangers, but psychologically it is very different. Why? Because I *chose* who I was going to have sex with when it was for free. I made some bad choices, thanks to beer goggles, but nonetheless I went ahead without being 'owned'.

When I fell for cocaine, I was prepared to do almost anything to keep our relationship alive, but I wasn't willing to mug, burgle or attack people. Instead, I decided that sex for money was the answer to my financial woes. Anyone who thinks that I had no choice about whether or not I had sex with men for cash because I was a hopeless cokehead is wrong. I *did* have a choice, because no one marched me off to a hotel room or flat to screw me; I went of my own accord.

Emotionally, however, it was different; I offered my body

to be used by strangers with a great deal of fear and very reluctantly. My compulsion to use drugs and to get the money I needed to use those drugs was greater than the feelings of self-disgust and anxiety that I went through prior to, often during and certainly after getting the cash. I'd zone out much of the time and wouldn't connect with the client unless I found him attractive, and then only sometimes. Nothing can remove the fact that your life is at the mercy of a stranger who has 'bought' you for the duration of the time you are with him. You are effectively his property, a slave.

I could hop on board a hard cock for money or not, as I chose. I could give the guy the whole eye-contact bit and I could occasionally even lose myself in a moment of carnal delight. But chatting and being physically close afterwards? Cuddling and lying still, close to someone, whether naked or not, was something I could not do.

Once I'd been in rehab for a number of weeks, I started to think about how my relationships with men were supposed to change. I'd heard a rumour that a lot of 'normals' get to know each other a little before they sleep together. They often form a type of friendship first, apparently, and only after that, if they choose to, they get naked.

I'd almost never spent time getting to know a guy as a friend before screwing him. Even my relationships had stemmed from one-night stands, with the exception of Jimmy, who insisted that we wait a month before we slept together. How very mature of him.

Perhaps, had I got to know the president's son better before flying off to Paris that fateful night, I'd have been willing to see him again even after the dismal events.

After he'd come on my hand, the guy seemed unconcerned

139

about what had happened. That, or he was a good actor. We climbed into the huge bath together and at one point he stood in front of me, hands on his hips – *cocky shit* – offering his erect cock for me to suck on. This time, I just about managed to get it inside my mouth before he erupted into orgasm once again. *Again!* Oh dear. He must be nervous, I decided. I still hadn't had a look-in. My genitalia had had no attention from him, and I tried to convince myself that now he'd relieved himself so speedily, *now* he'd run like a steam train.

Naked in bed, we began kissing. My pussy was ready for him.

'Does she want me?' he asked. Who? I wondered, then realised he was referring to my snatch.

'Yes, but use a condom.'

He ignored my request and entered me. Instantly, he withdrew and I watched him ejaculate his warm semen straight onto my belly button.

At that point, I'd lost the will to continue. I no longer cared about the flash hotel, the private jet or his big useless cock, I wanted an orgasm, and since I wasn't getting one, I wanted to go home. Had this been a job, I'd have laughed at how easy it was. But it wasn't work. I was supposed to be there for pleasure – mine as well as his. Joker.

How I'd achieve a new attitude towards sex, I had no idea. 'One day at a time,' I presumed. But I had no idea while I was in BCH what a difficult journey I had ahead of me. Prostitution and allowing myself to be used time and again had left me with immense scars.

CHAPTER 20

I was upstairs in the office hoovering when suddenly a hand cupped the crack of my arse. I knew who it was; I'd guessed this was coming. The moment I turned round, my mouth met Leon's tongue for the first time. It was noticeably soft and not too wet. I *'hmm'*d and so did he. I was more turned on than I'd ever been, but I also felt overwhelmed. The pulsating in my pussy was cascading throughout my legs. Was this the sensation that people talked about? There'd been no chemicals in my body now for nine weeks and I was shocked that for the whole of my life I'd been missing out on this.

This was my first sober and drug-free smooch ever. Even my first time, aged 14, had been lubricated with Merrydown Cider and Diamond White. (I'd forced this concoction down for its powers of inebriation, not for its sophisticated associations.)

Leon and I kissed self-consciously – a lot hung on this. This wasn't the time to lose our minds to our senses; we'd already crossed at least one threshold, and that was enough. My urge to consummate our thing was highlighted by the intensity of our goldfish-bowl environment. Still, though, I was nervous.

'I'm scared someone might come up here,' I said.

'Turn the Hoover off,' he muttered. I could feel his breath on the side of my face. 'Turn it off. Are you going to do as you're told?'

'Only if you kiss me.'

We both kept our eyes open. He looked blurred.

'We can't do this!' I said, more loudly than I'd intended to.

'Shh!' Leon gripped the back of my hair and his tongue took my mouth hostage. I pushed him off me.

'Stop. Stop. Is someone coming? Can you hear something?' I held my breath. I felt wired. 'You've gotta go!'

We kissed some more and suddenly his hand was inside my jeans and inside my knickers. I was immobilised. My entire world was that moment. I murmured.

'*Shh!*' Leon seemed fixated on the hold he had over me. I felt a rush of blood to my head. He pushed two fingers inside me. I gasped and he covered my mouth.

'That's it, baby,' he whispered. He was nuzzling my neck.

'Leon, please,' I breathed. 'I'm going to collapse, my legs feel like jelly . . . Please . . . go back downstairs.'

'I need to fuck you, Kate.'

'Stop, please, we shouldn't be doing this,' I croaked, not meaning a word of it. His mouth rotated onto mine. He pulled away, stared at me and left.

I felt disorientated. I buttoned up my jeans and bent over, taking deep breaths with my hands on my knees, desperate to find some balance.

I tried to ignore Leon as I finished off my duties back in the main room. Every part of my body was quivering. Surely someone knew what had just gone on? *Are people saying nothing for a reason?*

Suddenly, Maggie came up behind me and put her hand on my shoulder. I jumped.

'Ahh! Don't!' I snapped.

'I didn't mean to scare you, there. As soon as you're done, Katie, please come to my office.'

My heart leapt into my throat. I felt queasy. Someone knew what had just happened. I could feel it. I'd thrown my treatment away for nothing, not even an orgasm.

I glanced at Leon and he came towards me, but I couldn't stop and talk. I had to know what Maggie had to say. I rushed to her office, deciding to lie like a politician if she asked me about anything that was sure to get me the boot.

'Close the door, please.' *Fuck.* She looked stern.

'Are you OK?' she asked.

'What?'

'Are you all right? You look a bit worried.'

'Er . . . well, I'm just wondering what you called me in here for and what you're about to say.' I felt sick, sick.

'First, is there something *you* want to say?'

'Me? Oh God . . . well, not really . . .' I didn't want to play games. I just wanted her to hit me with it and have done.

'Maggie, please just say it.'

'Say what?'

'What you called me in here for . . . just say it.'

'OK, well, we've received the first payment from the social for your treatment, and what's more they've agreed to back pay the last four weeks. That's fantastic news, isn't it? So you don't need to worry about your funding. It's all in hand.'

'Eh?' Was this a ploy to sweeten me up before hitting me with Clause 4, Section 2.3, Paragraph 1 of the Laws of Rehab: 'No intimate physical contact'?

'You don't look too pleased.'

'Erm . . . no, no, I am, I just thought . . .'

'Katie, what's wrong?'

'Nothing. I don't know. I'm a bit confused . . . So is that what you wanted to say to me then? Is that it?'

'What more do you want? That's great news, isn't it?'

'Yeah, I suppose so.'

'You *suppose* so? There's clearly no pleasing some people. However, now I do have something else I want to say to you.'

'Oh no. What is it?'

'I want you to take that rabbit-trapped-in-the-headlights look off your face and cheer up! What's wrong with you?'

'I'm sorry, I'm just feeling a bit . . . So all you called me in here for was to tell me that everything has been sorted out with the finances? Is that it?'

'Well, yes. At least Jim will be pleased – even if you look a bit at a loss.'

'Oh, thank you! Jesus! Thank you so much!' I began to smile.

'So, you are pleased then?'

'I'm absolutely bloody ecstatic. You'll never, ever know what a relief it is to hear those words from you just now, Maggie.' *I certainly hope you never will.*

'So can I go now? Look, I didn't mean to sound . . . I just thought that maybe you wanted to . . . oh, never mind.'

Leon and I had evaded capture once again. Nothing, it seemed, could go wrong with our union.

Or so I thought.

CHAPTER 21

Camille left. We were told that she'd 'closed down'. In fact, she'd never opened up, and because of this few people cared that she'd abandoned ship. I hadn't clicked with her and neither had Tessa so, as far as we were concerned, if she'd decided to leave, that was up to her.

Anyone who thinks that anorexia is a fad is bonkers. I'm sure Camille didn't set out to restrict her food to one apple and one grapefruit per day, but that's what she was eating before entering BCH, she'd told us quite proudly. What may initially be perceived as vanity, or experimenting and fun in the case of drugs, can go too far – of course it can – but very rarely by chance. It's rare that anything in life is truly accidental. We subconsciously plan our route long before we reach our destination. But beware the potholes. Some can be harder to scramble out of than others. Undereating or overeating, or any other form of compulsive or obsessive behaviour, can easily go too far if you're predisposed to addiction.

Those who are emotionally well and who start a diet would never allow it to get out of hand. What stable person gets off on experiencing hunger pains and interprets these pains as an exciting form of control? This is masochistic, surely?

Who allows 'losing a bit of weight' to turn into a constant preoccupation with food? Now it's not fun. It's serious, it's secretive, it's no longer about body image. You can see you're not overweight. You may think you're heavier than others perceive you to be, but you know you're not fat. Now people are commenting about your shape for the wrong reasons and they just won't stop. You wish that people would keep out of your business and mind their own. 'Get some food down ya,' they squawk.

The thought processes, lies and deceit are the same with anorexia as with any other addiction, and it had been important not to alienate Camille because of our lack of understanding of how she used her drug. Again, it's not about substance or quantity; it's about attitude. Bearing this in mind, we didn't dwell on the specifics of food and eating but focused on the feelings of despair, fear, hopelessness and sorrow that we all shared.

Camille was possibly the most complex and sickest person I met in BCH. So where did she go when she left? Back to the husband who couldn't cope and had shared a bed with her for less than half of their eight-year marriage, back to a pretty stone house outside Bath, four acres, her chocolate Labrador – and back to starvation. That was all she knew. 'She succumbed to her demons' is the stock phrase. But what does that actually *mean*? It means nothing had changed. She was taking away all the emotional turmoil that had brought her into rehab with no tools to help her to cope.

There's trying and *really* trying, and *really* trying is painful, ball-breaking, excruciating work. Unhooking myself from the damaging attitudes I'd had since my teenage years, destroying habits I'd had for most of my life and dealing with emotions that had been kept buried for years was never going to be easy. No one ever said it would be. The power of compulsions, negative beliefs, habits and demons – whatever you want to call them – can easily outweigh that strand of sanity that suggests you continue to try to help yourself. I was both Nice Kate, the traditional girl whom Daddy had raised, and Goblin Kate, who was far more vocal, destructive and forthright than the quieter girl who shared the same space.

Two days after Camille left, Sabrina moved out of our room and in with Tessa, while Lisa moved in to share with me.

This was a sign that I'd been deemed 'well' enough to be placed with a newcomer. The arrival of a new face was a welcome breath of fresh air for me. Getting through every evening, stuck in a house with people whom I'd never choose to live with, was at times mind-numbing and frequently depressing.

'Oi, you two!' Tessa screeched one morning, before flinging herself onto my neatly made bed. 'There's no point in putting any more of that crap on yer face, Katie. It won't make any difference.'

'Did I tell you, Lisa, that Tessa would have won an award for her humour – if only she was funny!'

Lisa said nothing.

'Hark at you!' Tessa replied.

'Shaat iit!' I told her. 'I'm only putting on a bit of mascara, if that's all right with you. I didn't sleep that well last night.'

'Yeah, right. As if that'll make any dif– '

'Look, will you get off my bed, T. I've just fucking straightened it and it's taken me ages.'

'Ooh, sorry, Stroppy.'

'If I get pointed out in the cop group for having a crumpled duvet, I know where to find you.' I started laughing. 'Have you heard us? Going on about a bed and if the covers are straight enough in case we get ticked off by some fucking counsellor who probably doesn't even wash their hands after they've had a dump! Can you believe this is life?'

'I'm doing youse a favour by coming in here to get ya, cos you shoulda been downstairs by now.'

'Already?' Lisa grabbed her battered loafers (probably Hermès). Luckily for her, she didn't need to do anything other than wash that model face of hers.

'Don't worry, babe. Tessa's being a drama queen. Just ignore her.'

'I'm not, bab, honestly. Have you seen the time? It's nearly 8.45. Get a shift on.'

'OK, OK.'

I went into a frenzy, searching for clean socks and checking that my homework was in my bag, then going back to the mirror to check my make-up.

'By the way,' said Tessa, 'you know Stacey's getting her Step 4 today?'

'Is she?'

'Katie, come on, you've already got him, you don't need –'

I gave Tessa a hard stare to remind her not to say anything incriminating in front of a girl I knew nothing about.

'Got who?' Lisa asked. 'Should we go downstairs now?'

'Yeah . . . so, Stacey'll be off to secondary within a few days?' I asked, changing the subject – fast.

Tessa mouthed, 'Sorry.' I winked at her. For all I knew, Lisa might have grassed me up the moment she caught wind of any potential gossip about a guy and me, but I knew my friend hadn't begun to say what she had on purpose.

'Er, yeah, she'll be gone within a few days, I reckon, thank God. Good riddance to that miserable cow, I say. Oops, Lisa,

I'm only joking. She's not that bad. She's all right, really, it's just . . .' Tessa backtracked, for fear of sounding bitchy.

'You don't get on with her, Tess, be honest!' I said.

'You're right, I don't! She's got a face like a smacked arse.'

'So, anyway, who is it that you've "got", then, Katie?' Lisa grinned as we all marched out of the room.

'No one. Tessa talks crap to try and wind me up.'

We signed out of the house and started walking to the centre. Lisa was chatting to Sabrina while I stayed with Tessa.

'This thing with Leon is doing my fucking head in, you know,' I whispered.

'Bab, I'm really sorry about earlier. I wasn't going to mention Leon's name, you know. I just –'

'Oh, forget it. Honestly, it's all right.'

'I'm sorry.'

'Forget it. Look, I'm finding this Leon thing hard to deal with.'

'I know. I mean, this isn't an ideal place to start a relationship, is it? I have the same problem with Daryl. I mean, it's not as intense as you and Leon, but I can't stop thinking about him.' She paused, and then added seriously, 'God, I just want to get shagged rotten, you know.' We both burst out laughing.

Tessa and I had things in common. I knew she could keep a secret, but I didn't want to compromise her integrity by telling her about my encounter with Leon in the office. Even so, I wasn't really sure I could keep it to myself.

CHAPTER 22

'What are you two smirking about?' Maggie asked Tess and me after the reading from *Just for Today* had finished. 'I've watched you both grinning at each other as though there's something the rest of us don't know. So what's so funny?'

'Nothing,' I said.

'Well, something's up, so share the joke.' The way she peered down her glasses made me start convulsing with laughter. Tessa snorted and I didn't know what to do with myself. I couldn't stop.

In fact, we weren't actually laughing at anything in particular. Something Maggie had said had struck me as funny, I'd caught Tessa's eye, and that was that. We didn't just get the giggles, we were hysterical. It wasn't just excessive feelings of sorrow and regret that could be hard to manage in rehab; often things that would only have been slightly humorous in normal circumstances seemed absolutely hilarious.

'I'm sorry, I'm sorry,' I spluttered, shaking my head and fanning my hand in Maggie's direction.

'Just calm down, both of you. You're disturbing the group. Let me tell you this much, you may think you're comedians, and you may tell people that you are, but I assure you that to real comedians you're not!' Other people had also started laughing. 'Everyone, quiet! If the two of you don't take these sessions for what they are, precious time to gain understanding, it's not fair for everyone else here who does.'

'Maggie, please, I'm sorry.' I tried to calm myself. 'I do take this seriously. You know I do.'

'You could have fooled me.'

My mania subsided. 'Come on. That's unfair! Just cos we're giggling.'

'Please can I go and get a glass of water?' Tess asked.

'No, you can't!' Maggie snapped. How could a hippy-looking, tattooed, middle-aged ex-junkie be so grouchy all the fucking time?

Then the laughing started again.

'Get out of this group!' Maggie yelled.

'Me?'

'No, the Pope! Of course *you*! Stand outside and come back in when you can control yourself, Katie. This group is about Stacey and her Step 4, and you're turning it into a circus. It's so selfish of both of you, do you realise that?'

'I'm just feeling happy, Maggie, that's all. Is that such a bad thing? I'm sorry, but really I don't get what the big deal is.'

'People's lives are a big deal!' she shouted. I hated her in that moment. 'It's constant with you, and it's got to stop. You're laughing in groups, you don't listen to advice, you're playing with people's emotions in here. And while we're on the subject, let me tell you something else: you'll relapse if you go back to your flat. You can't afford to be there. You'll suffer an almighty tsuris. And for those of you not familiar with Yiddish, I'm saying she'll come a cropper. Mark my words, you'll end up selling your body to pay the rent, and your loneliness will overwhelm you. And before we get back to Stacey and her

Step 4, group, Katie needs you to remind her why exactly she'll relapse if she goes back to her flat.'

'Maggie, I'm here. You're talking to me as though I'm a plank of wood. I don't need you or anyone else to remind me of anything, because I'm not going to go backwards.'

OK, I wasn't a perfect specimen of sobriety, but the small steps I was taking were leading me in a forward direction, surely? If not, what was I doing there?

'Come on! Simon?'

For once, he looked lost. He blatantly had no idea what to say, but he had form for breaking the silence, so to save losing face he opened his trap: 'Well, I suppose she won't be able to afford it. That could be a problem.'

S.O.C.I.A.L. fucking S.E.C.U.R.I.T.Y. Was I the only person who'd ever heard of this? I smirked.

'Do you find this funny, Kate?'

'No.'

Sadistic Fantasy Part 1: Maggie is on the floor, begging me to stop kicking her in the ribs as I scream, 'Look what you've made me do to you, Maggie, you stupid thatch-haired cow-twat.' And when she won't shut up, I boot her in the groin.

'And what will happen if she can't afford her rent?' the Wicked Witch of Weymouth barked.

Tessa was about to say something, but Maggie spoke over her.

'Well, I'll tell you what will happen to you, Kate.'

'I think perhaps –' Billy started.

He was ignored. 'You'll be standing on a street corner, taking whatever cash you get offered for you know what. It will no longer be about swanky hotels and –'

'No I won't,' I said, seething. 'I will get social to pay the rent.' *Simple.*

Sadistic Fantasy Part 2: Maggie's nose is bleeding. I drag her up by her hair and, face to face, ask her if she's sorry for all the shitty things she's said to me before I start bashing her round the ears with a belt buckle.

'Look, I'm sorry for laughing, OK?'

'No you're not. It's written on your face.'

'What?'

'Just get out of the room.'

'Maggie?' Billy said.

'Be quiet!'

'I'm all right now, so, no, I won't leave the room.' I sat rooted to the spot.

Sadistic Fantasy Part 3: I'm standing in front of Maggie; she's sitting on a chair and I'm kneeing her in the face. When she squeals, I find a water pistol in my jeans pocket and a lemon, which I squeeze into the water, pips and all. I order my persecutor – yes, that's HER – to keep her evil eyes open as I continuously squirt the liquid directly into them.

'Katie, stop making things difficult for yourself. Do you hear me? It doesn't get you anywhere.'

'I'm not leaving the room, Maggie.'

'Why don't you just –' Sabrina started to say something.

'No! No!' I said sternly. Start a sentence with the words 'why don't you' and anyone would get defensive.

'Oh, bab, come on,' Tessa said, with a look as if to say 'Please just do as you're told'.

'Katie, come on, mate,' Slippery Simon chipped in. I rolled my eyes at him. *Mate.* He knew to shut up. I wanted to give him a blast of the water pistol too. Determined not to move a muscle, I couldn't understand how I'd gone from laughing like a nutter to fury in the space of two minutes, if that.

Suddenly, Maggie's tone changed. 'Would you please wait

at reception until we've both cooled down? Then I'll come and get you.'

Humility. She'd acknowledged there was a problem and that it wasn't just my doing. My pride was up. I didn't know whether to move. I glared at her and realised that she didn't know what to do either. I stood up and went downstairs. I was so angry I wanted to cry. I waited, in the kitchen, staring, deciding. *Leave now? Later?* I had to get out of there.

But I knew what would happen if I left now, carrying that amount of anger. I'd use for sure. I didn't want to run, but I felt I couldn't stay. Maybe I had gone too far – again – and the decision as to whether or not I would be allowed to complete would be taken away from me. I made my mind up. I had no option but to apologise to Maggie – grovel, if need be. I'd been out of order, and no doubt the Powers That Be would deem my behaviour to be threatening, even though I hadn't raised my voice. But what I thought mattered little. These were their rules and they were both the judge and jury, and I was determined to do whatever I needed to do to avoid being sentenced to expulsion.

'I'm really, really sorry for what happened in the group just now.' The only thing I was sorry about was the possibility of me being kicked out.

Maggie sighed. 'I'm going to talk with Lenny about this, because it's just not acceptable, Kate.'

OK, am I about to get turfed out? 'I'd really like to complete treatment properly, you know. But I've got so much on my mind. I can't seem to let go of that cruel comment that Sabrina made in my confrontation letter, amongst other things.'

'I know. I did speak to her about that. It was unnecessary. But still . . .'

I was in full-blown self-justification mode. 'I haven't been sleeping well and I'm also frustrated about this whole Step 4 thing, you know, cos you told me when I got here that I would complete after doing my Step 3, and that I could forget about secondary.' I'd recently been told that in fact I might have to go on to secondary after all, rather than being discharged when I was ready to work on Step 4 at home by myself.

'Who told you that?'

'Well, you did.'

'No I didn't.' Maggie scowled.

'Well, someone did. I thought it was you. Anyway, I presumed after –'

'Never presume anything.'

'God, Maggie, please don't be like this.'

'I'm not being like anything.'

'I mean, let's face it, if I went to secondary, which I'm definitely not, I'd be there for at least another three months, and I just can't cope with that. It's not doing the Steps that bothers me, it's doing more time that I can't handle. Look, I'm sorry for being like I was in the group just now. I am really, honestly.'

'You don't need to say "honestly" if you're already being honest, Kate.'

I wondered whether to mention the injuries I'd seen on Sabrina, to detract from my own wrongdoings, but decided not to.

'I may have hiccups but at least I'm improving, unlike –'

'Unlike what, or should I say who?'

'Sabrina.' I blurted it out.

'What about her?'

'Well, to me it looks like she cuts herself.' *What am I saying?*

'I don't talk about individual clients.'

'I know, but . . .'

'Sabrina's situation is being taken care of. If she does it again, she's out of here. No more chances. Now, back to you. I'm suggesting to you that you're not ready to leave here without doing secondary.'

Her stupid bracelets were jingling and pissing me off. I needed her to hear me. 'But, Maggie, do you really think I wouldn't have asked straight away if you'd consider me as having officially completed if I left in primary? Of course I did. The idea of doing secondary makes me want to throw myself off a bridge.'

Leaving without the total consent of BCH would be the same for me as not getting an honourable discharge. It's not that I'd leave *dishonourably* without it, but it's not a discharge with bells on. I wanted bells. I wanted the personal glory, the pat on the back, that would come with completing with the centre's full approval. I had to show myself that I could finish something good in my life.

Most of my fellow inmates felt the same. It's faintly comical how hardened criminals and ex-junkies can attach such importance to the opinions of a handful of people who've been strangers until weeks earlier, yet still their validation matters. We were mostly just regular people who'd dealt with life in a not-so-regular way.

'Maggie, I don't want to be harassed into –'

'We don't *harass* people into anything. We advise, and if you choose not to follow the advice . . .'

'OK, maybe not harassed, then, but pressurised.'

'There is no pressure,' Maggie snapped.

'Oh, come on. So you don't use thumbscrews, but you've got to admit that at the very least there's a *bit* of pressure . . .'

'Carry on.'

'Look, the point is I was told that I could complete in primary.'

'Who told you that?'

'Well, if it wasn't you, it must have been Lenny.'

'Lenny?' *Yes, fucking Lenny, Maggie. Don't act like you've never heard of him.* 'Well, I'll speak to him. But regardless, I think you would benefit from going to secondary.'

'I can't do it. I can't do it.' I was shaking my head. 'I can't do another few months here. Or anywhere. I just can't. I did six months in the last treatment centre I went to, and I'd rather leave right now than do secondary again. Are you saying all this because . . . because this place is a business? I don't mean to sound rude, but . . .'

'Katie, you know it's not about that. You sound as though I'm determined to make life difficult for you.'

I didn't say anything.

'Katie, do you think I go out of my way to make things hard for you?'

Weird question, but in the spirit of honesty . . . 'Yes.'

She looked startled and shook her head. 'I don't. You're wrong. I'm not sure why there's been some tension.'

This was embarrassing. 'Well, anyway,' I said, 'I'd appreciate it if you would talk to Len and ask him to confirm with you that he said I'd be able to go home after doing primary.'

'I will do. Oh, and I'd appreciate it if there's no gossip about Sabrina. Agreed?'

'One good deed for another,' I said, grinning.

'We don't barter here, you know that. I'll trust your integrity to help you do the right thing.'

CHAPTER 23

On the grass in the park with Leon next to me was my nirvana. Our hands kept brushing and I could feel his body heat as we spoke without saying a word. Life felt good in that moment. I had The Youth; I had a flat; I'd get the social to pay the rent; they'd also pay me a weekly wage, so I could eat and smoke fags; I'd go to NA meetings and hang out with 'sober' people; things would be fine. The only issue I had was sex, and getting some. That was all; nothing major. I didn't want to do drugs, drink, injure anyone or rob a disabled person of their life savings; I just wanted to get boned. And not by a random – I'd moved on from that. I wanted Leon.

'This is hard, you know, babes, get me? What's going to go down? I need to be with you, innit? Fuck, Katie, man! I'm feeling you big time, you know, and I can't even touch you. This is crazy shit, man.'

'There's only three weeks until I leave. We need to try to keep calm, baby, OK? Look, I can make everything nice for when you come out, and it'll go quicker than we imagine, I reckon.' Actually, I thought it would be the slowest three weeks of my entire life.

'I just want us to be together. You know that, right?'

He edged closer. How I stopped myself from kissing him I don't know. 'Come with me to the toilets.' I wanted to. Believe me, I wanted to. 'Come on, trust me,' he said, as he sat upright. 'We'll get Ozzy to come as well. Obviously we can't go alone.'

'Shh, baby, are you forgetting where we are? We might be in a park, but we're in fucking drug rehab, and what's more we can't involve someone else in this.' Leon started scratching the back of his neck. 'Oh my God!' I continued. 'He knows, doesn't he? You've told Austin what happened in the office?'

He didn't reply. He didn't need to.

'Leon, for fuck's sake!' I hissed. 'What were you thinking, and what if he says something? I can't fucking believe this. I'm reading this poxy letter that Maggie's made me write to my mum tomorrow and I'm worried enough about that and now this?'

'Allow it, babes. He won't say anything. You've got my word. I trust Ozzy, innit?'

'That's rubbish. You can't promise me anything. Nothing. Nothing at all.'

'I can promise you that I'm in lo– Look, I know 110 per cent . . . I trust him, innit? We're from the same manor.' *110 per cent*? I hate it when people say that. 'He won't say nothing to anyone.'

'That means he'd say something, then.'

'What? Just chill, princess. He'll keep it on the down low, get me?'

'Well, I thought *you* would, and look . . . so what were you going to say before? You can promise me that you what?'

'Nothing.'

'Tell me.'

'It was nothing. Babes, do something for me. Will you

consider us telling the counsellors about you and me? You know, just to –'

'Have you gone fucking bananas?'

'Just so it don't feel like we're holding a dirty secret, you know what I'm saying?'

I sat upright. 'Have you lost your mind? I mean, what the fuck are you on about, babe?'

He stood and walked away.

'Leon?'

I didn't know anything 110 per cent, but I knew 100 per cent that I wasn't saying anything to any counsellor about any of this.

For a moment, I imagined first telling the PTB about me and Leon, and second having sex with him in a public toilet. After that, we'd be packing our bags and heading for a cheap hotel for the night to try and screw our way through the shame. The reality was that, if they did find out about us, we'd almost certainly be discharged at different times and popped onto different trains back to London. Having said that, if we were found out and dismissed at the same time, it wouldn't officially be the centre's business if we left together and went to a B&B, a pub or the moon. OK, not a pub. *Silly idea.* I wanted intercourse, not a drink, although a tipple would definitely take the edge off the frustration . . .

Tessa came over. 'What're you up to?' *Actually, I'm baking a cake and about to serve dinner to my husband and kids.* She was lovely, but . . .

'Nothing,' I said. 'Just thinking.'

'You all right?'

'I suppose so.'

'You don't sound it, bab. You seem lost in your own thoughts.' *So what if I am?* 'You worried about tomorrow and reading that letter that you wrote to your ma? Or is it Leon?' She whispered his name as if she was talking about high treason. She was, in a way.

'It's everything, Tess.'

'I just passed him and he had a face like thunder.'

'Can you believe that he's just suggested that it might be a good idea to tell the counsellors that we're involved with each other? Can you fucking believe that? He's fucking stupid. I mean, what do you think to that for a ridiculously crazy idea?' Not a loaded question at all.

'I've heard worse than that in my life.'

'I know, but that's a pretty mad suggestion. You've no idea how much I wish we could both complete this, so we can be together away from all this horseshit. But for him to suggest we tell fucking Len and Maggie and them is barmy.'

'I know, I know.'

'The way he's carrying on, it's almost putting me off him.'

'He's just having a mini-freak-out, bab. You'll both be all right.'

I really didn't want to leave without him, but there was no option. Unless, that is, he left when I left.

CHAPTER 24

All five female clients and Maggie sat in a circle in one of the upstairs offices. I had the letter to my mum on my lap. Three A4 sheets. All six sides were covered. My arms were crossed and I desperately wanted not to be there. Maggie did the usual pre-group spiel and then spoke a few words about the purpose of my writing the letter. She was sounding very professional. I was embarrassed about having to read out loud this baloney about my mother.

'The idea of Katie writing this letter to her mother, a letter that she's never going to post, is to enable her to try and release even a small amount of those feelings that she otherwise has found impossible to articulate.' *I might have been able to if I'd had a fucking address for her*, I thought angrily.

I began reading, trying to be nonchalant. I read lines one, two, five, eight, then suddenly BANG! Halfway through the first page, I fell apart. There was no build-up to my tears. I simply crumbled. I sobbed and sobbed and sobbed and sobbed and sobbed, more deeply than I had ever done. I was shaking as I was crying, lost in my sadness. I might as well have been alone in the room as I wept freely from my core. I will never again reveal myself in that way in front of so many people. In those minutes, I wasn't aware of their presence as I expressed my deep feeling of loss at the absence of my mother in my life, my feelings of powerlessness and frustration at her disappearance, my hurt about her not appearing to have wanted me, my urge to feel her touch me, to feel her breath on my skin, to be loved by her, to feel that she'd wanted me.

For ten or fifteen minutes, I cried and cried. And then someone came over to me and held me. I felt as though I were five years old again. I clung onto the person until I became more conscious of my surroundings, and she must have been aware that I was and so she sat back down.

I came out of the state I was in and felt wiped out. The group was never discussed in detail afterwards. What was the point? The breakthrough had been made. After 22 years during which I'd carried those feelings locked away, they had finally been given a moment to breathe, and so had I.

Stacey went to secondary. For me, she couldn't leave quickly enough. Her departure showed that time was ticking and I was getting closer to getting out of there. Tessa did a 'good-riddance' jig and she was joined by Billy; he didn't like her either. The other, more hypocritical haters just grinned approval from a distance.

Maggie went on and on in one session about me moving to a dry house, a hostel where drugs and alcohol are prohibited. I imagined it would be similar to what living in a crack den would be like, with everyone constantly on edge, waiting for something to happen, a fight to kick off, a police raid, someone to snuff it.

'Often drug tests are done in a dry house, so that gives you a little extra incentive to be abstinent,' she continued.

Was she joking? I wasn't trying to change my life out of fear of some poxy test; I was doing this because I wanted to, and what's more if I planned on using, then I would. Nothing would stop that.

I had to tune her voice out of my head. I wasn't going into a dry house – ever. I had an empty flat waiting for me in Putney. Maybe I was being snobby, but I knew my limitations. Recovering addict, I was; totally stupid, I was not.

In the group, I became aware that Leon was staring at me maniacally. Suddenly he stood.

'Where do you think you're going?' Maggie sounded shocked.

'Downstairs.'

'Sit down. You know you can't just walk out in the middle of a group.'

'I can't stay in here.'

'Just sit down, Leon!' Maggie barked. He ignored her and half-tripped over a chair leg before belting out the door.

He needed to get a grip. Fast. We finished the group in the usual manner, eyes closed, hands joined, saying the Serenity Prayer, which I spoke from my heart. I then rushed downstairs to find The Youth.

Tessa and Sabrina followed, whispering sympathetic words. I didn't want to hear it, especially not from Sabrina. I went into the kitchen, but Leon wasn't there. Daryl was with Austin, who was making tea, and he told me that Leon had been crying. *Fucking fantastic.*

'Where is he?'

'Dunno. In the bog, I think.'

I told Tessa what Daryl had just told me.

'Give him a few minutes, bab.'

I had to know what was going on. The room filled with the usual faces and Simon came up to me. 'Bit of a tough group again there, Kate, mate.'

Whatever, arse bandit. 'Mate' sounded so contrived coming from such a posh person. I acted like he wasn't there. He was about to leave for secondary, and given a chance I'd have baked a celebratory cake. I wouldn't have to listen to that insipid voice coming out of that ginger head ever again. Even if I came for aftercare – which, at that time, I felt I would avoid – I'd ignore him.

Mysteriously, he'd managed to get his Step 4 quicker than anyone else and was seemingly ready to move on to the next stage of his rehabilitation. And it had all been kept low key. Word on the street was that it was because he'd been fearless in his openness and was completely focused on getting well. Fabulous. So what were the rest of us doing? Scratching our arses and killing time?

'What's wrong with you?' I snapped at Leon when he appeared.

He didn't say a word. He just stared at me. 'I want you,' he said solemnly.

'Look, you're going to have to get a hold of this.' I felt like a mother scolding her child. 'There's nothing we can –'

'Why won't you even –'

'Even what? Fucking hell. I don't get what is going on here. What the hell is wrong with you?'

Sabrina walked in. 'You OK?' *And she can piss off.* She quickly left.

'What's going on?' I growled at Leon.

'I'm not trying to –'

'You're not trying to behave like a normal human being, you're right.'

'I just think it might lighten the intensity with you and me if we tell the –'

'I'm not going to talk to you if you carry on like this. This is fucking stupid. I feel sick with nerves now.'

'But –'

'We should never have got involved in this.'

'Don't say that. Please don't say you –'

'What's going on in here?' Lenny scowled as he sauntered towards us with his hands in his pockets.

'We're just talking, that's all.'

'I'm sure you are. I didn't think otherwise.'

'I'd like to see you. Have you got a minute?' I said urgently.

'You're seeing me now, aren't you, Kate? I'm standing right here. Well, then?'

Clever arse. 'Well, could we go into your office, please?'

'You want to talk to Lenny *privately*?' Leon emphasised 'privately' as though I was about to cheat on him with a member of his family.

'Yeah. Is that OK?'

He stormed off.

'I'll have to see you later, Katie. This is about you not wanting to go to secondary, isn't it?' Lenny grinned. I didn't see what there was to smile about.

'Partly. It's about a few things.'

Leon reappeared, standing as still as a statue and staring at me.

'I'm sure your stress isn't helped by knowing that your friend Simon has got his Step 4 and is about to move on to bigger things,' said Lenny.

The guy belonged on the stage. He could make more money doing that than taking the piss out of his frustrated clients in a treatment centre. But I noticed that I wasn't as annoyed by his manner as I had been in previous weeks and also that I wasn't fantasising about doing him harm – a positive development.

'Come to my office in 30 minutes and we'll talk about everything then, OK? And by that I do mean everything . . .'

CHAPTER 25

RULE
- Clients who exhibit aggressive or threatening behaviour of any kind, including racist or homophobic speech, or who are violent verbally or physically will be asked to leave the programme and the centre immediately.

After my chat with Len, I bounded back into the group room feeling a little lighter. He'd told me that 'no one can make you stay if you don't want to'. I already knew that.

Tessa called to me, but she was talking to Daryl, so I left them to it. Leon was in a mini-group and I couldn't be bothered to listen. Billy was chatting to Austin and beckoned me over. I shook my head and said, 'In a bit.' I saw Lisa sitting in a corner looking lost, so I did what most people wouldn't do and sat somewhere else. But then I felt guilty for not reaching out, so I moved beside her.

'You all right?' I asked.

'Hmm,' she answered. That was good enough for me. We sat in silence, a glorious moment of peace. I might not have been much, but I was all I could think about.

It seemed louder than normal in the room. I watched people and imagined myself back home living a carefree life. I could cook whatever I wanted and spend as long as I wanted in the bath, and I would never have to sell my body again. But then a thought: how the hell would I get money? Anxiety welled up in me. I wasn't ready to get a job. Oh yeah, I'd get dole money: 67 quid a week. Or if I was lucky, I'd get 100 quid on sick benefit. This thought did little to quell my worry.

'Do you want a cuppa?' I asked Lisa. I had to focus my mind on something else.

'Nah.'

Fair enough. I headed for the kitchen and Billy tried to accost me again. I asked him to wait. Tessa appeared, chattering at me. I wished she'd pipe down. The constant background noise and my friend wittering on were enough to make me want to renounce the human race. She was saying something about Sabrina being told by Nick, her counsellor, that she had to stay longer in primary than originally anticipated. *Tough shit.*

I went to the bathroom. Sabrina was coming out. She didn't look at me. Inside, I saw drops of blood on the floor and on the door handle. This really bothered me.

I went back into the main room, leaving Tessa laughing with Billy and Austin, who'd gone into the kitchen with her. This time, curiosity got the better of me. 'Do you mind if I join this mini-group?' Leon looked up. I wondered if Simon, who was about to leave primary for secondary, had called the mini-group. If that was the case, I wouldn't stay.

'This one's for boys only,' Alan piped up. He was a new guy, overly cocksure.

'Ah, OK, then.'

'What're you talking about, bruv? She can join the group if she wants to.' Leon, my saviour, was here to rescue me from that mean and horrible ogre who wouldn't let me join in.

'Sorry, I didn't realise −'

'Get a chair and sit down,' said Leon.

'But this is my mini-group,' Alan said.

'Nah, man! This is bare madness. She can join the fucking group if she wants to. Mini-groups aren't meant to be divided between fellas and girls, get me?'

'Allow it, mate,' Daryl chipped in.

'It's all right, honestly,' I said. 'Sorry, I've forgotten your name.'

'It's Alan.'

'Well, sorry. I didn't mean to interrupt, OK?' I forced myself to smile at him.

Leon stood. 'Then fuck it. I'm not in the group if you're making new fucking rules about how all this works.'

Daryl also stood. 'Easy now, rude boy. Give the man a chance. He didn't know −'

'Well, he does now. I'm telling him and he's still trying to mug me off,' Leon growled. I'd never heard him raise his voice in this manner. He was usually so softly spoken. 'Mini-groups are for anyone, got that, mate? Anyone . . . all right?'

'OK, calm yourself!' said Alan.

'Fucking calm myself? You don't know who you're talking to, do ya, blood?' Leon was starting to sound like a Mafia don. I wanted to laugh.

Daryl placed his hand on Leon's chest to try to calm him.

'Don't fucking talk to me like that again, do you hear me? Go on, fucking jog on, mate!' The Youth continued.

'Or else what?' demanded Alan.

'Come on, now. Stop this,' I squawked.

'You're asking for trouble, mate,' said Leon.

'Come on, son,' Daryl muttered.

Alan stood up. 'Please sit down,' I said. '*Please*. This is my fault.'

'No it's not. What's this joker getting so excited about, making up the rules when he's been here five fucking minutes? Don't flex with me, blood. You hear me?' This level of aggression was totally uncharacteristic of my boy.

'What's going on?' Tessa came to ask.

'My man there needs to watch his mouth, innit?' Leon spat.

'*Please*, baby, don't say anything that you'll regret.' *Oops!* I'd 'baby'd him in public.

I felt like a gangster's moll trying to subdue her feral husband. My urge to kiss him was grotesque and I felt like screaming when I remembered I couldn't.

In the evenings, the time between dinner and TV was meant to be for study: therapy books, Step pamphlets, questionnaires, writing, writing and more writing.

I was sitting on one of the sofas, looking at nothing and trying to ignore the rest of the chatter going on in the room. Sabrina appeared and sat next to me. She started bleating on about Nick's decision that she needed to stay on in primary, and all I could do was stare at the blood that was seeping through her top.

'What's that?' I asked her.

'Nothing.'

'It looks like blood. Have you cut yourself?'

'I don't want to talk about it,' she snapped, then got up.

'Come back, Sabrina, sit with me,' I said, following her.

'Look, I'm really stressed right now, that's all.'

She'd already been there two days shy of sixteen weeks, but the PTB had decided that she wasn't ready to move on yet. Unless she walked out, she couldn't do a damn thing about it.

'I don't have a choice but to stay in this place. My mum

said that if I walk out without consent, she'll apply for guardianship of my daughter. So I have to do this, but I'm finding it really hard to cope. That's why I've done this.' She partly raised her arm.

'What *have* you done exactly?'

'When I find things hard, sometimes I get something sharp and pierce my skin.' I shuddered. 'That initial stinging brings me some relief. I know it might sound weird, but what feels better is when I see a line of blood pouring out. It gives me a sense of relief.'

Fucking grim. And I thought I had problems. 'You'd be better off taking some fucking downers or something, surely?' Oops, maybe that was an inappropriate suggestion.

I was watching Sabrina, amazed that she could sit and talk to me without mentioning the comment she'd made in my confrontation letters about me being sexually abused as a kid.

'So do the counsellors know?' I asked her.

'Hmm . . . But they reckon I don't open up enough, and I don't know how to open up any more. I mean, Nick thinks . . .'

'Maybe listening to the counsellor might be . . .' I wanted to say 'the best thing for you', but as the words were issuing forth from my mouth I realised giving advice I wouldn't follow myself wasn't clever, so I shut up.

'Kate!' someone shouted. 'There's a call for you! *Katie!*'

Leon had put on a stupid voice and called me at the house. I didn't know how he had the nerve.

'At least you didn't get a warning.' I'd thought he might get in real trouble over the row with Alan.

'Hmm.'

'You sound really down. What's wrong?' He was getting on my nerves.

'I'm OK, babes,' he snapped.

'You're so not. It's obvious. Fucking hell. Look, I don't really know what to say right now. Let's speak tomorrow, all right?'

Someone walked past me. I heard Leon mutter something, but I was too focused on grinning at the nosy passer-by – who'd suddenly got a suspiciously itchy leg and had stopped to scratch it.

'Babe, I'm going to have to go.'

'Don't go.'

'I have to.'

'Katie, babes . . . I can't do this.'

'Do *what*? Look, I'm off, OK? There are people around.'

'I'm going to leave with you when you go.'

'*What*? Say that again.'

'I'm going to leave with –'

'Ssh! Don't be stupid, for fuck's sake! Don't do this to me! I'm off.' I slammed the phone down and went into the sitting room. Sabrina had gone, thank God.

I avoided eye contact with everyone and sat on the floor by the sofa to stare at the television. I was scared that The Youth would call back and make an announcement: '*Sir Leon, white knight and keeper of honour, hereby comes to this kingdom in the name of love to claim as his own Lady Katie of Putney.*'

I had to speak to Tessa. Immediately. I looked in the dining room. She wasn't there.

Billy stopped me. 'Can I ask what you think about a letter I got today, Kate?'

'Later, OK?'

I went upstairs to Tessa's room riddled with anxiety. 'You in there, babe?' I heard a noise coming from the bathroom. I called her name and heard a muffled sound. I lay on her bed, my mind awash with Leon stress. Then I heard moaning. It was pretty loud. Maybe Tess was cutting herself open like Sabrina. Or was she in there with someone?

I listened hard and then I realised what was going on: my friend was fingering herself. It was quite a turn-on. The groaning was getting more rhythmic. I wasn't sure what to do, so I went out of the bedroom, loitered in the hallway, then stormed back into the bedroom and shouted Tessa's name loudly. As I did so, she came, very clearly. (I'm not saying that hearing my voice added to her pleasure, but I wouldn't be ashamed if it did.)

'Who's that?' She sounded flustered. The toilet flushed. *Her cover-up technique.*

'You all right, Tess?' I called, trying not to laugh.

'Great, darling.' Her eyes were cast down as she came out of the toilet. 'How long have you been in here?' she asked, trying to be blasé.

'A few minutes, but I thought you were busy so I just waited.' She looked startled and randomly started brushing her hair. *Avoidance.*

'I was in the bathroom.'

'I know you were. I heard you.'

'Oh, right. Did you?'

I smirked. I couldn't be bothered winding her up. 'Look, I need to talk to you. Leon is acting really fuckin' odd.'

'What's wrong?'

'He's falling a-fucking-part, babe.'

'Katie, look, bab, can we go downstairs, say, into the kitchen and talk about this? I've been up here at least ten minutes already, I'm sure I have, and I want to try and reduce the number of things I gotta cop to on Monday.'

'You must be constipated if you've been up here for that

long.' I decided I would tease her after all. 'Either that or you were having a wank.' I burst out laughing.

Tessa's face turned crimson. 'You fucking heard me, didn't ya? You silly plonker!'

'Babe, it was either that or you had Daryl in here giving you a rooting, but I guessed that since he's in another house there wasn't much chance of that.'

'I don't know if we'd be doing that anyway. I know I talk about it and I fancy the arse off him, like, but . . . well . . . he's HIV positive, innit? So . . .'

'What?' I froze. Goosebumps. 'No! Really? Oh my fucking hell, *is* he?'

'Yeah, I thought you already knew that.'

'No. Who told you?'

'He did.'

'Fuck, Tess. I'm shocked. I'm really taken aback by that.'

'I feel like I'm gossiping now I've told you, bab. I thought you knew. Please don't tell any– '

'What, like I'm going to go round talking about *that*? Course I'm not. Give me some credit. God, that's so sad. I feel really bad for him.'

'He's all right, bab. Don't start feeling sorry for him. He's not bothered.'

'Well, I'm sure he is.'

'You know what I mean . . . Anyway, I reckon that with a rubber I'd still do him from here to eternity given half a chance, like. I'm telling ya, he makes my fanny feel funny.' She cackled.

'I know, but . . .'

'Anyway, you friggin' perv . . .'

'Friggin', that'll be right.' I poked her, and we were pulling at each other's clothes and giggling like idiots as we both struggled down the stairs at the same time. For a moment, I'd forgotten about Leon.

In the kitchen, Lisa was in floods of tears. 'I can't do this any more. I just want to go home,' she wailed, her head in her hands, to four people who were sitting round her.

'You're going out to use, aren't you? That's quite obvious,' said Alan. He was brazen for a newcomer.

'Yeah.'

There was a stunned silence. No one had expected that for an answer. Tessa and I looked at each other.

'Go in the other room?' she mouthed. We left the mini-group to it. Lisa had enough people around her; another two would just crowd her. That was what I told myself, anyway. In truth, we should have stayed – but that was a matter between my conscience and myself. And anyway, there was a limit to how long I could hear the same tedious stuff from different mouths every damn day.

Tessa and I discussed Leon and my situation in the sitting room, after slagging off Lisa for shedding yet more tears.

CHAPTER 26

'It seems that Kate's already left us, group. You seem lost in your own world,' Lenny crowed.

'Eh? Sorry, what was that?'

'Ah-ha! You see.'

'I thought you'd like that one, Lenny,' I said.

'So, *have* you left us, Katie? You've been busy daydreaming. Have you already mentally unpacked your bags and rearranged the furniture in your flat?'

'A bit, I suppose . . . and of course I'm apprehensive.'

'She's apprehensive, group.' He raised his eyebrows. Leonard was up to something; I could smell it.

'Well, yeah. I would be, wouldn't I?' *Right now, I'm trapped between not daring to leave the security of this place and hating being here.* 'I haven't been back home for ages and, well, you know . . .' *I just don't know how my life will be from now on, or if I can do this, whatever this may be.* 'Things are a bit different now, I mean . . .' *My face was bloated and covered with spots, and I feared for my sanity – as I'm sure the two husbands I acquired on my journey to rehab would have testified . . . But can someone tell me, other than my putting on weight, what else has changed?* 'I have a lot of things to sort out still.' *In fact, I*

*don't even know what exactly I've sorted out in here, if anything.
I'm about to go back home, after supposedly leaving my crutches
behind me – with no skills to get a job and certainly no bridges
mended with my family.* 'But I'm sure it'll be OK.' *But it could
be a right balls-up, and honestly? I'm. Fucking. Shitting. Myself.*
'With some effort.' *But at least I'll be able to snooze whenever
I feel like it – and wank with no one to hear me and not have
to cop for anything . . . so, you know . . . it could be worse. But
I wish, I wish, I wish I had someone by my side to tell me what
to do and how to live.*

'So what are your plan Bs?'

What's he on about? Humour him. 'Plan Bs? You mean, am
I plotting anything? Well, no.' *Except to fuck Leon. But that's
not a secondary plan; that's a primary goal.*

Lenny raised his eyebrows.

'Sorry, I get the feeling that I'm not understanding the
question,' I said. *Why am I even apologising? You're humouring
him, remember?* 'Do you mean, am I planning to relapse?'

'No, that's not what I was asking, actually.'

'Cos obviously I'm not planning to use. I came here of my
own accord, don't forget. I want to get better.'

'That isn't what I was talking about.' His leg started
twitching. It was all about to come out now.

I said nothing.

'So?'

No comment, Mr Policeman.

'Group, someone remind Katie what plan Bs are, please.'

'I know what a plan B is, Lenny. I just said I wasn't –'

'Well, you don't seem to. You're finding it extraordinarily
difficult to answer my simple question.'

'I said I don't have any plan Bs.'

Lenny ignored me. 'Simon?' *Arsehole.*

'Maybe she's planning on getting with Leon. I don't know, I'm just surmising.' *Fucking surmising?* 'Maybe they're arranging to meet or something?' *Arsehole cocksucker.*

I looked at Daryl. *Please knock Smarmy Simy out, will ya?* He shook his head in sympathy.

'Maybe they've been plotting something all along.' *Arsehole cocksucker cuntface is on a roll.*

'Ah-ha! Spot-on! Why is it that it's only Simon who speaks up in these groups, eh?'

'It's not,' Daryl spouted. 'We all do.' *A simple but very fair comment there from our Daz.* A smile crept across my face.

This was starting to feel like a witch-hunt. 'Well, no, I haven't exactly got anything planned. I mean, obviously Leon and I will meet when he leaves, but that's it. It's no big deal, meeting for coffee or, er, something, is it? I'd meet everyone here, barring one.' I looked at Simon.

'Meow!' Lenny pawed the air. He was holding onto his handkerchief like a thespian giving a performance. 'Well, that's a plan B, then, isn't it?'

'I suppose so.' I couldn't be fucked to argue. *Plan B, sham tree. Someone please get me out of this place.*

'I told you yesterday that you weren't getting your Step 4.' *Thank you for piercing my heart by reminding me, Leonard.* 'We've strongly advised that you stay on here and go to secondary, but you've refused.' *Yep.* I nodded. No matter how many times they recommended this, I wasn't budging.

'We've suggested equally as adamantly that you should leave Leon alone.' I was refusing to change my mind on this just as obstinately, although hearing Len put it that way made me feel predatory and sleazy. 'And now you're telling us that you're going to meet with him?'

'You asked me a question and I've given you an honest

answer, this being an honest programme and all that.'

'Kate, this is very serious. If you leave us here planning a relationship, heed my words, this will be your downfall. Not just yours, I might add. It'll be Leon's life down the drain, too – or should I say back in the crack house? Do you understand? This relationship will ruin you both.'

I'd switched off. How could a relationship make me relapse? *Rubbish.* Surely two members of the same team were better than one person alone? I looked round the room. People were shifting uncomfortably. Simon was staring at me.

Sadistic Fantasy: I walk straight up to Simon with a glass of water and pour it over his head while screaming at him to poke his fat nose into someone else's business, otherwise I'll pluck that ridiculous bit of hair off his chin with my nails.

'You've pooh-poohed the suggestion that you get a plant and take care of it for a year before you get involved with another person. You don't even look like you're listening to me. You've clearly got your own agenda, but don't you care about someone else's life, Kate?' *Blah, blah, blah, blah, blah* . . . 'You know the state Leon's in. He can hardly cope with the situation.'

'Len,' I grinned, fuming, 'I don't know what to say any more, I really don't. This is getting silly.'

'*Silly*, is it?'

I sighed loudly. They had me by the balls. They weren't interested unless I said what they wanted to hear, and even then they wouldn't believe me. The thing was that I was involved with Leon, and I was going to see him and have a relationship with him whether they wanted me to or not. Screw them. The only thing I could do was try to talk him out of leaving when I left.

'We have a suggestion for you,' Lenny continued. Their suggestions weren't really suggestions; they were always really orders. 'Go back to your flat this weekend and see how you feel, and then come back here for another week before you're discharged. At least that way you can get a taste of how it will be at home alone.'

'OK. Is this some kind of set-up?'

'Of course not.'

'So you're saying that I go home, then come back here for just one week and after that I can leave here as originally agreed?'

'Yes.'

I felt like a bear that had fallen into a trap. 'This is a bit weird. Look, is this for any other reason than just –'

'She sounds very suspicious of us, doesn't she, group?' People grinned. I didn't smile until Daryl gave me a reassuring wink.

We gathered in a circle to say the Serenity Prayer and then the group was dismissed, so we could babble, smoke and curse.

Surely there wasn't an ulterior motive for Lenny's suggestion, was there?

CHAPTER 27

I didn't feel free as the train pulled out of Weymouth for my weekend of self-discovery. I didn't feel fear, either. I was just sitting on a train heading to London from Dorset.

I'd been given back my mobile phone. Maggie had suggested I switch it on before I left so I could discuss any awkward texts or voicemails while I had my comfort blanket around me.

There were a few texts from people to whom I had little or no emotional connection. I scrolled down the names in my contacts and felt very little. These people felt somehow alien to me. Perhaps I was kidding myself. I didn't think so, though. I deleted the messages and the contacts.

But I held onto Luca's and Petra's details. I'd been fairly close to both of them when I'd been doing a lot of coke. I wasn't planning on calling either of them, but they'd been a big part of my life, so keeping their numbers gave me a peculiar feeling of security. This may sound warped, given that I'd gone into rehab to escape that stuff, but I didn't want to eradicate every single thing that I'd once known. I wasn't ready to do that then.

I also had with me my flat keys, some clothes, the telephone numbers of two women in my local NA, which Maggie had sorted out for me, and my return ticket.

I stared out of the window and thought about Janet, who'd taken me to some meetings not long before I'd gone into BCH. I'd felt bad about disappearing after the last time we'd talked 18 months previously, just when I'd started to dip my toes into recovery's waters, but at that point I hadn't been ready to immerse myself.

My main concern on the journey back home was whether the flat would be full of empty bottles. I also worried that a zillion-strong army of flies and maggots would have executed a *coup d'état*, because I'd probably not put the bins out before I'd left.

As the train approached London, my (relative) serenity turned to acute anxiety. My heart was beating erratically. I became obsessed with the idea that my place was going to look as though it had been burgled. Thinking about this was my way of avoiding my fears about London, about bumping into acquaintances, about everything.

People looked stern, fed up, angry. Yet they all appeared to be employed, clean, well dressed. For years, all I'd wanted was the confidence to try to live a routine life like those of these glum folk. I wanted to tell someone where I'd just come from and how, despite the probability that they'd been getting up most days at 7 a.m. for the past 20 years, it could be worse. It really, really could.

At Waterloo, I got on a train to Putney and finally relaxed. I was trying to stop myself calling out the names of the familiar stations: Vauxhall, Clapham Junction . . . It was comforting to see them all.

I wanted to chat to some commuter – I didn't care who. I just wanted to feel part of my new world. I was no longer just a girl on a train from rehab; I was New and Improved Katie, striding out into pastures green. I wasn't an ex-coke whore, I wasn't a bigamist and I wasn't a bad person; I was just me, Katie, trying to move on with my life.

I got off at Putney station and couldn't stop grinning. I was home. Suddenly, I felt overwhelmed with hope. As I passed 'normals', I kept thinking, *You've no idea where I've just been for the past 12 weeks.* But this wasn't the time for me to inhale the delights of my neighbourhood. I had to get home and see what state I'd left it in.

I walked briskly out of the station, took a right and speeded up as I approached my building. My key slid into my front door. It smelled slightly musky, and I liked that. The communal entrance looked brighter and more spacious than I'd remembered, and I hadn't previously noticed the carpet was green. Perhaps it had been changed.

My heart was fluttering as I entered my flat. I squished my face up, waiting to be hit by an unsavoury smell, but there was nothing. In my tiny hallway were two pairs of trainers. I'd forgotten I owned them. I opened the door to the sitting room, holding my breath. There was very little clutter. I strode into the room and into the kitchen area, off the back of the lounge: *nothing.* It flashed through my mind to do my usual search. For months before rehab, every time I'd come home I'd done a systematic search behind doors, under the sofa, in drawers, in my wardrobe, behind the shower curtain, looking for people or things that could do me harm.

It seemed I'd disposed of the rubbish before leaving. I couldn't believe it. Either that, or someone had been in there. I wondered if the landlord had been round. Or maybe, just maybe, I hadn't been that fucked up after all, and I'd wasted three months of my life in an institution for no reason whatsoever.

I stared at the room, at my fluffy, cream Habitat rug by the fireplace and the red-wine stain that was close by. There was absolute silence. I burst out laughing; it felt surreal to be home.

A bird flew out of a bush directly outside my window, and I rushed towards the glass and looked at the grass outside. I'd never noticed the size of the garden before. I'd walked the length of it time and again, to the bins at the bottom, but clearly I'd paid no attention to my surroundings.

I suddenly snapped out of my trance, bounded towards my bedroom as if I were about to give someone mouth to mouth and flung open the door. My eyes quickly scanned the debris. OK there were clothes, lots of them, all over the floor and on the bed, but that was it. Nothing sinister. I shoved the things on the bed onto the floor and reached for the window to let summer in. I could feel the warmth of the sun streaming through the blinds and I knew everything was going to be all right. I just knew it.

I untied my Converse, clambered into the middle of the first double bed I'd been on in months and lay on my back. I laughed. 'Everything's all right!' I said out loud.

I was driven to an NA meeting by Emma, whose number Maggie had given me. It was the first time I'd been in a car for months. I hadn't been at all worried about texting a stranger; my confidence was up. Emma lived with two friends in Brixton and had been abstinent for some time.

We got to the meeting and I wasn't as nervous as I'd thought I would be. But neither was I confident. I knew I'd earned my seat there, and I wanted nothing more than to get cracking and get as much support as I could.

Within moments of arriving, Janet spotted me. I was embarrassed, but she was encouraging and pleased to see me. We both got our second cup of tea and sat together along with Emma near the back. Janet was in her late 40s, a teacher and mother of two who'd separated from her husband because once she'd cleaned up her act he couldn't handle her not being emotionally dependent on him any more. There is a name for someone who gets addicted to the pain that comes with loving a screwed-up person – co-dependent – and those who suffer this seriously need help in order to survive it.

Janet gave me her number and told me to contact her at any time, and so the next morning, while languishing in the comfiest bed ever, I rang her to see if she could meet for coffee. She agreed.

Things seemed easy. I could sit in the flat all day if I chose to do so. My phone no longer scared me. No one was after me for anything, apart from one or two debt collectors regarding non-payment of bills. But I chose not to worry about practical details like those. There was zero I could do about them. I felt I had few problems.

I walked into the kitchen with not a stitch on to make myself breakfast. I could do what the hell I liked. This was *my* day and *my* home, *my* life, and if I chose to mark my territory with my nakedness I could do so. I stared at the TV as I filled my face with toast with jam and too much butter, and felt totally satisfied. My mind was still and I decided to have a snooze, spreadeagled, right there on the sofa. I relished this freedom to do what I wanted, and dozed, guilt-free, with the fire on, which was delightful, all the more so because it was utterly unnecessary.

*

UNHOOKED

I returned to BCH hopeful that I could live my new life and that it wasn't going to be a struggle. In fact, I was certain it was going to be a doddle.

But when I got back to the centre, I found that something was frighteningly different.

CHAPTER 28

Lisa's urge to jack up cocaine and guzzle bottles of Jack Daniels had got the better of her. She'd buggered off back to Bristol, leaving her belongings without anyone seeing her go.

Four days later, her mother had found her dead from an overdose in her childhood bedroom. Twenty-five years old. Vomit was encrusted on the side of her pretty face, slate-grey bruising covered her body and a needle with congealed blood inside it was hanging out of her groin. When we were told, there was a group gasp and barely audible words were spoken. I got goosebumps and went cold, and in an instant tears filled my eyes.

Maggie candidly told us the details. I was blown away. We'd been warned. Here one moment, wiped off the planet the next, as a result of going back to something that she'd done for years. Just like that: brown bread.

'There are no guarantees with this programme,' Maggie began. 'Change can only happen with complete determination and conscious effort. Well-being will not come to you if you sit back and are not proactive. You must want to change more than you want anything else. Nothing can be put before your recovery. Not even your children.' Sabrina started crying.

'Without sobriety, you will never change, and without your sanity, you have nothing anyway. If you question this, you're in the wrong place.' I listened intently.

'You gave everything, *everything* you were and all that you had, to becoming an addict. It doesn't just happen overnight. It takes dedication, and each one of you proved your powers of determination by how avidly you tried to destroy yourselves. You're all experts at being utterly selfish. I know that cos I'm from the same tribe. Now you must do the same with regard to your recovery if you want a chance to get better. Continue to put yourselves first.' Maggie was very clear.

A sombre mood hung over the treatment centre. Lisa had stopped fighting the demons that were intent on seeing her destroy herself, and I prayed to a God that I wasn't sure existed for forgiveness for my glib attitude towards her tears. But even if I had been more patient, the course of events would have likely been the same. She was responsible for her own life. And what was the Almighty's role in this? Surely the girl was trying to help herself; that was why she'd gone into treatment in the first place. So why kill her off? Hadn't she deserved to live? Maybe she hadn't tried, or maybe she hadn't tried hard enough. By whose reckoning? Maybe she'd intended to top herself. Who knew? Lisa was gone, and that was that.

It was a matter of survival, and the rest of us were still in with a chance.

Tessa and I held each other, but she didn't cry. She'd had her face rubbed in the same stinking shit so many times that she'd somehow stopped smelling it. Her mother had died from a heroin overdose 12 years previously. Her father had followed shortly after that and wasn't found until weeks later, when the neighbours smelled his decomposing body. Her uncle had died in the same way three years before.

'This is what happens,' Tessa said. 'I've seen so many people snuff it over the years, bab. Loads of the brasses I worked the streets with, and a school-friend who had nothing to do with the scene, have passed on. We have to remember how lucky we are, do you know what I'm saying? That we've been given this chance to live.'

And as painfully tragic and shocking as it was that Lisa had died, it highlighted one thing: I had to be vigilant.

'Recovery must come above *all* other things,' Maggie said firmly. 'Katie, are you listening?'

'Pardon?'

CHAPTER 29

I was scared of going home and not having a clue about what to do with myself. Too much time on my hands, boredom and deep-down despair are not the best combination to keep one's sobriety thriving.

The days before I left rehab ticked by slowly. I gave feedback, but where in the past my comments had been blunt and opinionated, now they were much gentler. I liked that. I felt as though over a period of a few days I'd somehow grown up a little. Visiting home had given me some confidence.

I had to start creating lists and preparing myself for my arrival in unknown territory.

Things I need to do during my first two days at home:
1. Up early, shower, breakfast and *Just for Today* reading. Stick to the routine picked up in BCH.
2. Clear flat of rubbish – bottles, cans – and have a good tidy up.
3. Contact Janet to see if she'll go with me to a meeting.
4. Go to social-security office for housing benefit and income support applications. Ask about other support that I can get, financial or otherwise.

5. Buy food, more cleaning products and toiletries. Budget!

6. Phone Jim. Phone Maggie or Lenny. Write to Dad and Elaine. (Better than calling them.)

7. Go to meetings! Do not isolate. ESSENTIAL. *Avoid men.* Talk to women. Get their numbers. I need these people. My lifeline.

8. Every evening, as far as possible, write my plan for the next day down to the minute – and then FOLLOW IT as much as I can.

9. Call BCH or anyone from the Fellowship if I feel wobbly, uneasy, lonely, isolated, suicidal, weird or anything else negative. Use the phone. Speak to people. Everyone does it.

10. Keep referring to this note so that you don't forget that you do have some clear plans. Remember, 'progress not perfection'.

Simple as all this might sound, the more I read my list the more I questioned if I could do it.

When I thought about my future, I'd start fretting. Everything seemed like a hurdle. What would happen when I entered an adult world, in an adult body, but feeling like a teenager?

I was told I had to try my hardest to live in the moment. Who does that? It sounds good in a book or on a meditation course, but in reality? I felt stuck, trapped. One foot was in a forbidding past and the other in an unknowable future.

I'd been relaxed during my weekend at home and had felt ready to gatecrash normality's party, yet now that I was about to leave rehab permanently, I started to squirm – and badly. It was time to try out some of the skills I'd learned:

Positive self-talk:

- I can do this. *Breathe*
- Take one day at a time. *Breathe*
- It's all going to be OK. No, really, it is going to be OK. *Breathe*
- Don't forget that no one feels all right all the time.
- Be kind to yourself. This is not a race.

Speak to people, Fellowship members. Ask for help.

- Be honest about how you feel.
- Do not keep anxieties inside.
- Be conscious about how you feel throughout the day.
- Be vigilant. If anything bothers you, discuss it with someone as soon as you can, even though by the time you do this the feeling may have gone.
- Understanding yourself is the key to moving forward.

I was ready – sort of. I was up for it, I thought. I was optimistic, sometimes, yet utterly terrified, too.

My fears about seeing past cronies were negligible. I hadn't had contact with any of them for three months, and I wasn't about to bump into them randomly, not in Putney. Even in central London, it was unlikely, not during the day. They'd still be recovering from the night before, and I had no plans whatsoever to go out at night and celebrate my new life, unless it was at a Fellowship meeting. My old acquaintances were fickle; out of sight meant quickly forgotten. That suited me.

I was, however, concerned about Petra. We'd become close before I'd left London, entwined in a malignant embrace. I felt curiosity, and a desire to gloat about my change of lifestyle, but I knew that contacting her wasn't the healthiest of options.

*

UNHOOKED

I was hoovering the centre for the last time when Leon came into the office.

'I'm going to miss you loads, babes,' he breathed in between greedy kisses. I'd gone from zero to one hundred within two seconds.

'I'll be back in two weeks for aftercare,' I told him.

We looked at each other and said nothing. I felt bad about leaving him behind. There wasn't anything else I could say to make the situation better. All I wanted right now was for him to fuck me. Mercilessly.

CHAPTER 30

I despise goodbyes, and I said them quickly. I didn't know what to say to anyone except, 'See ya,' and, 'I'll definitely keep in touch.' Like I would. I dished out dry-eyed, robotic hugs to my fellow inmates, the PTB and Magda. In that moment, I felt pretty much the same about everyone; there was little preferential treatment. Of course, I felt something when I held Tess and lastly Leon, and when I bathed the two of them in explosive goodwill I meant every word. But my nerves were running riot. You know when you're setting off on a journey and you just want to get there? That was me. I wanted the next few days to zip by so I would be officially ensconced in my new world.

Nick and I took my last, and our first, walk together to Avalon, my home during the past three months. He was chatting, but I couldn't concentrate, consumed with mixed emotions about my upcoming liberation. I remember he didn't seem like 'Nick the counsellor' any longer. He was just a bloke, another citizen in recovery who was walking the same path as I was.

My holdall was in the porch. I shouted goodbye to Antonia, who duly stormed downstairs and gave me a motherly smacker on my cheek. I thanked her for the food and teased her about fattening me up, then Nick and I strode briskly towards the train station, where he bought me my single ticket to Waterloo.

That was it. He was gone and I was alone. I had palpitations and didn't know whether I wanted to cry or laugh like a banshee. I was free. I was free! Free to do whatever I wanted. I had no idea what that would be, but still, I could do it. I felt on high alert and adrenalin drenched my system.

This was what I'd wanted for months, and I'd earned it. It had to come at some point, and here it was. Freedom. I got on the train, sat down and, finally, I grinned. I breathed out. 'You fucking did it! You fucking did it!' I said under my breath. I suddenly felt ecstatic, absolutely swamped with endorphins. My first feelings of rapture. I kept knitting my fingers together and squeezing my palms to release some excitement. My dad used to do this.

Within days, the flat smelled like my home again. I didn't do much, except rigidly stick to my plan – although I ad-libbed long lie-ins in bed in the mornings.

I got back in contact with Janet, who arranged to take me to an AA meeting. At the entrance, a number of people were standing outside smoking.

'Hello, good evening,' someone said.

I murmured a reply and followed Janet inside.

'Are you OK?' she asked.

I told her I felt nervous and somehow embarrassed about sitting with a group of alcoholics and admitting to being the same.

'That's normal,' she said.

Two of her friends welcomed me, and the four of us got cups of tea. They were all different ages, and I felt I'd joined a sisterhood. I guess, in some respects, I had. Men were also allowed in this gang, but I wasn't supposed to be interested in them. People were friendly, too much so for my liking; I wasn't good at listening to, or participating in, talk about the weather or their kids, and certainly not 'spirits of nature'. Give me a fucking break. I'd just left rehab, and I didn't think people actually banged on about Higher Powers outside treatment centres. How wrong could I be?

'Thinking like that won't get you far, Katie,' Maggie would say to me when I talked about this when I called BCH. 'Don't forget, the first thing to go before someone derails is their attitude. So perhaps be grateful for folks' friendliness and don't take the piss out of them.' *Yeah, yeah.* I wasn't about to relapse. That was a fact.

The meeting room filled with maybe 30 people. 'We will be starting in approximately five minutes. Please find a seat if you haven't done so already,' some annoyingly cheerful soul shouted.

The four of us sat at the back – at my request.

'Welcome to the Thursday evening meeting of Alcoholics Anonymous. My name's Alice and I'm an alcoholic.' (Yep, that's right. Once an alcoholic, always an alcoholic. It's an attitude, not a behaviour, remember. Although I reckon 'recovering alcoholic' would be a more accurate label, but never mind.)

'Hello, Alice,' said everyone except me.

'OK, so this evening we're very lucky to have a gentleman here all the way from California, who has come to share his experience, strength and hope with us. Over to you, Hernie.'

Hmm . . . lucky us.

A cough, then: 'Hernie, alcoholic.'

'Hello, Hernie.' This time I joined in. I felt a bit of a twit. Not sure why. I just did.

Most meetings have a guest speaker. The things they usually cover in their talk are:

1. Past experiences. People need to hear they are not alone and that their behaviour isn't that of a weirdo. Addiction is a very solitary, thought-based illness.
2. What daily methods does the speaker use to stay abstinent from drugs and alcohol?
3. What motivates them to keep on believing both in sobriety *and* the programme, especially when things are difficult? Why bother to sustain a changed lifestyle? We need to remember what we would go back to.
4. What are the benefits of being sober and clean of drugs?

The speaker looked at ease, and I couldn't understand how, given that 60 eyes were gawping at him. I took it upon myself to feel awkward for Hernie.

'I'm over here on business from the States, but wherever I travel I feel safe, knowing my sobriety never needs to be threatened, because wherever I am in the world there are AA meetings I can attend. I thank you people for that.'

Grunts of 'hear, hear'. Thoughts of *yeah, OK*.

'It's been twenty-two years, but this programme is only relevant one day at a time, so the person who has been sober longest in this room is the one that got up earliest this morning.' *What absolute twaddle!*

Hernie spoke of feeling duty-bound to carry the message of recovery to other alcoholics and said that this was part of the reason he continued going to meetings. Besides, he sometimes needed 'reminding' that he was an alcoholic and that, although he no longer drank, if he did, he could go straight back to the emotional pit he'd left all those years ago. He talked for about 20 minutes, and then we all thanked him in unison.

More tea and a cigarette, and then the final part of the meeting, where people could share, basing what they said on some of the stuff that the old-timer had said. That or they could just babble on about their own lives.

I listened – when I wasn't fantasising about Leon fucking me from behind. I didn't see a problem with this. Usually, I imagined him ordering me to sit on his face. At least I was still in a meeting when I was thinking about this stuff. Surely I was doing everything I'd been told to do?

CHAPTER 31

I went to lots of NA and AA meetings before I opened my mouth, but I knew I had to start trying.

'I'm Kate and I'm an addict and alcoholic,' would have tripped off my tongue if I hadn't been cacking myself about speaking out loud in front of strangers who would be scrutinising me. But I wanted to do it. Well, I didn't, but it was part of what I was supposed to do, so . . .

Just cos we were in a 12 Step meeting didn't mean that the attendees had lost the ability to be snide and hurtful. So even if my sermon wasn't particularly informative, I at least wanted it to be audible, so I was seen to be making an effort to help myself. For the most part, people were genuinely there to try to change, but better not forget that a meeting is composed of rogues, former and current: thieves, liars, egocentric confidence tricksters, drug dealers, hookers, burglars and some violent thugs who would have held you up at knifepoint for your money. Many of these remained total arseholes whom I wouldn't have spat on had they been on fire. For sure, a meeting didn't teach you how to be a nice person; it only gave guidance about how to live differently day to day if you chose to. The only criterion necessary to be in a meeting was a *desire* to stop using chemicals. Nothing else.

And judging by the groups various people hung around in, some attendees took longer to choose their fruit than pick their friends.

'I'm Kate and I'm an addict,' I called out breathlessly. My heart was racing and my mouth was dry.

'Hello, Katie,' said Janet, grinning. She was sitting next to me. *My* Janet, my safety blanket. I glanced at her but didn't meet her eyes.

I was dazed. In theory, I could stop right now and I'd already have taken a personal stride forward, but I'd rather have taken a shit in public than cop out at that stage.

'Um . . .' I felt as though an electric current was sizzling through my veins. 'Er . . . I don't really know what to say . . . I just thought I'd open my mouth and say something, cos I've been advised that it might be good for me to . . .'

Suddenly, it didn't matter whether Janet was there or not; I was in this alone. There was silence except for some habitual throat-clearers. My goblin was screaming at me to shut the hell up. And then a very quiet 'thank you' came from the person next to me. Janet was still there. *It's OK; it's OK . . .*

'Well, that's it. Thank you.' I grimaced. I felt like a right dipstick.

Everyone had either spoken in a meeting for the first time at some point or hadn't done it at all yet, and it was remembering this that enabled me to sit back and grind my teeth less hard and allow some pride to rise within me. A small smirk, which I tried to stifle, was desperate to leap off my face in what I felt would have been an inappropriate show of self-satisfaction – given that I'd said bugger all.

But I was pleased with my bugger all, until, that is, Miss Self-Hater Extraordinaire spat that I'd sounded ridiculous. *Fuck you; I was all right*, I thought back.

Janet tapped my thigh. She looked as proud as if I'd received a knighthood for services to mankind. This silenced my goblin. My shoulders relaxed.

Before the meeting, Janet had told me, 'There's no pressure. It won't be an inauguration speech. This is *your* recovery. It's *your* life, love. Don't forget that it's only *you* who can take charge of it. But I assure you that your confidence will grow once you speak in a meeting.'

I'd proved to myself that I was trying. I thought I really was . . .

I hadn't yet decided what to do with my new life. The thought of getting a job was horrifying. I would start to get palpitations when I thought about this even for a second. I'd get glimmers of the vastness of the challenges that my new way of life would involve, and it was enough to make me do nothing or, if anything, go backwards. I cried very easily on account of being so anxious, and I threw myself into frenzies of self-doubt about my future.

I knew that it was acceptable, and even expected, that after rehab people who didn't have an established job took time before finding work or a course and expanding their daily routine. But when I'd heard this in BCH, I hadn't understood why this was so. Now I was living it, I got it. Some people I talked to were two years clean but still not employed. I could see why now: it was fear.

Luckily for me, social security was paying my rent, so there was no urgent need for me to throw myself into the ocean without protection against the rough waves. However,

I was worried about money. Dropping from £300 an hour as a call girl to £100 a week on sick benefit was hellish. Also, although in the past I'd spent virtually every penny I'd earned on my addictions, I had *earned* the cash, so mentally it was a strain to feel dependent on the state. I had to remind myself: one thing at a time, first things first, *breathe* and all that jazz – but still.

I knew I couldn't reorganise my life in one swoop. But I'd have come out of retirement and fucked a punter if it would have magically given me peace of mind. My brain had started chattering again in a way it hadn't done for some time, and I didn't admit to anyone how intimidated I was by this.

I hadn't yet met with my dad and Elaine, but we'd spoken on the phone. The call was civil, pleasant even. Wooden, yes, and stilted, definitely – but no change there. Speaking to my dad often shattered my heart and left me with fleeting visions of killing myself over the loss of the relationship we'd had when I was young. I felt it had been irrevocably destroyed.

I wasn't in a rush for us to get together – and neither, it seemed, were they. I'd leave the suggestion to meet up to them. No part of me wanted to cause them embarrassment or make them feel pressurised; I'd done enough over the years to upset them. Tragic as it was, I had to accept that all of us had suffered years of anxiety and that we weren't about to turn into the Waltons after just three months of my rehabilitation – if ever.

My first and foremost priority was to not drink or use a drug. That came before everything else, and the longer I was abstinent the more the self-belief that had sprouted as a result of my having completed treatment was able to grow. But there were nagging questions. For one, how the hell was I going to fill my days?

I focused on events, appointments with social security and

doctors, NA or AA meetings, fantasising about Leon and our life as a couple, and coffee dates with Fellowship members – female ones, of course.

This even though I'd noticed that caffeine seemed to give me the jitters. I'd meet whoever had tried to seduce me into believing that coffee was the new black and within minutes I'd start to feel shaky. I wasn't sure if this was because of the chat, which was too often 12 Step based, or the caffeine or just because my mind was constantly worrying. Regardless, I persisted, trying overly hard to fit in with my new norm. 'A person who wants sobriety will do absolutely anything to hang onto it,' Lenny had said. It took me ages to understand that not everything was meant to be taken literally all the time. Janet noticed I was struggling and talked to me about it. I decided it wouldn't harm me to stop drinking coffee, so I did.

I decided that, based on my inability to work out the issues surrounding the effect of my caffeine intake alone, I needed to get a sponsor. So I asked Janet and she agreed. She immediately talked about us going through the Steps together. I made all the right noises, but I couldn't have given a toss about going through them, not right then. Things weren't good, but they sure as hell could have been worse, and I knew it. So what was the rush?

There was no drama; quite the contrary – things were dull. As long as I didn't allow my fears to dominate my mind, everything was, well, as it was: pretty dreary.

CHAPTER 32

Alone on the train, twiddling with my newly extension-less hair, heading to Weymouth for aftercare, I thought about my first aftercare group in 1998. That time, when I left I relocated to the same town my dad had moved to after he'd married Elaine. I'd lived close to their home in a bedsit. He'd remained in Yorkshire, but 80 miles from the house that I'd called home, where he'd raised me.

Although my father was around, I felt I'd lost him – which meant I had nothing. He was married and I was deliriously jealous. My insecurities were crippling me, and my father offered me no sympathy or understanding. Any hint of grief that I displayed meant that I was lavished with threats of indefinite ex-communication from their two-person gang. That or they'd hand out lashings of controlling silence.

So what did I do? Fight – and loudly. I fought with every piece of artillery I had. I was confused about my status in my dad's life. He was childishly absorbed in his relationship, and since I didn't know how to deal with my feelings, I behaved in an equally selfish manner and attempted to make my presence known – by any means necessary. At this time, and for a long time afterwards, I would gladly have watched

Elaine being tortured with hot pokers and then strung up to die.

Instead of treating the situation with some understanding, my dad's new partner behaved as though she saw me simply as another woman who was vying for her husband's attention, ignoring the fact that I was his daughter. They cast me aside as a destructive force that needed to be fully banished from their lives. But I would not go away. My father was my only family, and I was willing to do anything to keep him in my life.

However, once I realised that my anger was rotting my soul and that obsessively fantasising about Elaine's death was doing me harm, I knew that, for my own good, not hers, I had to change my view. In the space of one year, there were lots of new additions to my life. I was sober, in a new town; I had a new home and no friends – and what had Daddy done? *Fucking left me*. And what was I going to do? Disintegrate in a corner? Nope, I was a soldier.

I was 21 years old. I tried to be happy with my damp bedsit and the sofa bed. I went to NA meetings and spoke the lingo, as I'd been told to do in rehab. I thought that abstinence was supposed to signify well-being, yet the fact was I was miserable and lonely, and I hated living. But I told no one. Did I have years ahead of me feeling like this? I was convinced that most people weren't walking round feeling this hopeless every day. Why would they bother if that was the case?

All that had changed was that I wasn't drinking or using drugs; internally I was exactly the same. For months, I gritted my teeth and tried, but failed, to believe that the way I was feeling would change at some point. I thought I'd been doing everything that the book had told me to do to stay sober, but in fact I was a walking time bomb. I was at the mercy of my goblin, who was being fed by my increasing self-doubt and thoughts of hatred and vengeance towards my stepmother.

I didn't know what to do to defuse the inevitable, or, indeed, what would ignite the explosives. No one ends up with a needle in their arm or a glass of pinot being poured down their throat by their own hand by coincidence; the journey leading to my relapse had started long before I picked up.

   • *to pick up* = to use a substance.

When I started drinking again, at first I couldn't get drunk, however hard I tried. I told myself again and again that as long as I stayed away from narcotics I'd be OK.

When it came to my first aftercare, convinced that I'd be ostracised from the community if I admitted to having fucked up, I felt I had to lie. So I did, relentlessly. I'd been trying to anchor myself to a familiar, safe environment, because away from rehab I'd felt alone and suicidal. In my first aftercare group, I was frightened of the consequences if I was truthful about what had happened, and I didn't think about the potential problems for my future if I wasn't.

Everyone in recovery fears relapsers, and even people who no longer attend meetings, presuming that they too have succumbed to their demons. Barriers go up, suspicion rises and gossip spreads at a terrifying rate.

Now my journey back to rehab for aftercare was different. *I* was different. I was sober. I had not drunk a drop or sniffed anything that could alter my state of mind, and I was no longer fighting a losing battle with my dad and his wife. I'd accepted years before that I'd lost him.

I was giddy about being allowed to take Tessa out for a

two-hour lunch once the aftercare group was done. And I couldn't wait to see Billy, Daryl and even Lenny. Of course, my biggest reward was that I'd get to hold Leon. I just hoped he still fancied me with my hair short.

I'd bought him a chunky silver necklace, which I knew he'd like, but I'd be keeping that private, and of course he'd have to, too. Still, I was no longer a client; surely there was nothing wrong with me buying a gift for a friend?

As the train to Dorset pulled out of London, I was the happiest I'd been since I'd left BCH, ready to pass on a message of hope from the great outside about a drug-free, sexless life. I felt alive; I felt healthy; I looked good. I'd lost some of the weight I'd put on during my three-month confinement, and I felt that the world offered me everything and I could gain it legitimately.

I practically galloped along the street from Weymouth station to BCH, with a smile welded to my face, and when I got to the centre I ran up the stairs in twos.

During the couple of weeks I'd been away, new faces had appeared. Billy and Leon had moved to Juniper, a secondary house, and Sabrina had finally moved on, too. But they'd be back at the centre for aftercare. Austin was still in primary; truth be told, I think that suited him. He'd spent so many years in prison that the longer he was institutionalised, the safer he felt.

There was an abundance of hugs, kisses, compliments and laughter. Billy asked me about what I'd been doing as though I'd just been on a trip to an ethereal universe that was only described in Holy Scripture. He was staring at me as though I was going to dispense wisdom that even he didn't already know.

Even seeing Stacey was pleasant. She was miserable as

ever, but who could blame her? She'd been in treatment for upwards of five months.

Austin grinned. 'Peace, lady,' he said, as he stuck out his hand to do one of those gangster handshakes that can cause embarrassment when you don't know what you're doing. I didn't, so I went to kiss his cheeks instead. As I went for the second peck, he moved and we clashed. 'Bless,' he muttered, and walked off.

'Where's Daryl?' I looked at Billy, who looked at Magda, who looked away. Then Billy told me that Daryl had absconded from secondary days before and had been seen 'looking rough with puffy eyes, but he swears he's clean'. My heart sank.

'But he's back, Katie, so worry not, darling. He's in there.' Billy nodded towards the group room. Neither Leon nor Tess had told me about this during our phone calls, but I knew Tessa had more immediate problems of her own to worry about.

She came towards me. My spirits lifted on seeing her, but I knew her jolly mood was a front.

'I'm so, so sorry, Tess. I really am.' I held her firmly.

She'd lost an appeal contesting her two children's adoption. There was nothing more she could do.

'Please let's not talk about it now. I'll tell you everything when we go for lunch, all right, bab?' Her eyes were watery.

'I know, but . . .'

'God, I can't believe your hair. It's weird seeing it so short.'

'Look, I'm desperate to talk to you, Tess. I want to know what's gone on.'

She pretended she hadn't heard me. 'I'd better fill my boots at lunchtime today, eh, Magda?' she said to the receptionist, who knew what a hard time Tess had been having and looked uncomfortable. 'You'd best leave yer tight Yorkshire ways outside the door when we hit that caff, Kate. I know what youse people are like.'

She was desperately trying to be jovial as she wiped away tears. I needed to hold her; I needed to show her some love. I pulled her close. I stroked her hair as she cried silently. A familiar voice postponed my tears.

'Is that Katie I hear?'

'Yes, Lenny.'

'Hi! Hi!' I waved as people passed by, whether I recognised them or not. I felt like a celebrity. Everyone was curious when someone came for aftercare, bringing news of the outside world. I wanted to rush into the main room to see Daryl, but I was enjoying catching up with everyone, especially Tessa, and I guessed that Leon was in there too, so I held back.

I heard Maggie's bracelets jingling before I saw her. She stormed over to me and interrupted my prattling on to Nick about how easy life was in a sober world. 'You look lovely. I like your hair shorter like that.' She said this almost reluctantly but at least she was trying to be polite. 'I'll catch you after the group, OK? Nice to see you, Katie.'

'You too,' I said, also reluctantly, also being polite.

I was trying to get more of the story about Daryl from Nick and Tess when I felt a perfect amount of pressure on my lower back. I knew who it was.

'I'm off. I'll see you in a bit,' Tessa said, and we kissed on the lips.

'Hello, you,' Leon smirked and pulled me close to him to sniff my neck before giving me a peck on the cheek. I could have screamed. This felt like torture. I wanted him to nail me right there.

'Hey, fella. I'm here too,' said Nick.

'Can you blame me?' said Leon, gripping my hand. *Argh! Jesus fucking Christ!* He looked better than ever before, and I knew that everything would be OK between us. I just knew it. I asked Leon if Daryl was around and his eyes dropped.

I headed to the main room and there he was: gaunt, ragged, spotty and downtrodden. 'I don't know why I left,' he said. 'I just did. I was missing my son, you know, and my head was mashed with the pressure of being in here, mate, and next thing I just fucking did one. And you know the mad thing is I didn't even get to London to see my boy.' He sniggered at the irony. 'Instead, I fucking rattled the fruit machine down on the front, then begged some moolah on the high street, and within an hour I'd scored, off this fucking minging bird whose yard I've stayed at for the last few days. Fucking stank in there, it did. Loadsa pillocks in and out. Her screaming kids running around the place where there are needles and pipes lying around. You know the coup.'

He looked a different person. His blond hair looked brown; his eyes were lifeless.

'I'm glad you're back,' I said.

'Ha! Yeah . . . I'm fucking trapped, mate. *Trapped.*' He looked broken. I rested my hand on his thigh. He continued talking. 'I had to come back here, eh? Or I'd have been arrested for breach of my parole.'

'Breaching your parole isn't the –'

'I know it's not the main thing. I'm just saying, you know. *Fuck, man!* Fucking shit life, this, mate.' He shook his head, furious at his situation. 'I'll tell you something, though, three days on the pipe and whacking up gear and I couldn't fucking take no more.'

'Babe, you have to talk about it.' I felt pathetic giving this advice when I knew full well how my goblin could not only silence me but also make me deaf.

'I have to do this fucking shite. I don't have a choice, you know, cos I've nothing out there for me. I can't even be a decent dad when I'm on it. But you know, the thing is I don't even know if I can do this, man.' He started rubbing his head anxiously. 'I mean, what if the urge comes on me for a pipe again? Then what? You know how it is. You can't fucking ignore it.'

The aftercare group was uneventful.

I announced that the social had agreed to pay my rent, but I didn't dwell on it because I didn't want to seem as though I was sticking two fingers up at Maggie, who'd dismissed that possibility.

After we were done, there was less than an hour before the non-residents had to leave the centre, and my boy and I spent most of that time sitting in a corner staring at each other and communicating silently. There was little to say. Action was what we really needed.

The centre was a hive of activity. Strangely, I missed being there. I missed the camaraderie; I missed the smokiness and even the boredom that somehow now seemed like decent meditation time.

I watched Alan, who looked a changed fella, nothing like the one who'd almost got into a scrap with Leon. He'd bulked out quickly. He came over and was chatty, introducing himself as though we'd never met. I didn't remind him that we had. He'd been on detox at the time.

'He's all right, he is,' said Leon when he walked off. 'He might be a bit posh, innit, but he's funny as hell. His dad works in the Government, you know.'

'Oh, right. My mind was on leaving when he arrived. What does his dad do?'

'Dunno.'

'Maybe he's just a janitor or something, and you're all thinking he's an MP,' I laughed.

'Maybe he's a what?'

'A janitor – a cleaner, you know.'

'Nah, he was on the back seat or something like that, innit?' Leon laughed and did his familiar shoulder jig.

'Back bench? He's an MP?'

'I don't fuckin' know. But it sounded proper.'

I thought it was time to change the subject. 'I've got something for you, baby, but you have to promise me that you won't mention it to anyone. No one, not even Ozzy, OK? We have to be really quick when I give it to you.'

'A pair of your knickers?' He grinned at me. I wanted him to penetrate me deeply with that big cock of his.

'No, but I could give you them too. They're moist.' They had been from the moment Leon and I had said hello.

He followed me into the kitchen. There were people in there. No one I knew. 'You need to hide it, OK?' Our noses were a palm's width apart. This was it. I was about to make a declaration of 'more to come'. 'I want you to be really careful when you open it.'

I placed the box on the top of my bag, not daring to pull it out. 'If someone comes now, pretend I'm showing you something that I bought for myself, OK?' He nodded. I opened my bag and leaned right into him. My pussy was throbbing. I breathed him in; I could feel him between my legs. He opened the box and a delayed, wide-eyed 'Ahh!' came from his needing-to-be-kissed mouth. He didn't have to say anything else.

'Put it in your pocket and leave the box,' I told him. Our hands clashed.

'Can you stop grappling with Katie, please, Leon, and get a move on?' *Fuck*.

'Ah, can't I just grab her a bit more, Len?'

Tessa came towards me and flung her arms round my waist. The Youth kissed my cheek and Lenny stood looking on.

I was glad to notice that Leon seemed to have binned the over-sentimental rubbish that he'd been churning out before I'd left. And I hoped to God the necklace wouldn't come back and bite me on the arse.

CHAPTER 33

Lunch with Tessa had been full of tears. I'd cried cos she had. Although of course I couldn't truly feel her pain, just seeing her suffering upset me. Her two children had been placed with a family who were to become their adoptive parents. Before entering rehab, she'd opted to put them into foster care, aware that she wasn't able to look after them. Her heroin and crack addictions had completely ravaged her ability to be a responsible mother, so she took what she saw as sensible steps to protect her children.

People say sorry when they spill orange juice onto someone's lap or brush past a stranger. But what do you say when you realise that you've imposed your own fucked-up life on your innocent kids? Partners and parents have the choice of walking away, but children do not; hence the massive disdain often directed at mothers who are in active drug addiction.

So, you're in rehab trying to change; what else is there? Is the word 'sorry' enough? If it's from the depth of your being, surely it is. The options are limited when it comes to showing adequate regret, and offering a pound of one's flesh in recompense serves no purpose.

Nearly all of Tessa's family had been drug addicts. Both

parents, both siblings, and some uncles and aunts. She'd grown up working the streets, screwing the state, and living by her wits, but she'd never robbed or stolen or got into trouble with the police.

Her cards had been dealt to her from birth, and although she could have taken a different journey, she didn't. Shoulda, woulda, coulda. The reality of the choices she'd made had to be faced. She followed the example set by those close to her, and no doubt sometimes she'd found her life exciting. She wanted to be away from her family home, where she struggled with her doped-up parents, and from her late teens she took to selling herself for money. With the cash she earned from prostitution, she paid her own way, and she felt she was being proactive regarding her future. She rented a flat, helped her parents financially and met a man. During the time she was in this relationship, she stopped working the streets and got onto benefits, while her partner worked on building sites. Together they had two children, and together they fuelled their heroin and crack addictions.

Tessa never kidded herself that the way she lived was right. But she lacked the confidence and awareness to live any other way. Drugs, hooking and struggling were all she had ever known. She realised her children were missing out like she had, and this she was not going to allow. So she contacted social services to explain that she was unable to manage and asked that the children be put into foster care while she went into rehab.

They were and Tessa did, for four weeks. Under the looming threat of having your children taken away from you, how do you begin to unravel a life like a ball of barbed wire? Even with a will to find the end, if you gently start to unwind the wire, what do you do when you reach a knot?

Give up? Continue? Each needle pierces your skin. You bleed. You grapple with the task, hoping there will be a great reward once the job is done.

You're disorientated. You haven't got the chemicals that enabled you to function normally. You're furious with yourself and search for people to blame for you having to sift through all this debris. And the more you face up to the realisation that you've screwed up monumentally and created a life every single aspect of which is drenched in degradation and chaos, with no one to blame except yourself, the more this causes you to feel despondency beyond belief. To cover this up, you display venomous anger, directed at anyone who comes near you.

If we are to believe people who say 'listen to your gut', how can it be right to ignore the constant churning in your guts and that internal screaming voice telling you you're not worthy of being a mother and not worthy of being alive?

As a daughter, you're a failure; as a mother, you're a failure; as a sister, you're a failure; and as a human being, you're a failure. And worst of all, you repeatedly tell yourself how loathsome you must be to impact on the life of your children in such a negative manner.

But you keep on pulling at the barbed wire. One moment, there appears to be movement, but the next there's nothing. The mesh is stuck. You forget what you're doing and why. All you are getting from this experience is blood on your hands.

Being the scum that you see yourself as, will you ever *really* be able to do anything good at all? I mean *anything*? Having destroyed everything in your life and even had your own children taken away from you, do you now have the strength to even try to change? I mean *really* try? *Why bother?* your goblin spits.

Having a drug constantly in your system is not dissimilar

to having cotton wool stuffed into your ears while wearing a wetsuit and goggles over your eyes. You're never going to get the full picture about anything. You can hear some words, of course you can, but you don't take in their real meaning. You can see, but your vision is blurred. You can feel. You're pretty numb because of the rubber suit shielding you from the sensations that most people experience, but you're still able to feel some things. So if users continue to feel, continue to see, continue to hear, what the hell is their reason for not getting their act together and stopping hurting those around them and themselves? How can a parent allow their child to be taken away?

No 'sane' person would live like this by choice, aware that their life is getting more and more complicated and more messy most hours of most days of every month of every year. No sane person would be willing to exist like this. Begging for money, living on the streets, selling your body, stabbing needles into your skin, drunk every day, sniffing chemicals that make you paranoid and smoking stuff that makes you twitch. And tell me, what sane person would allow their children to be adopted against their will, when they wanted to keep them?

So why then repeat the behaviour, if you suffered the same as a child? But look at Tessa's history; look at her influences. From an early age, she copied her mother. She did what was normal within her family. And when it came to taking care of her own kids, despite adoring them as much as the drugs allowed her to, she'd already screwed up. The cotton wool was already in her ears; the rubber suit was on; the goggles blurred her vision. Over time, she deteriorated.

Tessa was never evil. Sick, yes; unstable, definitely; but spawn of the Devil? Nope. She wasn't a bad person learning to become a good one. She'd been unwell and she was trying to recover from the sickness of her mind. If someone could have flicked a switch in her mind sooner and prevented some of the destruction, that would have been a blessed thing. But it didn't happen.

Previously, she'd tried and failed, and now her kids were about to be adopted. I'm sure I would have thought, *Fuck it, I'm going to escape this pain* – and used. But Tessa didn't. She was totally resolute she would stay clean so that when her children turned 18 she'd be able to face them and say sorry.

Really sorry.

PART 2

CHAPTER 34

What is the collective name for teetotallers out together? I don't know, but I imagined it had to be 'boring as hell'.

Emma, my new friend and an ex-user of anything and everything, seemed to know everyone in NA. She'd been round the block, and by that I mean . . . oh, never mind. She was the party planner for south-west London. Committee members would meet once a month to arrange socials and other Fellowship business, and it was with Emma that I went to my first NA party, held on a stationary boat on the Thames, very soon after I'd been for aftercare.

I hadn't wanted to go to the party; I wasn't ready to socialise straight-headed. The idea of going for a night out without alcohol felt fake, particularly when it was with other non-drinkers. But I felt under pressure to prove that I was able to live la vida loca even without booze. I also realised that this was a way to ingratiate myself with Emma and her friends, and possibly meet other potential mates, so I agreed to go. I couldn't imagine how it would be possible to enjoy myself without a little – *a little*? I'd never done *a little* – cocaine. But other people were managing. Apparently.

I was wearing a long, black peasant skirt that sat on my hips, a wide tan leather belt and a tight, black crossover top that stopped at my navel. Take my word for it, it was fashionable at the time. I got a lift to the party with Emma, and to me this meant I couldn't leave until she was ready to go. One of my fears was that I would feel trapped, but on the other hand the idea of getting a train home, alone, sober and dressed as I was, made me feel sick. I wasn't used to emphasising my shape.

Emma, her three friends and I got out of the car and walked towards the Embankment. I could hear music booming from the boat before we'd even boarded, and it just made me more nervous. I knew I looked good; I'd slimmed down after the rehab starch fest and my clothes were simple and a little bit sexier than I'd normally go for. But did I feel confident? Absolutely not. I wished to God I hadn't accepted the invitation, but I hadn't learned the art of saying no when I meant it.

We all marched into the bar. I hovered at the back and someone bought me a Diet Coke. It was busy but we found a table and sat down. I hated being there and was consumed with self-consciousness.

It didn't take me long to notice a guy whose cock I immediately started sucking – in my head. I knew nothing about his politics, if he had a job or had ever been convicted of a heinous crime, if he farted and sniffed it – all I wanted to know was whether or not he was circumcised. But I kept this to myself.

The girls seemed relaxed, like they were actually enjoying themselves. Life looked easy for them. They were open and optimistic, which made me wonder if they were all putting on an act. I listened to how they'd managed sobriety in their early days. One had gone to college; another had done an eight-week computer course before applying to be a National Rail administrator, then deciding to train to be a nurse. A third had spent her first two years recuperating before falling pregnant, getting married and setting up a babysitting business.

Interesting, interesting . . . I felt inspired hearing about the marriage and, more importantly, in the space of 30 minutes I had decided in which direction my future would go. Just like that! Failing at school was a big regret, so I made up my mind that I was going to apply for university. I wasn't sure which one, how, what course I'd go for or whether or not I'd get in, and I didn't know about fees or qualifications, but I was going to give it a whirl. I had nothing to lose. I needed something good to tell my dad about and to give myself credit for. Completing rehab somehow just didn't seem enough.

House music rippled through the battered wooden floors and I felt horribly uncomfortable as the girls danced next to me. I was way too shy to join them. As the bass got more intrusive, I decided without any doubt that I had to leave. I felt that it was expected of me to at least appear to be enjoying myself, but I wasn't.

'To be honest, I'm not feeling too well,' I told Emma.

She took my hand and led us out of the dance area. As we squeezed past people, I saw the guy I'd been eyeing up earlier. We glanced at each other and I looked away, then looked back, and he smiled. A burst of excitement lifted my spirits, but as quickly as it struck, it was gone.

Outside, Emma was understanding.

'I keep feeling rushes of anxiety. I'm just not used to this, ya know, so I think it's better I go home. I'll get a train or a taxi or something.' I was trying to be as calm as possible. That was better than saying, 'I'm fucking flipping out here. I hate all this noise and all these people, and I feel really fucking odd. To be honest, I hate every fucking second of this fucking experience. If this is sober living, I can't fucking do it! I want to go home immediately.'

'Look, babe, everyone feels the same the first time they come to a party straight.' Of course I didn't believe her. 'And you know something?' she continued. 'I feel pangs as well, but I try to ignore them.'

Pangs? Ignore them? Are we talking about the same thing? How could anyone ignore these feelings? They were as real as the pain and shock I'd feel if someone punched me clean in the face. Even so, I nodded.

'It does get better, you know. It really does. I know what you're going through,' she said tenderly. My eyes could easily have filled with tears, but I stopped myself. I didn't want my mascara to run. 'There isn't anything that can make you feel better quicker, poppet. It just takes time.'

Fucking great.

'I really need to go home,' I said to her again.

'Come on, you'll be all right. Just stay, just for a little bit.'

'I can't. Honestly.'

'Do you want me to come with you? Are you sure you won't stay?'

I was damn sure. This was the first time for years that I'd had a conversation like this. In my old life, if I wanted to go, I just left without saying a word.

The fit guy came over and asked Emma if she had a lighter.

'I don't smoke, do I, Gary? Have you got one, Kate?'

'I think so.' *Dear God, please let me find it quickly.* He said nothing. Added pressure. 'Here you go.' *You did it!* I felt pretty smug. I handed him my lighter and he offered me a cigarette.

'Cheers, love.' *Urgh! Love?*

'So how're you doing, gorgeous?' he said to Emma in a Liverpudlian accent.

I felt jealous. I was desperate for her to introduce me, but she didn't. Maybe she wanted him for herself. Maybe she'd already had him and still wanted to keep him for herself. I wouldn't blame her. He looked as good close up as he had done from afar. He was plainly avoiding looking at me. *Obviously not interested*, I decided.

They laughed together and I felt ignored. Then, as if he could read my thoughts, he said, 'Sorry, sweetheart, I haven't introduced myself. I'm Gary.' *Too late.*

I offered my hand, which he used to pull me towards him for a kiss. Our mouths barely missed. *Did he do that on purpose?* I knew he knew we'd near-missed. *What if he thinks I tried to kiss his mouth? Fuck.* We drew apart, holding each other's gaze, and I broke into an over-the-top grin, which I knew Emma had noticed.

CHAPTER 35

As I walked away from the boat, I heard someone calling, 'Katie!' I carried on, but my name was called again. I turned round and Gary was 20 yards from me.

'Where're you off to?'

'Home.'

'Where's home? Cos I could always take you.' He was walking towards me. 'I've seen you at meetings.'

He's seen me before tonight?

'Look, I'll drop you off if you like.'

'But where do you live?'

I felt awkward yet in control. I cared less about what he thought of me and how I looked now. I just wanted to get out of Dodge and back to my feather duvet to mind my own business.

'Honestly, it's no trouble driving you back, love.'

He was fit, but he'd have to stop calling me 'love'.

'It's better than you getting public transport or paying out loadsa wonga for a cab, you know what I'm sayin', sweets?'

Why couldn't any of these NA blokes talk normally? I didn't know how to handle this. *Should I smile? Act indifferent? Act indifferent*, I decided.

'C'mon, let's go!' he said. 'My car's not far from here.'

We started walking. I liked his imposing stature; not at all like Leon. Gary was big. He had his own plumbing company, he told me.

When I told him he couldn't come in when he dropped me off, he replied, 'Fair enough. Whatever you say.'

'It's only that my place is really untidy.'

'Who gives a fuck about that, like?'

'Me. I do. I don't want someone to come in when things are a mess.'

'Stop going on about it, girl. I'm just gonna –'

'I wasn't going on.'

'Whatever you say. I'm only gonna drop you off outside your place, all right? Fuck's sake.'

I didn't like the way he spoke to me. I started to over-think the fact that I'd be in a confined space with this guy for at least 40 minutes, which gave him just enough time to persuade me that it didn't matter how untidy my flat was, he'd pop in for a short time. Just for tea. It was way too late for coffee . . .

CHAPTER 36

I decided to apply to South Bank University, simply because I'd heard of it. I chose psychology because, well, like most people, I fancied myself as an amateur psychoanalyst. I wasn't scared of going for it; I was curious about whether I'd even be given the opportunity to do the degree with only two GCSEs, no A levels, no access course, no anything.

Just after I'd made my first phone call to enquire about getting onto the course, there was a knock at my door. *Who the fuck is this?* Whoever it was had managed to get into the building. *Leon? Surely not?* My heart was pounding, my mind was rattling. Then I remembered that he didn't know my address. Still, I went anxiously to open the door. It was Janet.

We drank tea and talked about men, our past experiences of addiction and our current situations. I didn't mention Leon and I definitely didn't talk about Gary. At first, I felt uncomfortable in Janet's presence. It was odd getting together without having a meeting to go to, and chatting for no reason other than to be friendly felt weird, but surprisingly I wasn't bored to tears.

There was a time when I wouldn't have answered a random knock at the door even if I'd been promised a lifelong supply of Häagen-Dazs. And now? The anxiety had lasted less than a minute. By the time Janet left, I'd laughed more than I'd expected to. I lay on the sofa, two cushions for comfort, and involuntarily giggled at my new-found normality.

JUDGE: Evidence of positive changes occurring. How do you plead, miss?

ME: Guilty, I guess.

JUDGE: And in the case of your soon-to-be-boyfriend Leon, how do you plead on the charge of infidelity?

ME: Do you have to burst my bubble like this?

The phone rang.

'Are you sitting down?'

'I'm lying down.'

'I'm leaving BCH tomorrow, babes,' Leon said quietly.

I sat bolt upright. 'What do you mean?' Gary flashed through my thoughts.

'I'm comin' back to London Tahn, innit?' he said, exaggerating his cockney accent. 'I don't know what more I can get from being here for another three weeks. It's pointless, right? I'll be back in my manor tomorrow morning, you feeling me, baybeee?' He burst out laughing.

'God, I don't know what to say.' I wanted to sound happy, I really did, but I couldn't.

'Ain't you pleased? What's wrong, princess? There's something up.'

'No! There isn't. Honestly, I just thought . . .'

'I don't see the point of jamming here. For what? For Maggie and Lenny to tell me that I'm suddenly straight enough to leave?'

'Yeah, but . . .'

'Nothing'll change over the next couple of weeks, you get me? It's proper mad just killing time in here when I could be on road getting on with my life, get me? *We* can start with our life together, innit, babes? I don't get why you're –'

'Leon, just slow down, will ya? I didn't expect this, that's all. I thought you'd be leaving in a bit, not now.' *What about Gary?* I didn't want to close the show after just one performance.

'Katie, man, tell me what's wrong. There's something up.' Leon sounded panicked.

'Nothing's wrong, OK?' I snapped.

'There is! You sound different, babes.'

'I don't sound different, OK? I don't sound any different at all.'

'What's happening? You ain't been with someone, have you?'

'Leon, for fuck's sake! Stop it! Look, I can't talk now. Call me later.'

'When?'

'I don't know.'

'Why can't you talk now? Tell me what's going on. Why aren't you buzzing that we can be together from tomorrow? Please, Katie, babes, just talk to me now.'

'I can't. I can't. I'm going out to meet Emma for coffee,' I said, worried sick.

'I thought you'd stopped drinking coffee?'

'Oh, fuck off, Leon! I said that as a figure of speech. I won't be drinking coffee, all right? Does that make you feel better? I might have orange juice or maybe even a cup of tea. Would that be all right with you?'

My mind was racing. All I'd been thinking about for the past 48 hours had been the image of Gary's perfect penis sliding in and out of my snatch. And now this?

I'd told no one about Leon and me and our flat-packed relationship. Now there was the plumber to add to the mix. I desperately wanted to talk to someone but feared being judged. How would it make me look? Not too clever. Although I was aware that Gary would get more 'blame' than me because he'd been clean longer, I wasn't one to stand back and let someone be slated for something I'd also been part of. Well, not usually.

There is a code of conduct for dealing with newcomers to NA and AA (anyone in the embryonic stages, within their first 12 months of sobriety, which, of course, included me), which people who have more than a year's sobriety are supposed (note the word 'supposed') to abide by. The 'advice' (allegedly not rules) includes refraining from what is commonly referred to as 'thirteenth-stepping', a colloquial term for 'taking advantage of a newcomer's vulnerability', particularly sexually.

No one could accuse Leon or me of thirteenth-stepping the other. Surely ours was a level playing field? Even so, I knew that we would have to keep our relationship quiet if we didn't want to be judged for 'not taking recovery seriously'. We were supposed to follow the 'no relationship within your first twelve months' protocol.

'I'm glad you got home all right after the party,' Emma said apologetically once we'd exchanged the usual pleasantries. *Do I tell her what's going on?* My face confessed I had a secret.

'What is it?' she asked.

I tried to assess how cross my 'big sister' was going to be about my flagrant embrace of a cardinal sin. I decided she'd be 'disappointed', which in my book means 'unexpressed anger'.

'Oh, babe, did you go back to someone's place?'

'Well, someone came back to mine.'

'Who?'

I grabbed my tea, attempting to hide my shamed smirk behind the cup. As if she could read my mind, Emma sighed and guessed correctly.

The look on her chops was the same as I would expect to see on the face of someone who'd witnessed a thief on a bicycle pedalling furiously away after having bundled somebody else's week-old kitten into their wicker basket. The reality of my situation, if I had told her the whole saga, including Leon, might have been worthy of such an expression, but since I'd told her only a part of the whole, I decided that she'd overdone it.

I'd had sex. With Gary. In my bed. Not on the bonnet of a car down a murky street while people were watching. I hadn't sucked him off in a toilet. No money had been exchanged. And I hadn't been a virgin until the said event. It had all been above board. I was 27 years old. He was 35. Neither of us had refused the deed of full penetration once an amount of foreplay had taken place.

'Katie, babe . . .'

I started laughing a little. I didn't want to, and I scolded myself for doing so. To make up for my bad behaviour I served Emma up some regret. 'I know, I know. Maybe I shouldn't have done it . . .' *Your Honour* '. . . but I have and, well, nothing can change that now.' I put on a forlorn expression to add to the drama.

'I'm only thinking about you, poppet. You know that, right?'

I wished she wouldn't call me 'poppet'. Not now. And actually, no, I didn't know she was thinking only about my welfare. Gary was a handsome chap. Maybe she was jealous. Or worse, maybe she'd been involved with him.

'I mean, where do I start with Gary?' she continued.

I interrupted her looming scaremongering by asking, 'Have you slept with him?'

'God, no. He tried it, though.' *Yeah, course he did.*

'Well, thank goodness for that. Listen, please, Emma, don't tell me stories about him, cos I feel OK about it right now . . .' *(Objection, Your Honour!)* '. . . and to be honest, I don't want to start worrying about what he has or hasn't done to Miss or Mrs So-and-So, you know? I've got enough on my plate at the moment. Unless, that is, you're going to tell me that he was lying when he said he was single.' I gulped.

'As far as I'm aware, he's single, very single . . . that's the thing, babe, he's known for being a real slapper.' *Bullseye! You had to say something, eh?*

'Well, as long as he's not with anyone, I can deal with it. Please don't tell me anything else. Honestly, I really don't want to know.'

'I hope you used something, babe.'

Bonus points to the lady sitting opposite. She had to get it out, she had to . . . Do you also want to know how many times I came? None. Too nervous. The sex certainly hadn't been how I'd imagined my first sober time would be. I hadn't had the pulsating sensations that I'd had when I'd kissed Leon. In fact, the experience had been a let-down.

'Hey, I thought you were concerned about my emotional well-being, not that stuff. I'm a big girl, you know. Everything's OK,' I said, smiling. *(Lies! Lies! Lies!)* I didn't want Emma to slag him off any more.

'As far as he's concerned, I'm worried about your emotional *and* physical health, Katie, to be honest, babe. I mean, the guy's been through half the girls in NA. I'm telling you, he's a dirty bastard. He disgusts me.' *Congratulations on a hat-trick. Feel better?*

Now I was definitely and unwaveringly going to keep quiet about Leon. I didn't want my friendship with Emma to be over within weeks of it beginning. I was sure to be excused for this one indiscretion soon enough, but more shenanigans involving other people – that is, men – and I was certain to be placed on a blacklist alongside other scrubbers, together with Emma's ex who'd cheated on her and who was Gary's cousin's best friend's best man at his brother's wedding. Or something like that.

JUDGE: The defendant goes against all advice and has sex within a month.
ME: Yes, that's right, and with Big Gazza, of all people.
JUDGE: That's not all. Not only does the defendant have intercourse with the aforementioned male, but her betrothed, who shall be known in this court as 'L', has now decided to leave a residential rehabilitation centre before his prescribed time is up, and he is due to alight at Waterloo train station tomorrow. Do you accept that this is partially your responsibility?
ME: No . . . OK, yes? Actually, not really.
The prosecution rests.

I scurried home, anxiously chuntering, 'Bollocks to Emma,' and, 'Viva sexual freedom,' after hearing but not listening to tales of folks dancing on boats, drunk on life's golden nectar. I knew now I couldn't be a sober party person. Not now, maybe never.

On the train on my way to meet Gary later that evening, instead of allowing myself to feel like a trollop, I concentrated my thoughts on him and his cock. This helped me to ignore Leon's calls and not dwell on the fact that he'd be back in London in 16 hours or so.

I arrived at Angel Tube station and texted Gary. '2 minz

babz,' he replied. That wasn't the best beginning. 'Babz'? He was 35, not 15.

I wanted him to get there so that I could get the initial 'Hiya-you-all-right?' baloney out of the way. I held onto my phone and looked at it every few seconds, just in case I didn't hear the text or call to tell me he was there. A minute ticked by – nothing. I wanted to leave. I'd had my mobile on the loudest volume setting for weeks so that I didn't miss Leon's calls, but now I worried I'd put it on silent by mistake. There was a first time for everything. I was shaking with apprehension. *What if this is some kind of wind-up?* My mind was racing, as was my heart rate. Hundreds of cars sped past – and more than I wanted seemed to slow down right by me. Still nothing. *Go home, Kate.* Then a horn. I looked up. Headlights flashed and there he was. My mind went blank.

I got into the car. 'Hiya-you-all-right?'

'Good, hon. You?'

'Fine, thanks.' *Hate the word 'hon'.*

He leaned in for a kiss on the lips and nearly made it; I just missed by a smidgen. *Now I must seem like an incompetent fool.*

I sat in his pristine, ten-year-old BMW, wearing a short denim skirt and boots. I've no idea why I wore a short skirt – I never usually did. I didn't know what to say. How the frig had I managed to be a hooker if I couldn't construct a worthwhile sentence in the name of conversation? And with someone I wanted to talk to, someone I'd already slept with. Gary smelled good. *Should I tell him?* I decided not to in case it sounded smarmy. I was a novice at this dating malarkey. He needed to take the lead. Thank God he did, chatting away, although it did little to help my anxiety.

From the outside, his place looked a mess. I adjusted my hair, which he made no comment on, although I'd had it cut.

We took an awkward lift ride to the 16th floor. He pointed out to me that his flat had been newly refurbished. We went into his white sitting room, where the obligatory 40-in. flat-screen TV sat on a glass table and that black-and-white photo of the 1920s American scaffolders sitting a million feet up in the air hung on the wall. As I searched through my bag for lip balm, I surreptitiously looked round, feigning being at ease. In fact, I couldn't have been more nervous if I'd had prior warning that my host was a misogynist with a penchant for talking to women as though he'd just wiped them off the bottom of his Adidas. At least he didn't wear Reeboks.

He offered me herbal tea. I took it. I don't like herbal tea, but I took it and tried to look sophisticated, reasoning that he was doing the same by offering me it. He sat me on a chair and took a seat on the sofa.

We babbled rubbish for a few minutes, until he asked, 'Are you going to sit over there all night or are you going to come here and give us a kiss or what?' I opted for the kiss. Getting straight down to business was what I knew best when I was alone with a man and sex was expected. I left the romance to him. Chitchat in pursuit of an end goal was not my forte; kissing, sucking, fucking was my comfort zone. However, when we'd last had sex, I'd been so nervous I felt I hadn't given him a good show. Now was the time to make up for that.

As his mouth sucked onto mine, there was a throbbing in my groin, a need to be touched and tampered with. Then he put my hand on his crotch. I took the lead, or rather I took *his* lead, and started to wank him off. I went into acting mode, toying with the head of his dick, and he was moaning.

'Come up here,' he ordered, and I did as I was told. I got a cursory kiss as my reward. He shoved his hand up my skirt, yanked my knickers down, and I spread my legs as he lapped at my cunt. I groaned to satisfy his ego. Was I acting like a whore, I asked myself? *Nah*. At least Big Gazza wasn't paying me. That was a start.

His technique was adequate, but a bit mechanical, and I knew I wouldn't come. He moved his face away from my vagina and gripped his cock, threatening insertion. *Do I say something? Don't I?* Why I even hesitated, I don't know, but I did.

'Wait, baby,' I said. 'I think we should use something.' I was expecting opposition, but instead he found a condom and whipped the little beauty onto his erect penis.

He dipped in and out of my hole a couple of times, which might have been horny if I'd been feeling in the mood for it, but wasn't because I wasn't, and then he penetrated me. He was into sex, I could tell. And it didn't have to be me lying there, I could tell that, too.

We made the same moves and noises as we had the last time, and thankfully it finished within half an hour. That was enough. I detest it when men go on and on as if we're partaking in a stamina test. I'm never sure who's being tested, them or me. And I hate it even more when I feel as though I'm being bullied into orgasm, which often goes hand in hand with excessive time spent banging.

After Gary had come on my tummy, I searched for my knickers and smuggled them into the bathroom, where I stared at my face. *Make-up slightly smudged – tick. Hair dishevelled – tick. Skin spottier than I'd realised in this God-awful light – tick. And, finally (bliss), now I can fart (quietly, if possible) and scratch that itch that's been bugging my fanny for the past couple of minutes – tick.*

Back into the living room after tidying myself up. *Now what?* The big man had put the television on and was lying flat, remote in hand, as though he'd been in that exact position all day long.

Where do I sit? On the sofa? On the chair? Yep, on the sofa. No, he might not want me to. On the chair . . . I perched myself in the armchair and wondered what to do with myself. In these situations a cigarette usually comes in handy.

'Can I smoke in here?'

'Yeah, course you can. I'll get you an ashtray. What do you think I do, go and stand outside every time I feel like a snout?'

'I wasn't sure if you smoked or not. I don't remember you lighting up when you came to my flat.'

'I probably didn't. I usually don't in other people's houses and anyway I'm trying to stop, kind of. It's a disgusting habit. It fucking stinks and makes yer breath rank. Here you go.' He handed me the ashtray before jumping back onto the sofa to stare at the TV.

I lit up and pretended to be interested in whatever it was that was on, my mind drifting onto Leon. I switched my phone on. Gary was quiet and so was I. I had to do something, so I decided to leave.

'Why are you off?' he asked when I stood up and started getting my things together. 'I thought we could get a chinky.'

'Er, I thought maybe you wanted me to go.'

He sat up. 'Why would I want that? I thought we were going to hang out and spend some time together, darlin'.'

This pleased my ego.

'Come on, let's go and get some scran.'

I wasn't hungry. I didn't want to stay another minute, but I would have felt an idiot if I'd just left. Besides, that was behaviour from my hooker days. Things had to change; that's why I'd spent time in rehab – for things to be different. And since fucking and then quickly leaving was a feature of my past life, it was a point of pride for me to prove that I could do things differently. *If nothing changes, nothing changes . . .*

We got into the car and Big Gaz placed his hand on my thigh. I liked that. He talked twaddle about his sporting activities, his dodgy workmate who got him cheap tobacco and who had him laughing almost all the time, it seemed. And then he asked me why I was so nervous.

Oh, I don't know. Maybe it's got something to do with the fact that I've just left rehab and that this is the first time I've been in this situation completely sober ever, OK? 'I didn't realise I was,' I answered defensively.

'Come on, babes! You were really jittery indoors, as though you were waiting for something bad to happen. Jesus, you were making me nervous an' all.'

'No I wasn't!'

'Yes you was. I was feeling para cos of you.'

'No, I mean, I wasn't nervous.' Then I remembered I was meant to be working an honest programme. 'Look, OK, maybe I am a bit, all right? I've been going through some big changes recently. Have you already forgotten what that's like?'

'No, course I ain't. I just don't remember being as twitchy as you seem to be, love, that's all. It's not that hard, is it?'

Fuck off. 'Well, I can't help it.'

'You just need to relax.'

Do you think I want to feel like this, you wanker? 'Hmm, maybe, yeah. I'm just not sure how.'

'Oh, fucking hell. Don't get dramatic on me, girl. You've been around, I bet you have, so don't play the damsel-in-distress card with me.'

I said nothing. Instead, I fiddled with my phone.

We ordered our Chinese takeaway. He paid, then draped himself all over me while we waited. I was surprised by his public show of affection, but I liked it.

We went back to his place, where we talked about what was on TV. Then my phone started vibrating. Leon. I didn't answer.

'You getting that or what?'

'I can't be bothered right now,' I said, as casually as I could.

'Why don't you just answer it? You've got that silly scared look on your face again, sweetheart. What's wrong with you, eh? You've got nothing to hide in front of me, you know. Nothing's going on here,' he said, while chewing his food and waggling a spare rib between the two of us to emphasise his point.

I really, really didn't want to answer the phone, but I did. 'Hmm . . . OK . . . Are you all right? *No, I'm not!* Stop it. I'm OK! Speak to you . . .' End of call.

'Was that your boyfriend?'

'I wouldn't be here if I was already in a relationship.'

'Cos I don't give a fuck if you're shacked up with someone,' said Gary, just before his food met his mouth.

'I only left treatment a really short time ago.'

'Yeah, well, you coulda met a fella there.'

'Well, I haven't.' *Honesty, Katie. Yes, sir.* 'Actually, I kind of did, but he's still in there, so it's not exactly like we're together or anything. It was just talk. You know how those places are, don't you? People are always saying stuff to each other about when they leave . . .'

'Is he a London boy, then?'

'Yeah.'

'So when's he coming back, like?'

'Soon.'

'Is he black, this fella?'

'No, why?'

'I'm just wondering cos these black fuckers can have some right nasty bastards behind them.'

'Don't say that, Gary. I'm black, don't forget.'

'No you're not.'

'Yeah I am. Just cos I'm mixed, doesn't make me not black.'

'You're fucking not, love. I don't do black girls, never have, and I ain't starting now.'

I wanted to leave.

'Anyway, I don't want any grief off this geezer, you got that? I don't want to be getting myself in a world of trouble for smashing some cunt's face in. Not again. I'm trying to keep my nose clean after last time. That fucking halfwit deserved everything he fucking got, mate, and the judge seemed to think so too, otherwise he'd have done me for more than community service and a poxy 250-quid fine. Silly bastard.'

Nice.

CHAPTER 37

I wanted to distance myself from Leon's decision to leave BCH early. His hot-headed action could mean one of only two things:

1. He was leaving so we could be together.
2. He was intending to relapse.

I couldn't sleep a wink. All I could think about was Gary. Why, I don't know. He was nice-looking, and . . . well, that was all. But he was showing me some attention. Of sorts.

The motto 'Keep it simple' had never been more apt during my fledgling sobriety than at this time. If I could have focused on my forthcoming university interview, that would have been something, but I couldn't.

I'd heard what Gary had said about there being nothing serious going on between us, but more than anything my ego wanted him to want me. We'd seen each other twice. We could have left it as a one-nighter, but we hadn't. I shunned the nagging voice of reason within me that understood that this made not a jot of difference to the reality of the situation. Why couldn't I just have waited patiently for Leon? Instead, I'd opted for some attention – an instant fix for a head swarming with anxieties. My urge to fill the void that abandoning my old life had left me with was greater than my desire to do the right thing.

In my turmoil, I plotted to use the fact that Leon had left rehab early as my excuse not to see him. At least not until I'd satisfied my craving for Gary's knob. I'd follow a faithful old trick: when in doubt, blame others. Since the damage was done and I'd already fucked the plumber, and therefore violated my tacit agreement with The Youth, I owed it to myself to get the big man out of my system one way or another. If this was an honest programme, I *was* being honest, at least with myself. Sort of.

I was supposed to have finished with complex situations, especially of the self-imposed variety. I felt sneaky yet exhilarated. I liked it, but I didn't.

I was dreading Leon's call and hating myself for what I was going to say.

'I'm at my brother's,' he told me.

'Right, OK. Er, so how you feeling?'

'My head's done in.'

'About what? Look, you've got to tell me if something has happened to make you leave early.' *Be strong, Katie. Focus.* As a result of his actions, The Youth had successfully made me feel responsible for him and our relationship, and I resented that.

'I'm worried about you, innit? About us. I don't get what's going on, Katie, but I know something's up. Look, can I see you later, babes?'

'No. I, er . . . can't.' *Don't crack.*

'Can't what?'

'I can't see you. I don't know what to say to you, Leon, except I'm a bit all over the place right now. I, er, I need a bit of space, that's all. Can you give me a few days?' *So I can fuck Big Gazza a bit more before I keep my promise to you.*

'OK, all right. Fuck, this is killing me, you know that? Do you know how I fucking feel right now?' I thought he was about to cry. I didn't want to deal with that, either. 'So can I call you tomorrow?' he asked. 'Maybe we can link then? God, babes, this is fucked up. I'm . . . I'm in love with you, and . . .' His voice was cracking.

I agreed to meet him to shut him up. But I doubted I'd keep my word.

I ended the call and panicked. I asked myself how I'd feel if Leon had done to me what I was doing to him. I was hurting him and I wished I wasn't.

After all the promises and declarations and the necklace . . . Maybe I really was the scum that I'd thought I was when I was selling my arse. *Don't even go there* . . .

I stayed at Gary's that night and I didn't sleep. The space between us could have fitted at least another person. Come to think of it, another body in the bed would have made things a bit cosier than they were.

At too-early o'clock, Mr Come-All-Night-But-To-Hell-With-You sprang out of bed. My eyes were partially sealed with crusty sleep, but I managed to watch him scuttle around getting ready for work.

'Yo, get up!' he shouted. 'I'm late! We have to go. Now, now, now!'

No climax, no cuddles, no affection and a 'yo'. I vowed never to do this again.

How much had I really changed? My head felt mashed from lack of sleep and regret. All I could think about was how cheap I felt.

'We offer progress, not perfection,' said BCH. *True*. But I'd thought, *hoped*, that I was better than this.

You're a fucking retard – Goblin.

You've made a mistake. Calm down – Nice Katie.

I needed to sleep. Two weeks before, things had felt easier, not like this. If it wasn't Maggie's nagging voice in my head, it was Lenny's – even when I was 200 miles away from them. Of course, this spurred my goblin on.

'Wherever you go, you take yourself with you,' I could hear Lenny bleat.

What do you know, Len, you fucking idiot? – Goblin.

Don't be like this. They really helped you – Nice Katie.

For a while, I'd had a reprieve from my goblin, but now it was reborn. Was it here to stay? I feared the worst.

CHAPTER 38

I spoke to South Bank University and asked for the lecturer whose name I'd been given when I'd made the initial enquiry about getting onto a psychology degree course.

'Name?'

'Kate.'

'Age?'

'27.'

'Why do you want to do a psychology degree?'

'I reckon I'd be good at it.' *A bit too full of myself?*

He laughed and we chatted a little more about God knows what and then I heard the immortal words: 'You need to get here during the next two days to enrol. You won't get onto the course if you don't make it here by either tomorrow or the day after.'

'Right.' My heart was racing.

'When you get to the main reception area, there'll be clear signs for you to get to the sports hall where enrolment is taking place. Your details will already be registered and you need to bring ID. Passport, driving licence, birth certificate will all do. OK?'

'Oh, but I don't have a birth certificate.'

'You don't have one?'

'No, I don't know my mum, and she had it.' I could hear some of the usual tedious sympathy brewing. Would people react as they did if I didn't know my dad? I doubted it. I continued quickly. 'Oh, and I don't have a driving licence. But I'll bring my passport.'

'Fine.'

'So is that it? I'm on? I'm officially doing a degree?' I could barely believe what I was hearing. Surely it couldn't be so simple? He hadn't even asked me about the qualifications I had – or, more to the point, the ones that I didn't have.

'Yes, so I'll see you during the first week in September.'

I was in shock. Maybe I would be all right after all? Fuck my goblin. I stood still, aware of adrenalin pulsing through my body; next thing, I burst into tears. This was the first time in my life that I'd cried from happiness. A stranger had given me a break. It had taken precisely two minutes for the lecturer to decide that I wasn't a hopeless case and I was worthy of doing a psychology degree. It didn't matter in that moment that I'd sold my body for money or spent years banging junk up my nose; I was about to go to university. Some cynics might think that anyone who was a mature student and therefore about to pay hefty tuition fees would be eligible, but I didn't see it that way. I'd sort out the payments at some point; I'd fill out every form there was and get all the funding possible. I wasn't sure how it would all work, but for now I'd been accepted, and that was all that mattered to me.

I thanked God, over and over and over. Call it what you will, but someone or something was helping me, I could feel it. I wiped my tears and made a cuppa . . . and in an instant, like a tramp pissing on the fire that was keeping him warm at night, my thoughts turned on me. Leon dropped into my head, followed by Gary, and I wanted to throw up, violently.

I knew I had to see the stumpy boy. And now, on top of man worries, I had the life-changing opportunity of going to university to think about. I was beset with anxiety and, right there, I made a promise to myself that, with this new beginning, I'd minimise my sexcapades so that my mind would be freer of unnecessary garbage.

It was up to me to do the right thing. I had to be brave and arrange to meet Leon for coffee or something, and . . . I wasn't sure what I'd say or do when I got there, but I'd have to do something. This wasn't fair on him, or on me for that matter.

My phone rang. It was The Youth. *Fuck. Why is he calling me? Do I pick up? Yes? No? Do? Don't? Shut up? Yes, please.*

I walked to Sainsbury's, and on my way I called Jimmy.

'It's me!'

'Bloody hell. You sound full of it today, pet. What's going on?' he said, laughing.

'Nothing much, our kid. Oh, I just, well, you know – got mesen into uni, like.'

'Uni? What do you mean? Not university?'

'Aye! That'll be reet!' I said, teasing him with a stereotypical Yorkshire accent.

'Oh, fucking 'ell, kidder! I don't know what to say, pet. You certainly don't waste any time, do you, eh? Bloody well done, you! That's fucking fantastic, innit? Fucking 'ell! Don't tell me what you're going to study. Let me guess.'

I knew he was about to make fun of me.

'Hmm, let me think. It must be a degree in something along the lines of sticking your middle finger up the arses of all those fuckwits who doubted you! Is that right?'

I laughed. He laughed.

'Not quite. But I might just stick my degree paper up their bums when I get it.'

'You do right, pushkin. You do right. Fuck 'em. You don't need cunts in your life who'll ever try and bring you down, our kid. Once they've been through what you've been through –'

'But I did it to myself.'

'Maybe you did partially, aye, but you didn't have the best of starts, eh?'

'It could have been a lot, lot worse.'

'I know. But still, regardless of where and how the shit hit the fan, the point is it did, and so until someone goes through that then comes out of the other side, then maybe they can say something, but, until then, tell 'em to fuck themselves. You got that? That African blood isn't for nothing, eh, kidder? There's some warrior spirit in them there veins.'

'Hmm, I suppose so. Anyway, Jiminy, how are you?'

'I'm all right.'

'Good. OK then, moving on, so what's the weather like up there?'

'Oh, please, *please*, let's not talk any more about me, I can't bear it,' Jimmy joked in a theatrical manner.

'We won't, don't worry!'

'Thank God for that!' We both laughed liked twits.

'Tell me about what you're working on, Jiminy. Will you be going back to France to that house to do any more frescoes?'

'It's a chateau, dahling, and no, that one's finished. They tried to contract me for two more. But can you imagine me signing a fucking piece of paper? I told 'em they'd need to tek my fucking word that I'll do it and that's that.'

'It's what business people do, Jim.'

'Well, it's not how I do it. So, anyway, back to this university thing. That's just bloody amazing news. Congratulations!'

'Oh, calm down, you!'

'Right, so if you've finished gloating, maybe I can go and get on with this painting I'm doing, eh?'

'Do I really sound like I'm showing off?'

'Don't be so stupid, pet. Course not. I'm fucking teasing you, for God's sake. You should know that by now. Come on, you silly billy.'

He was right. I was oversensitive, and I had every right to be proud of myself.

I returned home armed with camomile tea and food that actually needed preparation and cooking. I'd soon regret buying it. There was nothing to snack on and everything required effort. All this was to try and make myself feel as though I was living a healthy life and taking care of myself.

I had the radio blasting out some tunes as I began cooking. Life was simple and good during the moments I wasn't thinking about Gary or Leon. I could do what I wanted, and I didn't want much – and now I was going to university. I'd never have believed it possible.

I picked at my toenails, scratched my arse, stared at the telly, stuffed my face and decided to wash up later – because I could. And I could skip a meeting if I felt like it.

If this was sobriety, I'd no idea what I'd been so worried about. Everything was OK. *It is*, I'd tell myself. *Fuck Gary, Fuck Leon*, I'd say like a mantra. *No, really, Katie, it'll be all right . . .*

I was sitting in a workman's caff in Vauxhall, quivering with nerves and trying to recall my recent lies to get my story bang on for when Leon appeared.

He walked towards me, staring at my face with irritating tenderness, wearing his duffel coat and Reeboks. He was less handsome than my mental image of him, and guilt was making me feel hard. I didn't know how to be, so when he came to kiss me I gave him my cheek.

'Why? Why aren't you kissing me properly?'

'I don't know,' I said, really not knowing.

He sat down. 'Katie, what's going on, babes?' he asked as he took my hand.

'I don't know.'

He got up out of his seat and told me to stand. I did, and he tried to kiss me. Again, I turned away. Pain consumed his face and I burst into tears.

'I'm confused. I'm sorry. I'm not doing very well at the moment and, er, I'm going to see my dad for the first time since I got out tomorrow. Listen, baby, I'm sorry.'

'You nervous about going up north?'

'I'll be all right.'

'How long are you there for?'

'Just the day. But I'm worried about you, and us. I've just got so many things going through my mind right now. I'm really sorry for all of this.'

'What?'

'This. *This*,' I spat. 'You and me. I'm hurting you. I'm so sorry.'

'Give me your hand, Katie, and look at me. *Look at me!* Can't you see that I love you, babes? I'm in love with you, Katie.' He looked close to breaking down.

'Please, Leon, please don't. Don't say that.' I wanted to run, far from here, far from him, far from my feelings.

We sat. My whimpering was the only thing keeping us connected. I broke free from his hand and his gaze.

'Katie? I want us —'

'Stop it! I don't want to hear it!' I shouted through more tears. 'Right now, I feel that I hate you. I hate this situation.'

'But I love you, Katie.' Tears streamed down his face. 'I love you so, so much. Please don't do this. Please. I've left so we can —'

'Leon, no! Stop saying this. I'm sorry. I'm sorry. I have to go. I've got a big day tomorrow. I have to get up early and make sure I'm ready to face my dad and Elaine.'

'Don't leave yet.'

I stood, he stood and we held each other. Silent tears were tumbling down both of our faces. It felt surreal.

'Let's go outside,' I said quietly, leading the way.

I felt calmer now and Leon's tears were fewer. We stared at each other. I wiped his eyes and we kissed. Slowly. On the mouth. Softly. With meaning.

'I have a suggestion. Why don't you come to my place tomorrow evening and stay over?'

'Can I come now?'

'No, baby!'

'So tomorrow, then?'

'I meant the day after tomorrow. I just know I'll be drained after seeing my dad. I haven't been sleeping well at all. God, I don't know what's wrong with me at the moment. I feel tense about everything.'

'You're seeing your pops for the first time in — how long?'

'About three years. I can't remember.' At that point Gary did a streak through my head. 'Look, I want us to enjoy our time together, and right now I can't think of doing anything except sleeping.'

And Gary.

'OK, so we're going to start afresh, yeah, after I've been to Yorkshire? What do you reckon?'

'Sounds good, princess. We need some zeds, innit? It'll do us both good.' He stroked the side of my face. His softness

254

was killing me. 'It's been a strange couple of weeks, innit? You won't blow me out, will you?'

Again Gary flashed across my thoughts. 'Absolutely not. I *want* to spend time with you.'

I meant every word. At least I thought I did.

CHAPTER 39

On the two-hour train journey to Yorkshire to meet my dad and Elaine, I felt queasy. This would be the first time I'd seen them for nearly three years, and the first time since the age of 19 that I'd seen them without any drugs in my system.

I was a 27-year-old woman trying to convince herself that she was doing something perfectly normal: visiting her parents. The problem was that I felt like a scared little girl who was very apprehensive of what her parents would say to her. I was scared of how they'd judge me – because judge me they would. What if they still didn't like me?

I'd completed my time in rehab, and even if there was no other reason for me to feel pleased with myself, at least I'd achieved that. Daddy had always said throughout the years, 'I just want you to make a life for yourself, Kate. Not like this.' I knew what he meant.

When I got off the train, my mind was blank. I saw Dad and Elaine straight away, just as they did me. My father was wearing a thick coat and his trilby, while his wife wore a bright-blue wool coat, her face and hair groomed perfectly, as always.

They both smiled as I walked towards them. I barely

recognised my father. His appearance shocked me; he'd suddenly become old. I didn't know whom to kiss first, and since Elaine stepped forward I kissed her and put my arm around her. Warmly, she tried to talk to me as we hugged, but I pulled away, desperate to look at and touch my dad. We glanced at each other before we pecked each other on the lips. His were tight. His face looked strained. I felt self-conscious about throwing my arms around him. His hug was the same as it had been since I'd been a teenager: stiff and reluctant.

We started walking out of the station and somehow Elaine was in the middle. I wanted to be beside my dad. At least that way I could feel some sort of closeness to him. I also wanted to look at him, and look and look and look. I couldn't believe how his face had thinned and his skin looked like paper. He still had all his hair and all his own teeth, which he was very proud of, but he looked frail. As Elaine chatted and Dad concentrated on where he was putting his feet, I felt immeasurably sad. I could have cried and cried, but I fought the urge to do so and tried to be jolly. It wasn't working, so I became quiet.

This set the precedent for the rest of the three hours I was with them. We sat in a small, chic bistro, with me opposite the two of them. There was no deep conversation. Thankfully, Elaine took charge and nattered about everything except anything important. It was as though we were strangers. I answered superficial questions about my flat and friends of mine whom they knew, and they told me about their garden.

I asked questions about their travels and their daily routine, and the gaps were easily filled by talk of the food we were eating. Neither of them drank any wine, which made the lunch feel even more fake, and Dad and I said very little for the whole duration. Instead, we gave each other occasional heart-wrenching looks, and at other times I would smile at him, searching for forgiveness. In return, he gently nodded to reassure me that everything was OK.

It didn't feel it. It didn't feel OK at all, but what could I do? Start to apologise and embarrass him and try to find words to express sorrow that I didn't know how to access? Fling myself at his feet and ask him to break plates on my head as punishment for the pain I'd caused him? What was I supposed to do?

Back at the station, I kissed Elaine goodbye and then Dad, who smiled, nodded and winked concurrently. I began walking away.

I wanted to die. I turned around and waved, and my heart was crumbling. I wanted him so much. I wanted us to revert back to how it had been between us in my formative years. I was overwhelmed with sadness for the loss of our relationship.

I let go of the tears that I could no longer stop from falling and cried and cried.

CHAPTER 40

I sat on my sofa feeling nervous, so nervous. Leon was standing to one side on my cream sheepskin rug, a grey hoodie poking out from under his coat. I wished he wouldn't stand there with his trainers on. He looked like an animal stalking its prey.

We were finally alone. My heart was booming and my mouth felt dry. We stared at each other. Maybe I should have put on some background music to ease the tension, but I didn't dare move. Why wasn't I jumping on him? My shyness wouldn't allow it. Why wasn't he jumping on me? Did I look as though I'd had sex with someone else? Could he tell? Neither of us said a word. The tension was disgustingly heavy.

Right then, an orgasm wasn't my main concern, although the almost apologetic throbbing in my clitoris wouldn't take much persuading to burst into glorious, jubilant appreciation of his presence. I was ready for whatever was coming my way. I started to smirk. He kept a straight face. He was definitely going to put me through the wringer. It was written all over him.

For a second, I thought about this being one of those moments one remembers vividly, if not for a lifetime at the very least for a few weeks afterwards. I knew I'd messed up by sleeping with Gary, but if I could keep quiet about that, then surely everything between The Youth and me could carry on as if it had never happened?

'I'm feeling really shy,' I croaked awkwardly. I started to laugh inappropriately. Leon's cool broke and he started to grin. We looked like teenagers giggling about getting caught by our parents smooching.

The Youth thudded onto the sofa. I couldn't look at his face. He took my cheeks in his hands and we kissed and began clawing at each other, breathing loudly. Then his phone started ringing. 'You should get that,' I said, grateful for a pause. I got off the sofa and, with legs like jelly, went to the loo.

I closed the door more loudly than I'd meant to, mouthed an elongated, silent 'Fuuuuck!', shifted my knickers south and my arse in the same direction and breathed out deliberately. I felt delirious.

I dipped my finger into my vagina and introduced my tongue to it to see what he'd be tasting. A bit salty. Not my thing, but none too shabby. Everything was swollen. There was no smell other than a faint, almost metallic flora. I stood, flushed the loo, glared into the mirror. My lips were full. I didn't wash my hands. I was ready for combat.

My 'coy little woman' head was back on. Leon called to me from the bedroom. Finally. He was lying on my bed. No coat, no gross Reeboks, just a blue top, blue jeans and *that* silver necklace.

The bedroom was my territory. Shy or not, I felt confident here. I got on the bed and clambered towards him. He tugged at my belt. I pulled at his. He yanked my jeans down. I tried to do the same to his but rolled onto my back as he pulled mine off. He moved back towards my mouth and we kissed frantically. I was silent. He was groaning. He started rubbing between my legs with one hand and with the other took off his jeans and there it was, ready for action and proud as you like: an average-sized penis. He'd led me to believe it was *big*, but I didn't dwell on the lies I'd been fed for most of my three-month stay at BCH.

I was self-conscious about how wet I was as I rolled onto him, his cock barely pressing against me. Never in my life had I been so ready, even with Alex, an ex-boyfriend with whom I'd been infatuated. I straddled Leon. He was yanking at my top. I took it off. I wasn't wearing a bra. My nipples were erect. I shifted my weight and he gripped my hips, pulled my knickers to one side and thrust upwards. I gasped. We fucked ferociously, both of us grunting. All I felt was a pounding. Nothing was sensual about this. I came once, came twice, three times, and threatened to come a fourth, and then he spluttered, 'I'm gonna come.' He did. Again and again.

That was my brief intro to what became the most orgasmic sex I'd ever experienced. I hadn't realised until then just how numb drugs and drink had made me.

As for Gary . . . Gary who?

CHAPTER 41

I was having the best sex of my life. No doubt whatsoever. Leon and I were loving, loudly and violently, over and over. He made me question the quality of the 'professional service' that I'd dished out in my past. I could tell The Youth cared for me, and everything he did, he did with precision.

We spent the majority of our time together at my place because I wasn't comfortable with . . . well, he wasn't exactly my dream man and, to be honest, I wasn't that keen on going out in public with him. But he sure as hell kept me occupied. We usually went to separate meetings to avoid arousing people's suspicions and ending up on the receiving end of their opinionated frowns. But every day, we'd meet at my flat at some point and he'd stay over. He was living in a dry house, so it made sense for him to come to me. The two of us would have a giggle about some of the goings on at BCH, and, yes, we gossiped about people we both knew from meetings who didn't know that we knew each other.

I was happy. My new life was feeling easier to deal with now I had a man, in spite of that man being shorter than me. Most evenings, when we weren't at meetings, I'd cook. We'd eat and then make a nest of cushions and a duvet on top of my fluffy rug, where we'd lie together stroking each other's hands and snuggling and watching TV until we fucked some more.

Leon was different from anyone I'd ever had a thing with before. He came from an inner-city London estate and had grown up with gangs. For many of these youths, their mantra was 'survival of the fittest'. He didn't care about putting his knife and fork together after he'd finished eating. He'd spit on occasion when we were walking down the street and he didn't mind farting in front of me, from day one of us being together. Nevertheless, it was clear that Leon's family were decent, law-abiding people who'd worked hard for everything they had. He was affectionate and funny and softly spoken, and as the weeks rolled by I was really growing to like him.

My worries about work, university and my future life had diminished, and my sadness about my relationship with my dad had lessened. Now I had Leon around, everything else felt easier to cope with. Janet had suggested that we get together once a week 'and have an afternoon of food and talking about the Steps'. But every week seemed excessive to me. There was plenty of time. My mind was calmer and in many respects life felt simpler. I was OK as long as I thought only about the basics – sex, Leon, sex, staying away from drugs and drink, sex – and tried to avoid thoughts about university, grants, work, money or my future.

NA meetings were boring, but I went to show face, sitting as close to a back corner as I could manage, listening to 'My name is . . .', 'Hello, blah, blah . . .', 'Today I felt angry when such-and-such happened.' *Tedious.*

I'd always check the room to see who was there. Most importantly, was Gary? I could quickly tell if he was likely to turn up, as his equally dodgy mates would be lurking around.

Like other wild dogs, he rarely moved alone. I enjoyed the buzz I felt when he was in the vicinity, but the benefit of him not being at a meeting was that I could relax more. Even so, remaining focused was difficult.

Many people seemed to be just moaning in meetings. Every now and again, though, some golden nugget about how to cope with this or that would filter through. If only I'd listened more, I might have remembered what had been said after I left.

'Hey, hi, how're you feeling? Coffee later? Cool.' People trying to create and maintain friendships bantered and gesticulated. It was a chore spending time with folks I cared little or nothing for when I could be having a laugh and a, you know, with my boyfriend. And yes, by this time Leon was officially that. But only the two of us knew it.

Janet, who was chairing an AA meeting, asked me to do my first proper share. I had to sit at the front with her, facing the audience, and talk for 15 or 20 minutes about my experiences, strengths and hopes. I didn't include prostitution or bigamy when talking about my past; some stuff was between my sponsor and myself.

Experiences:
- My substance use.
- Desperation.
- The impact it had on my family.
- Why I chose to change and how I went about doing something about it.

Strengths:
- Asking for help and listening.
- Attending regular NA or AA meetings.

- Doing service. This is a year-long commitment to attend the same meeting weekly and carry out duties. For example, making tea, greeting people, chairing a meeting. (When I chaired my first meeting, I wasn't doing service, but it's said to be a good idea.)
- Reading the 12 Steps literature.
- Making a conscious effort to be a better person.
- Keeping in regular contact with my sponsor.

Hopes:
- Just having any hope is a miracle, and that shouldn't be ignored.
- Expressing gratitude for all or the very little that has come about as a result of recovering, and having faith that, taking things one day at a time, everything will improve.
- Personal hopes, plans, ideas, joys.

The main talk was always expected to be uplifting and positive. I was supposed to throw in some useful snippets of information that might be good for newcomers – on how I remained abstinent and why. But lecturing people, most of whom were further along the path than me, was not recommended.

Neither was turning up and relying solely on looking pretty and talking about having as much sex as possible with my fella. That would have been bad practice, to say the least.

Even though I was newly abstinent myself, I had to remember that there would always be people in the room who were even greener than I was. 'When you share, remember the newcomer,' Janet had said. As had Maggie, Lenny and Nick. It was essential that people new to the Fellowship heard a hopeful message about abstinence and the worthwhile aspects of change. Of course, a lot of people didn't do this. It's difficult to find a balance between speaking candidly about the struggles that are involved in recovering from addiction and not sounding depressed.

Before I started my share, I was so nervous I wanted to release a load of diarrhoea. I felt light-headed and sweaty, and my tummy was not at all happy with me. I'd been advised to focus my attention on one person to help calm me down. I chose Emma, whom I could see smiling in my direction. I didn't look round the room. I wasn't there as a professional after-dinner speaker; I was just trying to do my bit. Thirty minutes after I'd begun, I was still glaring directly at her as though she was on trial for shooting my puppy and running off with the only remaining tub of vanilla ice cream on the planet. I was done.

During the fag break, a few people thanked me for being 'brave and open', which was gracious. *But please*, I thought, *I haven't performed heart surgery*. One overly tattooed meathead said, 'Nice share, Katie, mate. Maybe next time make it a little bit longer, eh?' His sarkiness might have been amusing if I'd known him and liked him. And if I hadn't been as sensitive as I was at that time, I might have forgotten his comment. But years afterwards, I still haven't. Arsehole.

'Are you coming for some food afterwards?' Emma asked. As usual, I wasn't. I couldn't afford it, and more to the point I couldn't be arsed. I found the 12 Step chatter tedious. There were too many do-gooders who were very obviously, in my opinion, scared of life and hid behind a false veil of preachiness, constantly talking about gratitude for lives that stank and going on about their Higher Power (or worse their 'HP') and spirituality, probably before going home to fuck their neighbours' wives or husbands or something.

I was attending meetings. Surely that was enough input to keep me sober? How could eating, drinking coffee and talking crap to people I didn't respect help me?

Fuck 'em.

(Of course, I didn't think about the fact that 'fuck 'em' was only one letter different from 'fuck me'.)

CHAPTER 42

'Hey, how's it going?'

I saw a friendly face on the day of my first lecture. I recognised a guy from NA. Thank Christ there was someone from the Fellowship who didn't mind chatting – a bit of instant camaraderie. Some 12 Step troops get precious about talking to other members not in their immediate circle of friends outside of a meeting, because they think their anonymity will be blown apart. Why should it be? What makes *them* so interesting that anyone would give a shit if they were or were not part of a 12 Step programme? Someone who knows that another person goes to these meetings is likely to go themselves, so what's the issue? 'Anonymity is the spiritual foundation of our principles.' Zzzz . . . And so is being human and exhibiting some basic politeness by saying hello.

He and I sat together and nattered about stuff that didn't concern the Serenity Prayer or the expression of 'feelings'. I'd successfully applied for a grant, which was another bonus. I wasn't sure I was entitled to it, since my housing was paid for by social services, but I got it and accepted it. I'd face any problems if and when they reared their heads.

I was curious to be around lots of people in their teens.

Hardly any of them, perhaps none, would recently have left a residential rehabilitation facility; they would never have banged strangers for cash to supply a drug habit or have had their rent paid by a sugar daddy. It was more likely, however, that one or two might have swapped a spot of foreplay for a line or two of coke or accepted drinks from someone they didn't even want to speak to.

At times, I felt waves of inadequacy, and when I did I'd remind myself that the whippersnappers surrounding me might have got some A levels, but that didn't mean they would be able to be self-sufficient and survive regardless of the direction their lives took. I had never planned on becoming a hooker. It had happened.

In a way, my work in prostitution (since I wasn't forced into it) was an attempt at independence. It might have been a sick and dangerous way of going about it, but it was still a sign that I was being proactive, especially since I'd continued in spite of despising it.

I smiled at a mixed-race girl who was sitting behind me. During the break, she introduced herself as Natasha. OK, so I don't mind a bit of chat here and there, but I am not one to make friends immediately, and it takes something quite extraordinary for me to want to talk to a stranger at length. I'm all right being alone in an environment, at least until I've sussed people out. In this instance, however, I was polite. She seemed OK. A bit overly giddy – which irritated me – but she didn't strike me as being an undercover junkie, which was the main thing I wanted to avoid in potential new friends.

Day one over, and I waved goodbye to Mr NA and lost Natasha. I called my dad's house on the way to the Tube, feeling euphoric that I'd actually begun something so momentous.

'Hi, it's me. How are you?'

'Hello, Kate.' Elaine sounded subdued. That was usual, but still my spirits slumped. Even after my visit, there was so, so, so much work to be done to build a normal relationship with them.

Anyway, carry on. 'Well, I've just had my first lecture at South Bank, ya know, at the university. I'm really happy.'

'Gosh, that is exciting! How did it go?' *Surely there wasn't a lift in her tone there?*

'Good, it went well.' I really wanted to be having this conversation with my dad, but I'd learned, after years of fighting for the right to only ever be vague with my stepmother, that I was never going to get my way. 'It wasn't how I expected it to be. I'm not sure what I thought it'd be like, but there we go . . . I made it. And on time!' I laughed, trying to be jovial.

'Well, that's a good start, Kate. I'm glad you were on time.'

Sombre once again. She sounded tense. Couldn't they just relax a bit now they knew I was at least trying to sort myself out? They'd seen me; they knew I wasn't faking it. My reference to being on time was meant as a joke, not to be taken so blinkin' seriously.

Had I done my 'being polite' time yet? I would always talk to Elaine first, although I only ever called to speak to my father. They'd cultivated this ritual over the years – a vetting procedure – whereby Elaine would chat to me, get some info, check the mood I appeared to be in, and then pass on everything that had been said to prepare my dad before he spoke to me. That eased his fragile nerves, which couldn't handle the phone even ringing – another reason why she always answered the call. Of course, I was considered the sole cause of these ragged nerves. And this in spite of the fact that my father had lived for nearly 50 years and had other children and other wives before I came into his life.

'So, er, how are things with you, Elaine?'

'We're very well, thank you.'

I was actually only asking about you. I'm sure Dad can answer for himself when I eventually speak to him. They always spoke for each other and it always got on my friggin' nerves.

'We've been in the garden most of the morning. The pots are beginning to die off, now summer's over. If you can even say we've had a summer this year . . . So we've been clearing out the bits that are already dead, in order to have a fresh start for next year.'

Was this the type of chat most people had with their parents? I wished she'd talk about something relevant to things that mattered – like suggesting that we get together again, for example.

'I know,' I replied, agreeing with Elaine to keep her happy, 'the summer's been pretty poor this year.' Had I said that I thought the weather had been decent, which actually I felt that it had been that year, I'd have been considered argumentative. 'At least you got a chance to have a clear-out today.' *Like I give a shit about shrubs.* I wanted to speak to my dad.

Hordes of people were walking along the promenade towards the Tube station. I felt a part of something dynamic. I'd achieved something that day. But if anyone was able to put a damper on my meagre achievement and kick-start my anxiety, it was Dad and Elaine. So much thought went into a single sentence before I spoke. I would weigh up the impact of the tone and take into account the fact that they would not trust me one iota, so every word had to be carefully chosen. If I said anything that they could construe as inflammatory, they would revert to type. When they wanted to shut me out, their style was sneaky and dirty, like a stealth bomber. They might have seemed meek to an outsider, but their way of dealing with me could be harsh and unforgiving: 'Bolt the windows and doors. Pull the phone out of its socket. And whatever happens, don't let Katie in, emotionally, physically or otherwise. Don't let her in.' My modus operandi had always been more like that of a Catherine wheel: erratic, sparky, loud and explosive. Nothing was hidden. I had often been wildly aggressive and desperate for attention, and if our two worlds collided, both parties could attack and defend in equal measure. Each side blamed the other for our problems; no one was either adult or brave enough to try to face with honesty a destructive and bitterly painful situation.

In my mind, our conversations were a minefield that could lead to potentially disastrous consequences, and I'm sure they thought the same, too. Thank God I hadn't had to say much when I'd gone for lunch with them. My primary concern was that they might ostracise me because, well, just because they didn't feel like 'dealing' with me. If I said something that disagreed with their ideas, I'd be marked down as a 'problem' within seconds, without being able to plead my case, and Elaine would point her witchy finger and snap her old faithful line: 'Your father's terrified of you. You've caused him nothing but . . .' *Change. The. Fucking. Record. Please.* But they didn't know how.

Finally, Dad came on the line. 'Hello, Kate. Elaine tells me that you've just finished your first lecture. How was it?' He sounded distant. Going through the motions, I felt.

'I really enjoyed it, thank you.' I smiled as I spoke, trying not to sound gutted.

'I'm pleased. So when are you there next?'

'Tomorrow afternoon.' *When will you invite me to visit you again?*

'Ah! So you'll be able to get there on time, then?'

This got my defences up. 'Well, I was on time this morning and the lecture started at 9.30.'

'Kate, I wasn't suggesting that you hadn't arrived on time today. I was simply remarking that tomorrow it should be easy for you to arrive on time.'

My anxiety had gone from manageable to off the scale. I had to breathe. 'Yeah, OK, I'm sorry.' Now my head was rattling as I tried to think how to fill in the silence. *Ask him about the garden.* And so I did. I zoned out as he said exactly what Elaine had just told me.

I rang off, devastated that Dad hadn't said that he was proud of me. Then a rational part of myself made me aware that actually I hadn't yet done anything for him to be proud of. All I'd done was go through rehab and attend a single lecture.

I had to believe that things would get better between us. After all, we'd got through a few consecutive conversations without anyone slamming the phone down – and that was a great leap forward.

I got a break from NA chatter when I was with Natasha. We gravitated towards each other for a number of reasons: she was a mature student and, like me, she'd lost her African mother aged five and had been raised alone by her English dad. I'd never come across this before.

I felt safe in her company. Sometimes after a class we'd go to the campus bar, but I felt uneasy there. Yet because I was determined to appear to be just a regular student and member of society, I tried to force myself to feel comfortable. It wasn't working.

'If you sit in a barber's shop long enough, you'll end up getting a haircut.' Lenny's words haunted me and I was pissed off by the extent to which I'd been brainwashed. 'Your brains need to be washed!' BCH and their preaching seemed to have robbed me of free thought. *Fucking bastards.*

CHAPTER 43

'Come meet my mama,' The Youth had suggested time and again. I was reluctant because:

1. I knew that his mum was worried about her son being involved in a relationship at this early stage in his recovery. He'd told me so.
2. I wasn't certain if Leon and I would be together for long. I've always made it my business to avoid meeting parents unless the boyfriend and I both believe we have a sustainable relationship.

I'd felt impatient with Leon for some time, and the reasons weren't obvious to me. But since it was approaching Christmas and I'd run out of feeble excuses not to go with him to his parents' place, I felt I had to join him. Dad and Elaine had gone abroad for the holiday, as had been their custom ever since I'd been 17 years old, so I decided some festive cheer in a family environment might be pleasant.

Leon's mum's flat in Stockwell was small and cluttered, but obviously kept by someone who was house-proud and had plenty of time on her hands to keep the scores of trinkets looking dazzling. The company was serious. Mama bear barely spoke five words to me. But her husband, who clearly knew about his wife's objections to my fling with her son, tried his hardest to be jovial, as did I, when we weren't staring at the television.

The Youth's relationship with his parents was fragile. Apparently, he'd threatened them and stolen from them countless times, at least so his dad had indiscreetly told me. I already knew all this from rehab.

Still, I was on Leon's side. Like me, he had to battle to reclaim some respect from his parents, and I empathised with him. Somehow, it made me want to try harder to make things work between us. After all, marauders and courtesans had made effective unions throughout history. Maybe there was a chance that I really could be happy with Leon. All 5 ft 8 in. of him.

We bought a fake Christmas tree, baubles and lights from a local pound shop. Not at all classy, but nevertheless we were participating. We'd been to the supermarket and bickered about the excessive amount of vegetables he insisted we bought and about whether to eat turkey or goose. As if there's a contest.

How could I have gone from all-consuming desire for this man to feeling aggrieved because he preferred turkey to another bird? The way he spoke was getting on my nerves, too: 'innit' this and 'get me' that. I couldn't hold his hand in public because of his height, and the way he walked got on my nerves. I wanted to yell at him to stand upright and stop acting as though he wasn't worthy to pound the streets of London. His texts were annoying because he didn't spell things out properly. The long showers he took pissed me off;

he never cleaned the bath afterwards and, worst of all, every morning he blew his nose with his fingers while he was in there. His quietness and non-committal attitude to most things were bugging the life out of me. I hadn't realised that I cared about his financial status, until he wouldn't stop rabbiting on about how broke he was.

But the sex remained filthy and bewitching. He smelled good on every level, better without deodorant. He'd grip me hard, fuck me harder and if I'd been particularly nice to him he'd restrict my air intake at the point of orgasm. He would come twice, sometimes three times, in one session. In fact, the sex was the only thing (other than when he tucked me into bed and stroked my hair when I was on my period – they'd finally started again) that was keeping me wanting him in my space.

Over Christmas, we didn't leave the house for days, and for days I left my phone off. Everything outside of sex that The Youth did was irritating me, and that included when he did nothing.

We'd spent more time than this together before and all had been good, but now something was different. I felt different. I had done for a while. I was worrying about my course, my future, my father, my lover and everything else.

The more I looked at Leon and heard him putting himself down, the more convinced I became that he was right and I'd never really fancied him in the first place. He was still my secret and I wanted to keep it that way.

All Leon had was an average-sized cock. At least Mr Average's presence helped me not to obsess so much about my own failings, but what else was he providing? Was having a TV-watching pal and a handful of orgasms reason enough to be with someone? I'd fallen into this same trap with Alex, years before. So when the physical began to be a little less frequent – meaning less than three times a day – I actively began to dislike him.

What was he doing in my place if he wasn't going to screw me? Eat the food I bought, sleep, take week-long showers and lounge around scratching his bollocks. He already had a mother. He was tactile – credit where it's due – but this lessened as I'd push him away. Now there was *really* no point in us being together.

I'd always been used to transactional love, ever since I was five years old; when I passed my piano exams, my dad gave me a prize. Usually money. The higher the grade, the more cash I earned. When I did well in swimming competitions, again I'd get rewarded.

I wanted Leon to make me feel good, and to see action from him to reassure me that everything was OK, but there was nothing and I deeply resented him for this. I chastised him for what I saw as his inadequacies, to avoid my own fears about myself.

We were cold towards each other during the weeks following Christmas. I used this as a control mechanism. I knew I was becoming hateful, and I didn't know how to stop myself. I found his hesitance to make an approach towards rectifying the clearly dismal situation abhorrent, and my ego wouldn't allow me to reach out to him.

We had yet another blazing row, or, more to the point, I was ranting loudly and in his usual docile manner he said little until I smashed a glass against a mirror, spilt blood onto my cream rug and began screaming. He tried to grapple with me to calm me down, and when I wouldn't, he left. He just left. All this and neither of us was even using drugs.

I knew that I was slipping. It was obvious and I didn't know what to do about it.

The days ticked by slowly. My mind felt fiercely alive. Obsessive fury towards every person I'd ever met now tempered my boredom. I was forced to face my reality alone. I had no one to watch telly with, eat with, cook for, cuddle, and no dick to round off the edges of this new life or enable me to feel like an attractive woman. Whispers in my head began to suggest that I should have a drink, just one. But who ever has just one drink? Not me. But maybe this time I could?

I called Leon and we screamed abuse at each other, before I vowed never to see him again. He called back. I didn't pick up. I called him. He didn't pick up. I didn't want to leave the house. For what? A meeting? I couldn't face people, and I most definitely did not want to be preached at.

I kept thinking of elegant wine glasses filled with Sancerre. That or a chilly vodka with tonic and a fat chunk of lime. And when I did my heart would race. I was desperate for something to ease my persistently nagging tension.

I had to find someone to fuck . . . that was my only realistic prospect to release the pressure. That, or drugs. And I didn't really want those.

I sent Gary an innocuous text.

He replied: 'Y dnt U cum ova 2nite. I wnt u 2 wax all ova n cum n suck mi big cock.'

I couldn't refuse his charming offer, could I? The trouble was I didn't wax, I shaved, and I told him he'd have to take me as I came.

'Uh, reali? Duno bout dat babz,' came the reply.

I didn't respond.

He called me. 'If you get waxed for me today, how about next time you're due a defuzz, I'll give you the money for it, eh?'

'Oh, right . . . er . . . OK, then . . .' I took his comment to mean that he wanted us to start seeing each other more often. *Balls to Leon.* I hadn't heard anything from him for nearly 36 hours, and this was making me feel queasy, even though I'd told myself and him that it was over.

'By the way, sweetheart, wear something sexy, eh? I love a bit of saucy lingerie, me. Fucking love it,' Gary continued. The way he said 'lingerie' sounded ridiculous. Natural, it was definitely not.

I followed orders, and arrived at his flat having spent over two hours trying to get the hair on my head to cooperate with me. I wore black skinny jeans and a slinky black V-neck jumper.

'Oh, I thought you'd be wearing something see-through or lacy, and maybe red. I love a bit of red,' Gary said when I stripped as he sat back on his sofa with his cock in his hand. He hadn't even had the decency to put some of that slimy gunk in his hair that he usually never went without.

'That's a bit trashy; I thought I'd stick to standard black.'

'Yeah, it's *standard* – you're right.'

Once and for all, I finally admitted to myself that I couldn't stand the guy, but still I fucked him and ignored his offer of a lift to the station as I left. I felt like a whore. He offered me the taxi fare home, but taking cash after soulless sex would have upped the feeling that I'd behaved like a hooker.

I left his house feeling exposed and angry with myself. Why had I just done that? Seemed like a good idea at the time, but that just wasn't a good enough reason any longer, surely? I'd spent my adult life – shit, longer than that, since my teenage years – doing things that had 'seemed all right', and quickly afterwards discovering that they weren't, yet repeating the same errors over and over. That's one definition of insanity, apparently: performing the same action and expecting a different result.

During the next few days, my mind was screaming at me to drink, to use, to do something to try to ease my relentless anxiety. I was feeling manic and more than a little crazy.

I dodged Janet's calls and Emma's daily knock on my door. I knew that doing this was not the right thing, but even so I couldn't view it as 'wrong'. I just didn't want to talk to anyone. I wasn't interested in TV or reading, and if I wasn't wanking, I sat and stared at the carpet. At times I tried to sleep away my worries, but nothing changed when I woke.

I decided to go to the doctor for a chat. She was kind but hurried; she clearly hadn't looked through my notes.

'I need you to help me. I'm slipping backwards and I don't know what to do about it. Please help me, please. I need someone . . . I need something to calm my head, before I totally lose it.'

My goblin had taken over. I wanted what I wanted and I was steering her in the right direction.

I left the surgery and went to the chemist with a prescription for two weeks' worth of Valium. I'd got what I wished for. There was no fear, and no internal voices doing battle over whether I should or shouldn't do what I knew I was about to.

I cashed the prescription and felt nothing as I walked up the street to a shop, where I bought a bottle of Sprite. My mind had been decaying for some time, and it wouldn't have taken a genius to guess that I was about to screw up. Big time.

I took two pills, then another two, then four, then more. I was empty, thinking nothing, nothing at all, and I was feeling the same. All I wanted was peace. I just wanted some peace in my head. And for the anxiety to stop.

I'd relapsed; it was official. I'd ingested a substance with the specific intention of altering my state of mind. I'd phlegmed on rational thought, or any thought, and ground whatever was left of it into the pavement.

I glided past my flat to another shop, where I bought a litre of vodka, tonic and fags, and went home. I still wasn't thinking anything. My mind had not been this quiet for a very long time. I had no goblin bullying me, no questions, no anything; there was silence in my head. I was at peace.

As I poured that first drink, still nothing changed. I glugged it down and the vodka tasted as it had always done: nothing special, nothing different. There was no great release; it was just vodka and tonic. Vodka, tonic and Valium. The combination kicked in and I was soon wobbling all over the place, talking to myself and chain-smoking as I played loud music.

I'd forgotten Leon. I'd forgotten my dad, forgotten university, forgotten NA, forgotten Janet and Emma and Gary. I did, however, remember Jimmy and knew he'd still love me, and I muttered constantly about BCH fucking themselves.

I smoked more, drank more, and then decided that I needed cocaine. Just like that. The thought, the phone, a call. I didn't think twice. In fact, if anything, I couldn't wait to get some.

I spoke to Petra. It had been nearly a year since I'd chatted to her, but it might as well have been the day before. I was slurring in the way I'd always done. We squealed and laughed, and arranged to meet an hour later. I got a taxi into central London.

I was off it. Void of all anxieties. My plan was to rid myself of my unstable mind, and it had worked.

I felt free. I was finally home. How could this be wrong?

CHAPTER 44

I gave Xavier, the suave, Latino-looking dealer, two twenties and a ten and he handed me a wrap. I watched excitedly as he racked up lines from his stash and invited me and Petra to help ourselves. He and his friend joined us. I knew then that the coke he was selling to us would be crap, cut with speed or bicarb of soda. If he was getting high off his own supply, he'd be keeping the good stuff for himself.

That first line, cut or not, after three months of intense therapy and a total of ten months' abstinence, felt like I'd slipped on a pair of jogging bottoms that still fitted absolutely perfectly although they were nearly worn out. *Whoosh!* Straight up my nostril. I sniffed and pinched my nose and grinned at Petra. Within a couple of minutes, I could taste it sliding down my throat. Adrenalin flooded my cells. I took a glug of wine, chopped up more lines from the gram I'd bought and offered them about. And again, *bang*! The rush was forceful. Deep, slow breaths. I had another line, convinced that it would have taken two just to straighten me out after too many pills, and then, right there, within ten minutes after that third one, I was no longer drunk. I'd found what I'd been searching for: clarity.

I felt powerful, overwhelmingly alive and in control – of myself and of the moment. I felt warm in my shielded world. This was it. This was everything. All that mattered was on that table in front of me. I lit a cigarette and blew out slowly. The tornado that was rippling through my blood was authoritarian. I was untouchable. I wanted to growl and release my elation at being back in this exquisite world where no one could hurt me. There was only me and the powder, and it felt biblical, pure and eloquent, as though cocaine was genetically programmed into my system. Petra was clearly thrilled that I was back on the sauce. I could see it in her smile. She couldn't stop talking about the usual bullshit – clubs, people, bars – but I avoided conversation in favour of focusing on sensation.

This is what I'd craved and denied myself all this time. I should never have persecuted myself in the name of abstinence. For what? I felt on the precipice of a climax. I didn't know what to do with myself. I stood up. Sat back down. Lit another Marlboro, bit my bottom lip to try and contain my euphoria. I leaned back, away from the table, and felt unquestionably turned on. I took my drink. Laughed at nothing. Right then, I would have allowed Satan to open me up and impregnate me if it meant I could stay high, constantly, for the whole of my life.

'Have another line, Katie,' said Xavier. I started chatting animatedly. I felt no guilt. Why should I feel bad about feeling *this* good? Surely I'd been through enough? Xavier's lines were generous. Tactics, to ensure that I became a customer.

'So why have we never met?' Oh God, was he flirting with me? It was the last thing I wanted. I just wanted to get wasted. I glanced at him to try to read his face.

'Are you both Spanish?' I asked.

'Latino, sweetie. Me, I am from Paraguay.' He touched his chest proudly.

'Really? OK, well, I've not been around, so . . .'

'Katie's been away for a while,' Petra said.

Don't say it. I was certain she was about to drop me in it. I mean, the guy may not have cared if I'd been in rehab or on Mars, but I felt stupid admitting to having been in a treatment centre. That would have left me feeling as though I'd just confessed to working for the CID as a honey trap and that I'd actually come to investigate Xavier and his cronies for a future arrest.

After a while, I asked for his number.

Petra and I left. We were high and I was ready to get higher. But I began to feel uneasy – a change in dynamics.

I was wearing my usual jeans, a boring top, and Converse. Petra had the tiniest of skirts on and her boobs were heaving over the top of a cropped Versace offering. Four-inch Stella McCartney heels finished off her look.

'Jimmy Choos are so not ethically viable any longer,' she spouted in a transatlantic accent. I laughed out loud. I couldn't help myself. She ignored me. She'd apparently become vegetarian. She waffled on about having Botox and how she was sucking off the doctor so she could get it for free.

'You call that free? *Really?*'

'Don't start!' she snapped.

The excitement of that evening for me was not the bars, the people or the chance to chuckle at Petra's new role as a pseudo animal-rights activist. The thing that interested me was in the side compartment of my bag.

After drinking anything but Chardonnay in wannabe-hip bars, I left my friend with her latest banker, kisses and promises of more good times to come. I texted the dealer and went back via an ATM to his place and picked up another two grams.

Xavier, his odd-looking mate and I talked about guys and dolls we claimed to hang out with, and Judased others who were not worth kudos.

Drinking in a smoky room with two strange men, I became convinced that they expected me to suck or fuck one or both of them to justify my presence, although, looking back, I might have been imagining it. My saving grace was that these guys would never have suggested this outright; that would have seemed uncool. I needed to leave, so Xavier ordered me a cab.

Underlying my high, the ringing in my ears and the weird drunk-yet-alert sensation, the anxiety was impossible to ignore. I knew what was to come and feared it, badly. I apologetically asked him to tick me one more gram of charlie and told him that I'd pay him over the following days. I was trying to delay the inevitable, but it was coming, and there was nothing, no one, and no amount of money, no amount of powder and certainly no amount of wishing, that was going to alter it.

At some point I would come down. *Fact.*

I grumbled my way down the many stairs leading outside, trying to tell myself that despite my vision being blurred and feeling unsteady on my feet all was OK. But the reality was I didn't feel it. I felt utterly alone. I gave myself a pep talk and reminded myself that everyone is walking the planet alone. Only problem was a bit of self-talk at the start of a come-down can turn into babbling, over-analysed confusion that can only lead to paranoia.

I felt uneasy next to the taxi driver, with whom I was

desperate not to have a conversation. My mouth being dry as a rock in a desert (a side effect of being out of my skull), my voice was hoarse, and as soon as I realised that I could smell my own breath without cupping my hand over my nose and mouth, I knew that it reeked.

On the drive home, we stopped at a garage. I needed some water and fags. I hated having to go in, under those bright lights, and trying to avoid eye contact with a stranger who'd be looking straight into my face as he asked for payment.

And when I came out . . . that's when I fell off the edge of my reality and into a new world of pandemonium.

I was trying to remember which car was the taxi I'd been in. I stood staring for ages, zoned out. All I could see were dazzling lights until some random bloke approached me. As he came closer, I freaked. I started backing off in a panic, convinced he was about to attack me. I could see he was saying something but I didn't know what. He kept coming towards me. I shouted at him and asked what he wanted. Directions, apparently. I didn't believe him. I didn't know what was going on and I remember ordering the man to leave me alone.

At this point, the taxi pulled up beside me and the driver beeped his horn. I took this as a sign that the guy who claimed to be asking me for directions was going to bundle me into the boot of the car. I was frantic. I ran to the exit of the forecourt and was then confronted by the main road, which stopped me in my tracks. The taxi again came up alongside me, and this time the driver opened the door.

'Go away. What do you want?' My heart was pounding. I kept looking around me, searching for my would-be assassin.

'Please, madam. Please. Just get in the car and let me drive you home.'

I glared at him. I vaguely recognised his face. He assured

me that he was legit, so I got into the car, because one thing was certain: he was definitely not the guy who I thought was about to kidnap and attack me.

For the entire 20-minute drive back to my flat, I believed to the point of 'knowing' that the guy who had approached me at the garage was following us. I kept asking the driver if he could see a car behind us that I couldn't, and he kept denying it.

'Are you working alongside him?' I asked him.

When we got to my block, I didn't want to get out of the taxi. Through the wing mirrors and the back window there was no obvious sign of anything sinister, but still I begged the driver to walk me to my door. I was absolutely certain that the man from the garage was creeping along my street through the bushes.

The cabbie refused. Instead, he told me he'd watch me go inside. I yelled at him for being entirely responsible for my death if I now got ambushed and I threw his fee on the floor of the car, then ran to my door, where I tried to insert the key. I rushed into my building, then entered my flat.

My mind was squealing like a siren. I crept around as light-footedly as possible, barely breathing as I systematically checked first behind doors, then inside cupboards, inside drawers, under the bed, in the wardrobe, under the table, behind the sofa, in the shower, to make absolutely sure I was alone – a ritual I'd grown used to before going to rehab.

My eyes were darting; my ears echoed. I sat still, fixated on my rug – and then I had a line, and another, and another. I sat on the floor listening to Alicia Keys: *Songs in A Minor* over and over and over and over.

I awoke at some point to a voice message from Tessa, whom I'd recently been avoiding talking to.

Leon had relapsed.

CHAPTER 45

At some point during the next 48 hours, Leon and I got together. We decided to get out of London for a weekend. Of all the places in Britain we could have gone to, we found ourselves in a hotel in Weymouth. Don't ask.

In the hotel bar, we tried to ignore the fact that we were both getting drunk. Considering we'd met in drug rehab in this same town, this was at the least unusual. And at the other end of the scale, it was totally preposterous. Looking back, we were both in an emotional state and in going to a place that felt safe we were perhaps inadvertently asking for help.

Leon was fidgety and getting on my nerves.

'What're you doing? What's wrong?' I asked him when he stood up.

'Getting another drink. What's wrong with you?'

'What do you mean?'

'You sound edgy as fuck, babes. I'm only getting up, all right? I'm not waiting for that dizzy waitress to look over cos I'll be here all night otherwise, get me?' He shrugged. 'We need to get some rock or sniff or something. I'm mashed up already.'

'Yeah, me too. You said you'd score some here.'

'Fuck's sake, man, look at us back in Weymouth. Jokes,' The Youth laughed uneasily.

'Baby, sit here next to me, will you?' I patted the chair.

'I just said I'm getting a drink, innit?' He walked off.

'What's up with you?' I asked him when he came back with two double vodkas.

'I'm fine. Fine.'

'Is that fine, *fine*?'

'Fuck's sake, babes, chill out.'

'Or Fucked-up, Insecure, Neurotic and Emotional?'

'Don't give me that treatment fucking bullshit, sweetheart, please!'

Ouch! Where was the softly spoken boy I'd fallen for months before? He was more pensive, abrasive and louder than he'd been at any time since I'd known him, except for that one time he'd nearly had a scrap with the new boy Alan in rehab.

'Sorry, OK? I was just teasing. And listen, don't talk to me like that, all right? I don't like it.'

We finished our drinks and got a taxi into town.

Leon paid – with my money – and took my hand as we ran across the road and into the nearest bar. Maybe now we'd both lighten up. The music was loud and tacky, catering for people who weren't there for anything other than booze and a fight.

'Hang on a minute,' he said, handing me my own cash so that I could order the drinks.

'Where're you off to?'

'Just shut up a minute, will you?'

'You can't just walk off and leave me in here by myself!' I called after him.

But he could and he did.

The Youth had bought a gram of charlie for each of us with

part of the 250 quid I'd given him to hang onto for us to spend.

The dabbling would last for a few days, only a few days, that's all, nothing more, it was OK, I told myself. This would be a blip in my real life, which was now about abstinence.

No, it is, it really is.

The mood between us lifted and the music boomed. Leon and I were kissing continually. We couldn't keep our hands off each other and we were drinking like there was a drought.

There were very few people around. We talked excessively about our relationship and how we 'have to make this work'. Our love for each other would get us through any tough times, we decided. I stumbled to the loo for another sniff, and a guy who was walking out of the men's toilets tried to chat to me. I didn't stop, but I could still look. I felt wasted as I bumbled back into the bar.

And right in front of me there was my fella, the man who'd just been telling me that he 'needed me in his life' and 'I'll do whatever it takes to keep us together', with his hands on another woman, laughing with her and her friend.

'What're you doing?' I snarled, hitting his hand off one girl's back.

'Hey, what the –?' Leon snapped back.

'Come on, let's go! Let's go!' I shouted, pulling his arm.

'Just a minute, Kate, for fuck's sake, man.'

'And you two, just fuck off, do you hear me?'

'Who do you think you're talking to?' one of the girls snapped.

'Sorry about her,' Leon said, as though I wasn't there. He leaned closer to them and said something else.

'Leon, I swear to God, don't you dare be doing what I think you're doing. I'm. Not. Fucking. Joking. Right? You'd better not be buying drinks for these fucking bitches, and with my money.'

He scowled, pointing upwards. The music was too loud for him to hear me. Apparently.

'I said, "Don't you dare buy these fucking girls a drink," OK? Do you hear me now, you fucking bastard arsehole!? Or shall I shout it again and again?'

'Don't you fucking talk to me like that in front of people, pussyhole!' Leon barked as he grabbed my wrist. I flung my other arm back, ready to launch at him.

'Stop it, Katie, man!' He held onto both my wrists.

'No, no, I won't, I won't fucking stop anything!'

'Look at the state of you!'

'That hurts! Let go of me! Let go of me now, Leon! And what the fuck are you two still doing here?' I screamed at the girls.

'Go to the bathroom and sort yourself out, Katie, mate, for fuck's sake.' He gripped my face with his hand, forcing me to look at him.

'Mate? *Mate?*' I slapped his face. 'How fucking *dare* you talk to me like you don't even know me?!'

He raised his hand, then stopped.

'You'd better stop that, love, or you'll get yourself into trouble,' one of the girls squawked.

I went for her. Leon yanked me back. She yelled. I screamed at her friend, who tried to get her to leave.

'If I wanted your fucking opinion, you fucking dog, I'd have asked for it, and since I didn't, you can just fuck off! Just fuck off!' I bellowed at the peacemaker.

'Go away, you stupid idiot,' the girl answered back. She then started pointing at me, and they both started laughing.

'I'll fucking knock you out, you fucking trollop. Go and

find your own man and stop sniffing round mine, d'you hear me? And as for you, Leon, you fucking prick – give me my money back.'

Leon tried pulling me towards him. 'Katie, go to the bathroom, now. Go and wash your face, for fuck's sake. Your nose is bleeding.'

'Just give me my money back.' I leaned towards the girls. 'Have you got something to say, eh? Have you got something you fucking want to say to me?'

'Yeah, your nose is bleeding!'

It was, too; it was pouring with blood.

CHAPTER 46

'Just fuck off!' Leon shouted at me after he'd downed two double shots of brandy as we stood together at the bar. He stomped off towards the exit.

I guzzled my drink as fast as I could, trying to keep an eye on where he was. I threw my head back to finish my vodka and when I resurfaced he'd disappeared. So had the girls he'd been talking to. I ran in the direction that he'd taken, ignoring a couple whom I knocked into.

'Excuse me!' the guy spat at me sarcastically.

'You're excused, you dopey fuckwit,' I called back at him.

I didn't have a clue where I was, and outside on the promenade I couldn't see Leon anywhere. Livid, I paced down then back up the street, steaming drunk. I stumbled into a virtually empty bar, but couldn't see him. Instead someone stood right in front of me. It was the guy I'd seen before who'd said hello to me when I went to the bathroom before The Youth and I had started arguing. This was my chance, if I wanted to take it.

'Hello. We meet again,' he said in a foreign accent. 'Are you alone? Would you like some company?'

'No, I'm all right, I'm looking for . . .' I didn't want to say my boyfriend. '. . . a friend.'

I suddenly remembered my nose had been bleeding. Was it still? No.

'You look lonely by yourself. Are you OK?'

'Yeah, I'm fine. I just don't feel like talking right now.'

'A girl like you shouldn't be alone. Look, how about you come with me to another place?'

Go with it? Not? Leon? Where's Leon?

'Look, it's nice of you to offer me a drink –'

'I'm not offering you a drink, sexy, I just think you should be careful in your state, alone.'

'What do you mean by the state I'm in? I'm all right. There's nothing wrong with me.'

'Let's get out of here. What do you say, huh? Maybe we could go to a B&B or your place?'

'No, piss off.'

'My wife's at home, I can't take you there.' He laughed.

'I'm not a fucking hooker, you know.'

'Who do you think you're –? Well, you look like a whore to me.'

'If I look like a whore, what do you think your mother looks like? Go and jump off a bridge, you fucking dickhead. That way you can save your wife having to live with your horseshit.'

I started to walk away. I still had to find Leon.

'Bitch!'

I turned round and rushed right up into his face. 'If you call me a bitch or a fucking whore once more, I'll, I'll . . .'

'You're slurring. Speak clearly!'

'Listen, you fucking ugly arsehole, *please* go and harass someone else with your beaked nose and your small cock.'

'Small dick? Nothing small about this,' he said, grabbing his crotch. 'You want to see it, you slut?'

'Oh, fuck off.'

'And why are you so angry? Is it because you've got no man?'

I stared at him, and the truth be told I'd forgotten why I was so mad. I found a cigarette. He lit it and within seconds his slippery hands began groping me and we kissed. When I stopped for a puff of my fag, I dried my face and he took my hand and tried to lead me with him. I pulled away and started running.

I got to the hotel and went straight to reception to ask someone to let me into the bedroom, as I couldn't find the key.

'Your husband is already there.' My heart leapt.

'He's not my husband, but anyway, when did he get here? Is he alone?'

'I think so, yes. I don't know when he arrived back, madam. Maybe an hour ago. Is everything all right?'

I didn't know. Hearing that Leon had arrived back at the hotel should have pleased me, but instead my anger exploded because he'd left me – to go off with two random women. I crept up to our room, holding my breath so that I could hear what was going on inside. I rested my ear against the door and knocked. I decided that if he was in there he might open the door, thinking it was the hotel staff. But there was no response. I couldn't hear a sound. *He's got a woman in there with him.* I banged on the door and called his name. I still couldn't hear anything except my own heavy breathing and ringing in my eardrums. I became hysterical and began to kick the bottom of the door. Leon flung it open, and I charged inside screaming, 'What the fuck is going on? What're you doing in here? I've been knocking –'

'Shut up, Katie,' he said, surprisingly calmly.

'Don't fucking tell –' I lunged towards him with my fists.

He grabbed my arms. 'What the fuck are you doing here?' I screamed. 'Let go of me. Now! Fucking let go of me!'

'Are you going to be sensible?' Leon asked. He didn't even look that angry – fed up, maybe. Even though I was wasted, I noticed this. He let go of me and turned his back.

I followed him to the bedside and watched as he snorted a line.

'What the fuck are you doing?'

'What the fuck are *you* doing?' he shouted back.

'Why the fuck did you leave me at that bar? Where's the rest of the coke?'

'In the drawer. Anyway, you've got some.'

I opened the drawer. 'I've done mine, and the rest of it isn't in here! You'll have caned it or hidden it or something, you fucking sneaky twat. I can't believe you left me by myself in this fucking town. How could you do that? Where's the fucking coke, Leon? Tell me! Where is it? It's not in the drawer!'

'It is.'

'So what did you do with those fucking hags that you were chatting up?' I screamed, moving forward to whack him again. He ducked.

'Stop it, Katie! Just stop it and shut the fuck up!' Leon shouted. He got off the bed and started to pace.

'Don't fucking tell me to shut up! And stop what? I'm not doing anything. It's you, Leon, it's you. You're fucking with my head.' I wanted to hurt him, to show him how I was hurting. 'I can't believe you fucking left me, you bastard! Where's the coke? Where's the fucking coke? Where is it?' I screamed, close to tears. I was trashed.

Leon rushed towards the wardrobe, grabbing the rucksack he'd brought with him. He started to throw his things inside it. 'The charlie's in that fucking drawer. I've told you and I'm not telling you again.'

I again searched inside the drawer and found it. Without saying a word, I racked up some lines on the bedside cabinet. I rolled up a £10 note and sniffed hard: a line up each nostril.

'What are you doing?' I asked Leon. He didn't answer. 'Hey, have you got some fags?'

He still said nothing. I went to the bathroom to get a tissue.

'Are you listening to me, you skinny arsehole? Have you got any cigarettes or what? And what the fuck are you doing?' I slurred as I passed him.

'I'm gone.'

I didn't want him to go but I didn't know how to be softer. I was fucked, the relationship was fucked, everything was fucked. I knew I'd gone too far to change the inevitable, so instead of calming down I turned up the aggro.

'You've been boning one of those girls, haven't you?' I taunted him.

'Shut up, Kate.'

'What was that?' I bellowed as I stormed out of the bathroom. My nose was bleeding into a tissue. 'You fucked one of those fucking girls you were speaking to earlier, and I bet she's in this fucking hotel somewhere waiting for you, the fucking slut!' I said, and started to prod him.

'Katie, shut up. I haven't,' he said firmly.

'Yeah you fucking have, and you've had this planned all fucking night, haven't you, you fucking, fucking . . .'

'I haven't fucked anyone, but I almost wish I had.'

I lunged at him again.

'Stop it, Katie, man! Leave me alone, you fucking nutter. Fucking stop making all this fucking noise or I'll knock you out.'

'No you won't.'

'OK, OK, I might not knock you out, but if you touch me again or follow me now, I will hurt you.' He nodded his head slowly. 'I promise you that.'

He left and I flung myself on the floor, wailing hysterically.

CHAPTER 47

I was woken up by Leon nuzzling my neck. 'Get up,' he said. 'I want to take you somewhere.'

'What do you mean?' I was dazed. At first I didn't know where I was. I sat up. Lightning erupted in my skull and the grimness of what had happened bombarded my stomach.

'Get up. Let's go, innit?'

I imagined him taking me away and murdering me, then chopping my body into tiny pieces and leaving it to rot as compost. Maybe that would be a worthy punishment for my behaviour. Penance for all the shit I'd ever done in my life. I got off the bed.

'What's going on? Are you OK?'

'Yeah, I'm fine,' Leon answered matter-of-factly. 'C'mon.'

My nerves were destroyed. We left the hotel and walked into absolute darkness. He led me in silence. I didn't ask where we were going. I couldn't think clearly. I was weary and accepted the idea of being pushed off a cliff, if that was what The Youth had in mind. At least that way I wouldn't have to inflict myself on anyone else ever again.

We reached the beach and it was cold and windy.

'I was saving these for a quiet night in, but I think we'd

better take them now.' Leon put his hand in his pocket and pulled out two tablets. Whatever it was, I didn't want any. I looked at them; they looked like Ecstasy. I was already in bits.

'Open your mouth,' Leon demanded.

I wanted to sleep or something. I didn't want whatever he was offering, but felt I had to take it.

'What is it?'

'Trust me, babes. Just open your mouth.'

I did, reluctantly, and then closed it quickly. 'What is it, Leon?' I asked urgently.

'You trust me, don't you?'

Not really. Was he trying to feed me cyanide?

'Look, are you having one of these?' I asked. 'You do yours at the same time.'

He placed a tablet on his tongue and kissed my dry mouth to deliver it. It *was* Ecstasy. That bitter, foul taste was unmistakable.

I tried to swallow it, but couldn't. I spat it out into my hand.

'Do it,' said Leon.

I gathered some spit on my tongue, pinched my nose, scowled, and jumped up and down as it partially dissolved and disappeared down my throat. Leon effortlessly swallowed his.

'Come on,' he said, taking my hand. I was cold, and the sea was rough and loud. We continued walking in silence until we reached some sand dunes. In complete darkness, we trudged up into the sandy mounds. Suddenly, The Youth turned and kissed me with such urgency it took me off guard.

'I love you and I want this to work,' he said quietly.

I couldn't see his eyes, but I could feel the determination in his touch.

I started to cry. 'Baby, I'm so, so sorry. I don't know what else to say. I feel awful. I'm sorry about everything. I want this to work, too. I want us to be together.'

'We'll be OK.'

I nodded and squeaked, 'I hope so, I really do.' And in that moment I wanted him more than anything. The effects of the Ecstasy were kicking in, and what felt like intense feelings of love coursed through me. We began to kiss again. His warm breath was flowing into my lungs and joining us. I'd have cut myself open and told him to climb inside me if that could have brought us closer.

My snatch was wet. We were both groaning. Our mouths joined like leeches. We were pawing each other, taking whatever we could. We collapsed onto the sand. He bit my nipple hard and I slapped his face. Leon's cock, hard as a rock, rammed inside me. I grunted, and within moments he was thrashing deeply, perhaps seeking some revenge for the drama that had happened earlier in the night. He came inside me. I was disorientated, and before I had time to register what was happening, Leon had got up and zipped up and without a word he ran and ran and ran . . . and vanished.

CHAPTER 48

It was getting light as I waded through the sand back to the hotel, feeling as bad as I'd imagine I'd feel had I been made to have sex with an Alsatian while people watched. I squeezed my arms around my chest. My body temperature had dropped due to the come-down and I was shaking.

Confused, I began asking myself or an imaginary friend about Leon's whereabouts. Suddenly, my stomach churned, I heaved and stinking water burst from my trembling lips and hit the sand below.

I got to the hotel and somehow remembered where the room was. I went straight there and tried the door. It was open.

Paranoia hit me. Had an intruder been in there, or was Leon back? I called to him. No answer.

My heart dropped; I held my breath and stood perfectly still. I didn't dare enter. But this was counteracted by another urge to vomit.

In the bathroom, the light had been left on, but I managed to miss the toilet bowl. I stood up to wash my mouth out with water and felt as though I was about to collapse. I sat on the floor and slumped my head back onto the wall.

'Leon? Are you here?' I tried to call out, but barely a whisper came out. Nothing.

'Fuck, fuck! What have you done, Katie, you absolute fucking idiot?' I blurted out loud, convinced that whatever was going wrong was definitely my fault. We'd had sex; everything had been all right, hadn't it? But he'd disappeared. I cried with no tears.

Leon was gone. He was gone. As gone as he possibly could be, even though some of his belongings were still there. My ears were ringing and my body was numb. I was shaking as I climbed under the duvet.

Things around me seemed to consist of massive detail that I wouldn't normally be able to see. Shapes in the carpet and on the ceiling seemed to be moving like lava. I turned my head to listen to a buzzing sound. My eyes felt as though they were nearly popping out of my head. I held my breath. There it was again. I jerked for cover. There was another noise.

Was that Leon? What is that buzzing? Is it a wasp? There's no wasp, Kate; you're imagining it; you're safe. Where's Leon? I started laughing.

'Yes?' I said out loud. I stopped breathing and lay still. I felt something on my skin. I sprang up and screeched. Insects, there were insects crawling over me, I could feel them. I started giggling for no reason and quickly stopped.

I got out of bed and stared at my hand, which looked as though the veins were moving under my skin. I held it right up to my face and prodded it. *There's that wasp again.*

'There isn't anything in here, Katie. It's OK, it's OK,' I said, once more talking to myself. 'Where are your cigarettes? Go and see if the fags are in the bathroom. Mind the cup of tea. I haven't drunk any tea. It's sick. You were sick. Find some alcohol, some wine, beer, anything . . .'

'Where's Leon?' I asked the walls as I searched for a drink and cigarettes. I laughed like a clown over nothing and then slumped onto the bed and started to sob, but no tears came.

My world felt lopsided. 'He's left you, he's left you cos you're a dirty, useless piece-of-stinking-shit slut,' I told myself.

Then I spotted a wine bottle. I stopped whimpering and got up.

'Where are my fags? Where are you hiding? Let me find yoou-oou-oou!' I started singing. 'I'm going to find you!'

I stopped and stared. I searched everywhere, all the time holding onto the virtually empty wine bottle. My only comfort.

I woke up at 2.30 p.m. The reality of what had happened slammed me.

With every realisation, it was as though someone had grabbed the back of my head and was bashing it into a wall. I was in Weymouth. Alone. I was trashed and alone. I now had to get back to London. Alone.

I turned on my side. Bad move. I felt my blood was boiling; if I moved again, it would pour out of my eyes and ears to release some pressure. I sensed a shadow beside me. My heart beat in my throat and I froze.

Images from the previous night flashed before me and fear surged in every molecule of my body. *Fuck*. I wanted to throw myself off the pier with a ton of rotting fish strapped to my middle – and not be rescued.

'You stupid, stupid fucking cunt, Katie. You stupid, stupid fucking idiot,' I said loudly, again and again. I needed painkillers. Lots. Them or arsenic. It was happening all over again.

Had I ever had a time of 'wellness' during those months after rehab? No, I decided; I hadn't. It confirmed what I'd always suspected: that I was pathetic – a failure in every way possible.

I spoke to the hotel receptionist, who told me that they'd tried to wake me, but I'd been comatose. They didn't need to tell me that; I'd been there. So I was charged for an extra day because I'd left the room after the official 11.30 a.m. checkout time.

Without arguing, I paid the money. I wasn't in any state to do battle over it; I was just grateful I'd managed to cling onto my bank card.

I left Weymouth on the train with no phone, no Leon and no clarity of thought. That had left me weeks ago.

What I did have was a queasy tummy; a nervous system in pieces; a head that, given the option, would gladly have taken a bullet if it meant no more pain; and an honorary PhD in how to screw your life up.

However, I'd miraculously managed to retain my return train ticket back to London. But this joy was abruptly cut short when I realised I had no keys to my flat. My only option was to get to the estate agent's before they closed. Surely they'd have a spare set?

I was utterly shattered, but panic was rising. I wished I had a blanket to cover my face so no one could see me. My goblin was back in business, rubbing its hands together, believing that once again I was batting for its team.

On the train, I thought about university and how proud I'd been to get onto the course, but I knew I'd not be going back. I recoiled. I couldn't cope with it. It had been too soon after leaving BCH.

UNHOOKED

What would my father's response to my recent failure be? He must never, ever know.

And what about Jimmy? I'd speak to him soon, but not yet. He'd never turn his back on me. Would he?

CHAPTER 49

I arrived at Putney station dreading the idea of walking amongst people. I looked a wreck. I felt a wreck. I was a wreck – and I had to get to the estate agent's. Fast. I was obsessed with the idea that I might not be able to get into my flat. But there was no time to dwell on the matter. I decided to jog. Thankfully, their offices were less than a ten-minute running distance away. On my way, I stopped at the cashpoint and got a statement, which I stuffed into my pocket. I'd deal with that later. I arrived at the estate agent's panting. I felt like kissing the woman who confirmed that there were spare keys and that I'd be driven back to my flat.

The driver was overfamiliar and asked me how I'd lost my keys, with a corny wink. Did he do that because he could smell sex on me? I was trying to calm my overactive mind. Again, I thought about my dad and what I'd say to him about this relapse. *Not a word.*

In BCH, I'd been told that this meant I was being dishonest by omission. Fuck that. This was the real world, and saying nothing was exactly what I was going to do, to save wrenching open my father's already fragile heart. If he found out about my recent set of calamitous events, I was certain he would

309

never regain any faith in me. That wouldn't be fair for either of us. I could be better than this, although I wasn't sure how. Besides, I couldn't face being served my parents' tough-love regime again, and I knew that it was very likely that my relapse would make them shut down completely. 'Tough love': what a stupid, incongruous expression. Love is love, surely? By making it 'tough', isn't the perpetrator of this 'loving' behaviour being controlling and patronising towards the recipient?

My reality was grim. But thankfully I hadn't taken the final step to take me to my personal Hades: I'd not sold my body. Not yet. But I wished with everything that I was:

- that I'd never got involved in a relationship so soon after rehab;
- that I'd listened more and genuinely integrated myself with the Fellowship and its members, especially at the beginning of my recovery, and not taken the piss out of people in my mind or scoffed at the goings-on in the meetings;
- that I'd asked for help and been more honest about how I was feeling and what I was thinking.
- that I hadn't ignored the advice to go through the Steps with a sponsor, because I couldn't be bothered and saw no point. In fact, I'd ignored any advice that meant I had to actively make an effort.
- And I wished, desperately, with every cell in my pointless body, that I hadn't relapsed.

But wishing wasn't going to change a thing.

On my way home, I spent some change on two bottles of cheap wine and twenty Marlboro Lights. I had to do something to shut my head up, and I didn't know what else to do, except possibly lie in the middle of the road and wait for a car to finish me off.

CHAPTER 50

I woke, fully clothed in the night, to a banging at my window. My first thought was Leon, then a punter, then a dealer, then a punter's wife, then Leon again, when I realised my ex-clients didn't know where I lived. I put my fingers into the blind and peered out. It was The Youth. Before I'd had time to contemplate the meaning of this, he was in my room. I wanted to know why he'd left me.

He came with fags, Jack Daniels, an eighth of charlie and downers. The conversation was on hold. I didn't ask how he'd got the money to get the gear. We sniffed, drank, sniffed, smoked, sniffed and fucked like beasts – with some hatred.

Then he left. He walked out. One minute he was normal – well, my idea of normal during that session – and then he just buggered off. *Again*, without saying a word.

This time, I was determined to get him back. I slid on my flip-flops and burst out onto the street. Through the drizzle, I spotted The Youth's duffel coat, with him in it waddling up the road.

'Leon!'

He didn't turn round.

'Leon!'

This time, he did turn round. I was running towards him and he started running away from me.

'Please, please wait! Where are you going?' I yelled.

I stopped still, breathless.

'Leon!'

He looked at me again, and then he started walking. I was in pieces, wrecked, light-headed, and I felt very, very sick. I needed him to be with me.

I screamed his name hysterically. He carried on briskly. I ran towards him and called his name. He turned round and, when he saw me running, he started to run again. I was crushed.

'I want to talk to you,' I mumbled, knowing he couldn't, and didn't want to, hear me. I stopped and bent over, heaving for breath. I watched The Youth as he turned to look at me with a hateful smirk. I didn't want to see it.

I began to run slowly, and he mirrored my actions. As a test, I stopped and began to walk. I began screaming loudly and screaming madly. My life was in pieces. I wanted some help. No one came. Certainly not Leon.

'Please wait,' I called in his direction. He didn't stop. Not for me.

I collapsed onto the pavement, my legs tucked under me, and I beat my head with my fists and I screamed.

In my flat, in my thoughts my world had come to an end. I sat on the edge of the sofa. I felt dead. There was silence. Complete silence. No birdsong, no tears. I wished I would die. I felt I might. I couldn't even feel my own breathing. Surely God knew that I couldn't take much more? Surely he'd be merciful and pluck me off the planet to stop my pain? My body and my mind were ready to combust.

I felt lifeless. I imagined a blade smoothly slicing deep

into my wrist, upward, and feeling the excellent relief as red treacle poured down my hands, releasing me from the world, allowing me the freedom to rest.

I stared at the carpet, and imagined myself lying comfortably on my Habitat rug, my 400-quid beautiful cream over-priced shroud, having never felt such peace, and knowing that I'd soon be free. I would go to a place where no one could harm me, where I would feel equal to everyone and where no one could leave me. I could cause my father no more pain and not contaminate everything I touched with disaster. I wanted to claw open my stomach and pull out my intestines. This would be an offering for my mother. If only I could hand her my weeping insides, a part of the body she'd created that was joined to hers, so she might understand how her absence had made me feel.

After a long time of sitting motionless, I found myself fiddling with a piece of paper. A bank statement – *my* bank statement. It said there was £2,200 in my account. I froze. I stared at the figures. Was the Devil toying with me and lulling me into a false sense of security? I scrunched my eyes into slits to see if the numbers altered. They didn't. Had I made a mistake? I checked the date. It was the statement that I'd got on my way to the estate agent's after I'd left Weymouth two days previously. £2,200 was in my account. My university grant. I felt nothing and thought very little. But one thing was definite – I now had a choice. I could score some coke, buy some alcohol and forget everything once again. At least for a while. But this realisation did nothing to alleviate my dense sadness. I was tired, tired of existing. I had cash waiting to be spent and I could continue to try to hide.

Why not? What else was there?

Life.

CHAPTER 51

'Honesty is the backbone of recovery,' I could hear Len's voice chanting. I wanted to scream, 'Yes, I've fucking got it! I've got it!'

I had to contact Janet. What would she think of me now that I'd relapsed? I'd been dodging her for a while, so she'd probably guessed I'd fucked up. It was time for me to get real and if she didn't approve then I'd find someone else to guide me. What would Tessa think of me? I grimaced. And Maggie? Lenny? Emma? They mattered. The rest could get to hell. But when I thought about Jimmy and my dad, I put my hands over my ears and started humming out loud. I couldn't bear the thought of hurting my dad in this way. Not again.

I texted Janet, who immediately called me.

'If you want to go to a meeting, I'll pick you up and we'll go together. Come on, you're going to be all right. You haven't given up, Kate, don't forget. If you had, it's more likely you'd be in a mortuary right now and not speaking to me.'

My back was up against the wall and I was finally ready to listen. This was no time for false pride, only humility. And this time I couldn't ignore my reality, jump over it, tunnel underground or flirt my way out. *And yes, yes, yes, I will stick with the women.* That penny had finally dropped. I had to surrender wholly and be willing to admit that I didn't have the answers.

However much I didn't want to sink back into oblivion, it was what I knew best and the thought of abstinence terrified me witless. I was officially in no-man's-land.

What would I do? How could I live in this world? How would I earn money? I had no qualifications, no skills. I could forget university. *One day at a time, remember?*

You won't manage to stop, Kate. Don't waste your time trying. Just do yourself in. You know you want to. Part of me did want to carry on drinking and taking drugs. But I couldn't cope with the mental battering that came with it. I couldn't manage the constant tension between the opposing sides: my actions versus my upbringing.

I crept into the meeting and hoped to God that very few people I knew would be there. The ones who were were OK, a bit more distant than I recalled them being before. It was obvious I'd relapsed before I said it. They made the right noises, but whatever their thoughts they'd have to deal with them. I was there fighting for my sanity, not their approval.

'Do you want to go for coffee with some of the others?' Janet asked me at the end of the meeting.

'I want to, I really do, but I can't face hanging out with people at the moment, and I can't even invite you to my place cos it's a tip. I'm sorry. I think I'll just go home. I'm tired.' I felt totally incompetent; I had no energy and I couldn't even keep my home tidy.

'It's fine. I understand. Why don't you come to mine and I'll take you back later? Let's go.'

I told Janet that I wanted to call BCH to apologise for having been such a chump.

I wanted to call Jimmy and confess all, but being stuck between rage and tears left me worn out. Janet reminded me that I could do the apology stuff further down the line. There were provisions for this within the 12 Steps. How would I explain Leon to my NA mates? *You're as sick as your secrets.* Fuck, yes, OK, OK! My priority for now had to be *me*, to the exclusion of everyone else. This was my life, and my need to find some stability had to come before everything: my father, Jim, friends, a boyfriend, university, sex and anyone's opinions. I'd already tried to avoid myself through being intimately involved with others, and I was now reaping the grim rewards of that.

I was constantly anxious. I didn't dare go out, but I didn't want to be at home. I didn't want to be with people, but I was afraid to be alone. My flat was a mess, but I felt too shattered to tidy it up. I was having nightmares, when I was able to sleep, and panic attacks that would come and go and leave me feeling battered.

I'd jump at nothing and my inner voice was rabid, relentlessly screaming obscenities and suggestions that I should get trashed with the money I had. But rule number one was: DO NOT PICK UP A DRINK OR A DRUG. In my head, Len would say, 'These negative feelings will change sooner than you may think. Just stick with it. Don't be afraid of how you feel.'

The dark shadows that had haunted my periphery were back with the power to make me stop perfectly still and hold my breath until I sensed movement, and then they'd vanish for a while. I was at war with myself. I felt as though my actions were being controlled by an entity outside of me. Some might say this was psychosis. I didn't have a name for it, except 'absolutely shitting myself'. I was no longer certain if I could ever rid myself of whatever it was that made me do things that caused me chaos and pain, and I certainly couldn't take on anything more than just keeping myself sober from hour to hour and day to day.

So this is a relapse? I'd messed up after my first rehab, but then I hadn't sunk as quickly as I had this time.

I'd never bonded with the AA Step 1: 'We admitted we were powerless over alcohol and that our lives had become unmanageable.' I'd therefore overlooked the most vital, essential part of the whole programme, the very basics of why I'd ever gone into treatment in the first place. I felt embarrassed and ridiculous.

I listened to Janet on the phone, at her house, at my flat, in cafés, in the park, wherever she could meet me. Most days I saw members of the Fellowship; we talked and talked and I heard what was being said. Every day I went to an NA or AA meeting, sometimes with Janet, sometimes with Emma, often alone, and I ranted shamelessly about the confusion in my mind.

I shouted, 'I'm Katie, and I'm an addict,' and whatever anyone thought about me speaking up I couldn't have given a toss. No one was going to get in the way this time.

I chose different meetings to where Gary would be. The few times I saw him, I avoided him, and I didn't feel weird about it. He sometimes said hello, and I sometimes replied, and that was that.

For weeks, I was close to exploding at any moment, over anything, with anyone. My jaws were constantly grinding, even when I was at home staring at the TV or taking a bath, but rage at my situation kept my tears away. I needed affirmative action to get me through this. I was overwhelmed with hot flushes, palpitations, inordinate sweating and self-consciousness. I was as good as back at the very beginning.

I soon came to accept that I'd made some very basic and fundamental mistakes leading up to this point:

- I'd not followed the suggestions I'd been given in treatment.
- I hadn't been honest, and had therefore not expressed the depth of my fears to people who could help me.
- I'd continued to do my own thing, not believing that the consequences would affect me.
- I'd immersed myself in another person – Leon – to avoid looking at myself.
- I'd expected sobriety to take hold magically.
- I hadn't *really* tried. Simple. I hadn't consciously tried to become better.

What made me so special that I should think that the patterns of behaviour that had always led people to relapse, well before I ever came into the Fellowship, would not take me down the same path?

Addicts suffer from terminal uniqueness, the belief that individually we're vastly different from the next person. 'This attitude will keep you sick and also isolated!' Nick used to say in groups.

I decided that shopping might give me a lift, and it would also rid me of some of the money the presence of which in my bank was stirring more doubt. I spent 900 quid on a bag, a pair of boots and a coat. It did nothing. Nothing at all. All it did was confirm that I had no interest in stuff.

Everything seemed to take me a long time to do, perhaps because I over-thought things. I didn't just act; my lack of confidence made me over-analyse every action. I eventually got antidepressants from the doctor after years of refusing them and for the first time in my life I took a prescribed medication as it was meant to be taken. Within a month, the tablets kicked in, and as my thoughts became clearer I realised I had to regroup immediately. The cotton wool began easing out of my ears and I was more able to see through the murky goggles that had covered my vision.

Taking the tablets was my way of doing something necessary and practical to help myself, and if anyone from the Fellowship considered my taking these pills to be a relapse, they could kiss my arse.

I wondered if how I was feeling then was how 'normals' felt, most of the time, and, if so, why had a deranged inner goblin tried to batter me down for most of my life?

If I continued to try, people in meetings promised me, this difficult time would pass. They *promised*, not suggested it might. I had no other option but to continue to try.

I asked Janet if she'd once again consider being my sponsor. Her response: 'I never stopped. You just didn't use me when you most needed to.'

Together and through the Steps, we continued to unravel my attitudes and behaviours to help me learn more about what I had become and why. This way I could arm myself better against another relapse. On a good day, I wanted to know all there was to know; other times, I would wallow in bed, cursing myself and sleeping and trying to ignore the world. This was OK, but only for a designated amount of time. Janet suggested no more than two days.

'You have to remember that it's OK to give yourself a break, Kate, and not constantly persecute yourself for what has happened. And smile! What's happened to that cheeky face, huh?'

'I don't feel I have anything to smile about.'

'You're breathing, Katie. That's not to be dismissed. And, for today, you're sober!'

'Yeah, but . . .'

'Katie, think about what I'm saying. You. Are. Alive. You still have a chance.'

'Yeah, but what about Leon and what went on there? I mean, was that my fault? I don't even know if he's alive or dead.'

'Look, if someone relapses, that's their own responsibility. You were both vulnerable.'

With Janet, I was more honest than I'd ever been, and as a result I admitted that I'd been heading for a relapse before I'd left treatment. The PTB at BCH had been right all along, and this stung me and left me feeling stupid.

'I want you to write three affirmations on some card, do you hear me?' Lenny said when I called him. I couldn't yet bring myself to talk to Maggie.

'I don't have any card.'

'On some paper, then! It's good to hear you haven't lost all your spirit, there, Kate!'

'Hmm . . .'

'And every day I want you to repeat these a few times throughout the day, OK? So, for example, every morning as you're brushing your teeth, or whatever it is you ladies do, try chanting your affirmations out loud. You might laugh, Kate, or feel silly while you're doing it, but this will help you a great deal.'

'OK, but I don't even know what to write.'

'Here's a suggestion. Think of a friend and jot down three good things about her, and then make them about yourself. That's one way to start. Don't expect the habits you've formed and the damage you've done to yourself over the years to be healed after just months. That's not realistic.'

I'd have paid to have my life fast-forwarded right then. Paid with literally anything.

CHAPTER 52

During the following three months, I stayed close to AA and NA. My life was simple but surprisingly full. I got close to Sophie, who'd been abstinent for a year and was the same age as me. In her I found a confidante and someone I could have a laugh with, who appreciated men in the same way I did. Had we known each other when we were both using, we'd have got into a lot of trouble together – that was certain.

As the anger that had throttled me during every waking moment began to subside, I noticed the pendulum swung heavily the other way. Many days, I experienced profound moments of exhilaration in doing nothing. My evenings were spent mainly at meetings, or with Sophie at her flat, or at home watching too much television. The first film I watched during this period was the first time I'd ever watched a movie from start to finish and remembered it after the credits. For me, such things were notable achievements.

Very minor things were events that could create elation. One of the most obvious changes was that I was able to be home alone and not be scared or jumpy. I didn't need to switch the TV on to dampen the persecutory voice in my head that in the past wouldn't let me rest. The shadows weren't around so much and when they were it was late at night when I'd been alone for too many hours during the day, or I couldn't sleep for tears, images of Leon, sadness for my dad and anger towards myself for acting like a fuckhead throughout my life.

The demons came for me while I was under my duvet via unidentifiable noises and a relentless sense of unease. I'd often sleep with the light on, which barely soothed my fears, but usually I'd feel relief in the morning when I'd remember that I could now control at least a part of my own destiny, if only I could remain abstinent.

CHAPTER 53

I was 28 years old and qualified to do sod all except give good head. I was single, not that that was a huge issue (but, truth be told, I'd have loved a secure, healthy relationship. Whatever that was. It sounded good), and I was living on social benefit. Not at all sexy. But that was my life and for now I had to get used to it. Jim put money into my bank for me here and there, which I was grateful for, and he agreed to help me deal with paying my bills. I'd never done it before. I wasn't yet ready to try and find a job or get myself on a course of any kind, not then. I felt as though a sneeze in the wrong direction could blow everything apart if I didn't take each moment as it came.

Like many people, I'd hoped that once I'd stopped using drugs and alcohol, everything would be good very quickly after I'd recuperated for a while. It. Really. Does. Not. Work. Like. That.

The scars that had developed in my mind had to be worked on; habits had to be broken and new ones created; attitudes had to be altered. 'Change your behaviour and your attitude will follow.' Hearing this and the reality are two very different things.

The more ashamed I felt about how I'd lived, the more

I began to stay away from meetings and new friends. I still hadn't been able to confess my bigamy secret to anyone, and this was wearing me down. The idea of going to jail was more than I could bear. I thought I'd been all right for a while, but now I questioned if I was. The smallest things – making breakfast and washing up – left me exhausted. Again. I was sinking. Again. In spite of taking antidepressants, I was losing my grip. I thought the tablets were supposed to help me. Initially, they had, but now I'd hit a wall. A dismal fog had settled. Depression was stopping me from staying awake for more than four or five hours a day.

Sophie suggested that I begin to attend daily meetings as I had done immediately after I'd relapsed. I needed a goal for each day. I began to struggle to keep my dates with Janet, and when I did see her she knew that I wasn't all right, and I tried to brush it off. My ability to be honest with myself was getting swamped by my goblin, who'd re-established its rent-free home in my head.

The fewer meetings I went to, the more I started to fantasise about drugs and drink as a means of getting rid of my heavy feelings. Again I started ignoring phone calls from Fellowship members and even Sophie.

I knew I'd relapse if something didn't change, and I really, really, *really* didn't want to. So I went to my doctor, who upped the antidepressants.

'In my opinion, you've suffered from depression and anxiety for most of your life. It's all here in your notes, stemming back to you being around 15 years old.' She shook her head. She handed me a prescription. 'Take two of these tablets a day. That will be 200 mg. This is the highest possible dose. I'm going to give you some beta blockers for your anxiety. Take no more than 100 mg of these per day. If these don't help, we'll re-evaluate your treatment and send you for some tests. But after so many years of suffering, Katie, you need as much help as possible right now so I'm putting you on a waiting list to see a psychologist.'

I'd gone from 50 mg to 200 mg and while I waited for the pills to take hold, I kept a low profile, started eating properly and tried to attend a meeting daily. Within two weeks I felt a shift in my mood, and quite suddenly my drive to keep sober was the greatest it had ever been. I started seeing Emma and Natasha and told Sophie about my secret marriages.

'Really? You have been a busy girl,' she said with a straight face as she clutched her cuppa, and then we both cracked up laughing. She could relate to madness. She'd chosen to live on the streets for two years while addicted to crack and heroin, despite coming from a well-to-do family who'd always offered her a bed. She shared some of her secrets with me and I didn't feel such an oddity when I discovered that some of her own actions when she'd been using made no sense to her.

I was nervous but excited about my first sober night out in central London. I wanted to see how I'd fare booze-free around men and people drinking in a bar swimming in alcohol. Sophie looked confident in jeans, like me, and heels, not like me. We chatted animatedly about men, men and sex on our way to meet Natasha, who was glamorously dressed and already tipsy.

The West End was buzzing as it had always done and expectancy was in the air. The three of us took a rickshaw to The Sanderson hotel bar, which was one of my old haunts. We arrived at the glitzy entrance and I led the way straight past the smiling doormen. I could tell that Sophie felt uneasy. She needed me to be sure of myself. I knew I couldn't wallow in the simmering feelings of inadequacy that lurked in my belly. Natasha, on the other hand, was full of it as we edged our way up to the flash long bar. There I froze.

'You order,' I told Natasha. Bottles of spirits mesmerised me, and so did the hordes of slick men who were checking out anything with tits.

The brightly lit room was too much. Then a guy smiled at me. Had I fucked him, I wondered? My mind went into overdrive as I stood sipping my slimline tonic water, trying to calm myself with statistics about how unlikely this was considering the millions of men in London. But I couldn't get the thought out of my head, so I told the girls.

Sophie had already known that I'd been a hooker, but this was the first time Natasha was hearing it. I cringed.

'All the stuff you'd told me before, Kate, don't take this badly, but I'd already guessed. I'm not that naive. It's the only logical explanation for you to be able to afford the life you described to me.' She smiled. 'And something else – that guy? He keeps looking at you cos he fancies you, sweetie, nothing more than that.'

It seemed so simple. Until, that is, he and his friend came over. I didn't fancy him, so talking wasn't too difficult, until he asked *that* question: 'So what do you do?'

Arrgh! Fear overwhelmed me. My God. *What do I do? Shit.* It was a perfectly ordinary question that had me in a spin. Natasha began with her marketing spiel, and I immediately left to go to the toilet. I had to. I had to get away from there. I excused my way through heaps of people just so I could stand in a toilet cubicle to pass some time for no reason other than freaking out because I'd been asked what I did for a living. If they were still there when I returned, I decided, I'd lie. I'd claim to be a student. Fuck it. I felt bad enough as it was without admitting to doing jack shit to boot. Well, that wasn't strictly true. My truth was this: 'I'll tell you what I do . . . I've actually recently come out of rehab, and I'm now on powerful antidepressants and I'm not working cos it takes all my energy just to keep myself from cracking up every few minutes, goddit?' *Brilliant.*

After fretting like a pig heading to a slaughterhouse, I rejoined my friends only to discover that the guys had gone and my worry had been pointless.

I'd had enough. I needed to go home. I just couldn't carry on. Sophie decided to leave for the suburbs too. Natasha was gutted. She wanted to stay out but I had to do what I needed to do for me and not to please someone else.

The night out was all right. It was what it was. Just spending time with two friends and drinking pop. But that was the crux of the situation. I'd done it. I'd made it through a night out without getting plastered.

I'd been finding it difficult to get hold of Natasha and I began questioning if this was because I'd told her I'd been a prostitute, in spite of her being so dismissive of it being a big deal. 'It's more likely she's sulking cos we left early,' Sophie said.

I was feeling stronger, thanks in part to the tablets, and as a result I was allowing myself to face my past as a hooker in more detail. This wasn't easy, but it was necessary. I shuddered, however, when I thought about the time I went to the house of a married man who wanted me to flog him with a cane while wearing high-heeled boots, a coat and a balaclava over my face, nothing more.

'Hit me harder, please, Mistress, and tell me I'm a naughty baby,' he breathed when I tested him out with the first lashing.

Mistress? Please! A naughty baby? Cunt, more like.

I stared at him as he was bent over on the bed, his arms attached to the headboard with wire, which I'd tied. The guy's pornographic groans made me snap, 'Be quiet.'

'Yes, Mistress. Sorry, Mistress. Harder, please do me harder.' *Right, you fucking grotesque horrible shyster, I will.*

I turned my head away from him, and, ignoring the fact that it was a person I was beating, I put all my weight into it until he yelled out that he was going to shoot his load. He slumped forwards. I knew the game was over but I hadn't quite finished. 'I want you to lick your come off the covers while I go to the bathroom, and then I'll untie you. Do you hear me? And don't stop until I say so.'

'Yes, Mistress,' he said, and got to work.

I left immediately.

CHAPTER 54

Tessa was training to be a therapist and she was living on an estate close to where she used to use.

'It's not ideal, bab, obviously, but that's what the council offered me, and if I hadn't taken it they could have made me wait at least another year, and I'd have been stuck in that dry house for even longer,' she said as she stuffed some lemon cake into her mouth in a café at Clapham Junction.

'Guess it's up to me if I spend time with those pricks down there, though,' she continued.

'Yeah, well, look at me. I fucked up, and I was out in the suburbs.' We both laughed. 'Bet Maggie had a field day when she heard I'd proved her right. Remember when she was banging on about me relapsing if I went back to my flat?'

'Yeah, but it's not about location, bab. I've spoken loads to my sponsor about this and it's really not,' Tessa said with a very straight face. As I stared at her, I couldn't help but think about how different she looked from when we'd first met. She looked younger and more poised, and she was more confident than I was.

'Anyway, listen, I've finally decided to do a computer

course. I applied through the adult education centre and I'm in and I'm bloody crapping it now.'

'You'll be all right.'

'Well, after my last fiasco, a couple of years ago, when I didn't know what the return key was, course I'm more than a bit apprehensive.'

'Not too sure I know, myself, bab. It's the big button on the computer, that thing that makes things move?'

'Er, kind of. It's something like that.'

'We're a right pair, aren't we?'

'Speak for yourself!'

'Har har.'

'I feel ready to try and do something, now. I need to get a bit more . . . well, more of a life.'

'It ain't easy.'

'Thanks for the encouragement.' I started laughing, as did Tessa.

'I'm just saying that at times it feels like you're trudging through treacle, you know . . . It's really tiring just being a-fucking-alive. Don't you think so? Just don't rush yourself or give yourself a hard time if you find it difficult – that's all I'm saying. After a relapse you need time.'

'It's OK now. It's OK.'

'I'm saying this as much for me as I am for you. I'm trying to be honest with you, cos, truth be told, I'm struggling right now. I mean, there are times I just feel like jacking this fucking counselling thing in and jacking up some smack, you know? I feel guilty for saying it cos of the kids, like, but you know sometimes I don't even know who the fuck I am any more, and that's weird and scary.'

'I hear you.'

'But no one said that any of this would be easy, eh?'

Tessa told me about two tearful meetings she'd had with her social worker and her daughters. We talked about this at length and as usual cried together.

We later chatted and giggled about Billy, as we walked towards a local park. He'd decided to take his self-discovery further and live in a Buddhist retreat for a year. We also commiserated about Daryl, who had been spotted looking 'in a right fucking state by the sounds of it', according to Tess.

Strangely, neither of us mentioned Leon. Not once. My soldier sister guessed correctly that the whole tawdry affair was something that I wished to put behind me. He was off doing something, somewhere – and with whom was none of my business. I didn't want to know anything about him.

At my computer course, I mixed with people who knew nothing about me or the things that had once consumed my life. I felt as though I needed to keep relatively quiet and not mingle for fear of exposing my past. I looked at my classmates and imagined that they all had their lives in order, were in balanced relationships and came from uncomplicated families and weren't battling depression. If this was the case, good for them. My time would come.

Things were changing, but slowly. Arriving at the course on time was a big thing for me. My confidence was growing in all areas, and after months of procrastinating I anxiously went to see a solicitor, with Sophie, for advice about my marriages and how to free myself from them.

'Well, I've certainly never come across this before,' he said. 'Try not to worry. Act as though they are both legal and apply for one divorce and then another. But apply for the second divorce petition in a different court, OK?'

'Please don't go to the police about this, will you? I'd never cope if I went to prison.'

'I absolutely won't be talking about this to anyone outside of this room, and you won't be going to prison, I'm positive about that. I advise you to drop your idea about handing yourself in to the police and confessing. See your priest about it if you feel so inclined. Otherwise, be calm, do what you need to do, and then put it behind you and laugh at it.' *Right.*

The next day, I went to a county court and asked for the forms to apply for a divorce from Sam. We'd had no contact for more than five years, so I didn't need him to sign the papers. I couldn't believe how easy it was to start the process. I felt a healthy portion of relief, but I still had my marriage to Hassan to deal with.

And then a gift: Ivan, a school-friend from Yorkshire, announced he was moving to London. We'd been close since we were 12 years old. Our parents were friends and he was like a brother to me. The first words that came out of his mouth after not having seen me for years, but knowing all about what had gone on, were: 'Looks like you got away with it then!' If only he knew . . .

We decided to rent a place together. We moved into a two-bed, furnished, high-ceilinged flat in Kentish Town. Ivan paid the deposit and put his name on the tenancy, since I couldn't do either.

Ivan was my six-foot, blond electro-music lover and all-round super-friend, who'd come to sprinkle some magic dust over my life at a time when I needed it greatly. Spending time with him, cooking for each other and laughing about old times made me feel safe. OK, so I was told to be careful not to become emotionally dependent on him. Some people needed to lighten up – oh, and, if my recent past was anything to go by, I needed to keep an open mind about what they were saying to me. Oops.

Ivan was a friend and our friendship wasn't any different from other people's, in spite of the fact that I'd had some problems. It didn't mean I'd be clinging onto his skinny legs to prevent him from going to his graphic design job or that when he gigged with his bandmates, who were trying to make it in London, I'd be begging him not to go. It also didn't mean that I'd ask him if I could go with him to the local shop when he popped out to buy rolling tobacco or milk. Although we did go to the supermarket together, as if we were a long-established couple. But then I suppose we were.

I continued to practise my computer 'skills'. I still hung out with Sophie, who Ivan wished I'd see more of, at our place, since he fancied the arse off her. I still went to meetings. And then I finally decided to attempt a job. A taxpaying, smiling-at-people-for-no-reason-and-pretending-to-give-a-shit-about-one-another-and-the-minutes-would-be-counted-until-lunchtime job. Things seemed to be working well and I praised my doctor for upping my pill intake.

The first job I applied for and got was basic: no computer use was a major result and absolutely necessary in my situation. Seemed that someone was looking after me. I was paid £6.60 an hour to answer calls, transfer those and say hello to anyone who came within spitting distance of me. That was it.

Going into the small, old-fashioned office on my first day, I was not especially nervous. Dressed in smart trousers and a shirt, I didn't feel like I was entering a new world. It all seemed quite uncomplicated, and I liked it. The job was ten minutes away from where I lived, on a standing-room-only bus, and inwardly I was grinning. At work, I tried overly hard to please everyone. Part of me was terrified that someone would suss that this wasn't my usual form of employment and I'd be rumbled for having a fake CV and no experience. But in spite of this, I was doing what I had set out to do. I was living my dream. I was sober and I had a job. I had a flat and I was paying my way. The weeks went by more quickly than I'd ever known time to move, and when I got my wages at the end of my first month I don't recall comparing the money I earned in the office with my previous line of work. Maybe at times I did, but not enough for it to have an impact on me. The two jobs signified such different lives that it was of no relevance.

So what was missing? A relationship. Was I ready for one? Was I hell. *One thing at a time.* Amen to that. Kissing men usually led me to obsessiveness and emotional turmoil, and I could only just about cope with what was in front of me. Of course, sometimes I felt lonely, and my goblin would suggest that I bang someone just for a quick release, but I followed my gut and stayed clear.

In the evenings, I'd hang out with Ivan, who, like me, was a homebody. He did drink alcohol but didn't in the flat, which made things easier for me at that stage. I spoke to him about my marriages, but couldn't dwell on it for long; the thought made me want to puke. He wasn't shocked; in fact, he started to laugh, just as Sophie had done. But Jimmy didn't find my marriages at all funny.

'I mean, what can I say? What's the point of trying to rationalise something that manifested in an irrational mind?'

Er . . . none whatsoever.

'Now, had you killed someone in the process, then fair dos, they should throw the bleedin' book at you. But I'm sure that's not necessary for a silly sausage like you.'

Ivan could see how anxious I was at the prospect of dealing

with both divorces in England, and the idea of flying to Gambia, the scene of the crime, was beyond frightening for me. So he agreed to help me deal with the marriage to Hassan by flying to Africa and representing me in court.

Within days, we found a solicitor in Gambia, via the Internet, who agreed to act for me. I told him nothing about the Hassan marriage being illegal. Around the time that I received the decree absolute for the divorce from Sam, I received the decree nisi for the Hassan caper. There was a six-week cooling-down period that allowed my second husband to contest my petition. He didn't, of course; he didn't even know that a divorce was taking place, which was perfectly acceptable, according to my lawyer. Now he'd got his papers allowing him to live in Britain, he wouldn't give a toss anyway.

I borrowed 500 quid from Jimmy to help pay for the trip and I signed power of attorney over to Ivan. He then jetted off for a week towards the sun, buxom beauties and half a day in a magistrates' court.

'You'd better get Sophie to agree to let me sleep with her now!' he laughed as he handed me my decree absolute.

I'd always believed I'd feel tearfully ecstatic on this day, but I wasn't. In fact, I barely registered the event emotionally when the finale came.

'You're getting closer all the time to reclaiming your life,' Jim told me on the phone. 'You should be bloody thrilled!'

I should be thrilled! Should I? By whose laws? God's? The laws of sanity? There was a helluva lot more work to do yet. I'd barely begun. The external stuff was easier to sort through than the emotional cack that needed resolution. But at least I was now calling my father and Elaine weekly. As long as their faith in me had not diminished – and it hadn't, because they knew nothing about what had happened – then at some point time would bring us together again.

One year's clean time was not to be ignored, and Ivan, Sophie, Emma and I celebrated with a stir-fry and Diet Coke. No, no fancy non-alcoholic cocktails. That would have felt contrived. I wasn't ready to wave the 'I'm sober and lovin' it!' flag. However, I had to remain vigilant. Addiction doesn't sleep, and the likelihood that I could find something other than drugs or drink to pin my obsessions to was high.

I was now beginning to live a life that I'd always believed was unobtainable for me. My goblin lies dormant, for the most part. It lives deep in my core. It is a part of each of my cells and it waits for lack of focus, self-doubt, cockiness or difficult feelings to arise, so that it can try to persuade me to take a well-trodden route or a yet-to-be-found road back to its comfort zone: the mental anguish I lived with for so many years. But with absolute determination and an acquired self-awareness and practical steps, it didn't take long for something to click, and I realised I was no longer fighting a daily battle. My goblin had retreated. The bloodiness of the war I'd been fighting had mellowed.

I wasn't suddenly 'healed'. That never happens. But addicts can recover. Leopards *can* change their spots. All that is required is a heartbeat and a willingness to try. I mean really *try*. And, in the words of a wise, moustached man I once knew, 'seek progress not perfection'.

Nuff said.

EPILOGUE

After my eight-day relapse, there was a major change in me; it was my turning point and I have been abstinent ever since. Through six and a half sober years (it would have been seven and a half had I not messed up for those eight days, but still, it can't be ignored) I have made some bad decisions with men, college courses, and saying yes meaning no. But I no longer need to escape when emotions feel difficult to manage. A fear of my past and an understanding of my susceptibility to chaotic, damaging behaviour also help me remain abstinent. However, temptation comes in many forms, therefore self-reflection and fearless honesty must be a personal, ongoing commitment.

Of course, life can be difficult, as it can be for everyone, but not drinking and not taking drugs is *not* difficult. Now, it's just what I do. I simply don't drink or use drugs. No biggie. Of course, there are times when I see a bottle of cold beer on a hot day and I think, 'Mmm, that looks good.' But I don't pick it up. A thought never killed anyone. Instead, I order a bottle of Coke and I think, 'Mmm, that tastes good.'

I haven't turned into a robot since becoming abstinent, therefore I'm still sometimes attracted to doing things that could emotionally damage me. But I no longer have a compulsion to act on those thoughts.

Susceptibility to craziness never leaves a recovering addict. Acceptance of this is essential when the whispers do come. I now know that if it takes one hour, one day, one week, one month or more, I *will* reclaim my peace of mind. And knowing this is invaluable.

So would I change the past if I could?
Damn right I would.
Even if it meant I had less understanding of people and life?
Absolutely. Even if it meant I was more of an arsehole, I'd still go back and change it all. I went through too much and caused too much pain.
Why do I remain abstinent?
I'm happier like this. I make choices based on rational thought rather than impulsive fervour. That's empowering. And I finally began to believe that I deserve to live better than I did.
Why do I believe that?
Because anyone who suffers from emotional or mental-health issues deserves to live just as well as you do.
Who keeps me clean?
Me. Although I need other people in my life – friends and the Fellowship, and there have also been many professionals such as doctors, therapists and psychologists who have helped me. But the incentive to reach out to others comes from inside me.
So how do I feel about my mum now?
She's fine, I suppose. And that is fine as in she's all right. Not fine as in I think she's Fucked-up, Insecure, Neurotic and Emotional. Although I'm sure she's those things too. Sometimes I'd like to punch her, other times I'd like to hug her, and I'm all right with those fluctuating feelings. But right now, yep, she's fine . . .

UNHOOKED

People are sometimes puzzled when they realise that I don't drink. 'Of course I *drink*,' I tell them. 'Just not alcohol.'

'Why not?'

'I just don't.'

'Not even one? Never?'

'Nope.'

'Would you have a sneaky tipple if no one knew?'

'That's like asking if I would chop off my own arm if no one found out.'

What others don't know may not hurt them, but the consequences of your own lies can sure as hell hurt you.

TWENTY-ONE-GUN SALUTES TO:

People in rehab and recovery – keep on truckin'!

Isabel Atherton – for your support.

Loulou Brown – for your expertise and good humour.

Claire Rose – for your astute eye and understanding, and everyone at Mainstream for being on the ball.

Bill Campbell – for taking a second bite of the pie.

Katharine Scott, Jo Morris for your comments, and to those who know and who kept an open mind – thank you.

Natalie and Julian Fox for the cheesecake, and to Likinopolvs – just because I can.

Claire Martin – for being inspirational.

Mark Ibson – for being a rock star; as you know, this won't be the last stone I'll throw . . .